SOULLESS

ALSO BY THE AUTHOR

Turn On Your Mind: Four Decades of Great Psychedelic Rock

Let It Blurt: The Life and Times of Lester Bangs,
America's Greatest Rock Critic

Milk It! Collected Musings on the Alternative Music Explosion of the '90s

Staring at Sound: The True Story of Oklahoma's Fabulous Flaming Lips

SOULLESS

THE CASE

AGAINST

R.KELLY

JIM DeROGATIS

ABRAMS PRESS, NEW YORK

362,76
DER

ABRAMS The Art of Books
195 Broadway, New York, NY 10007
abramsbooks.com

FOR THE GIRLS

Sometimes this versatile musician
Snatches up a pretty gal.
No town has offered him admission
Where he found no girls to beguile.
And even if the girls are dim
And all the women are too prim
They all together lovesick long
Enchanted by his strings and song.

—Johann Wolfgang von Goethe,
from *Der Rattenfänger* ("The Pied Piper")

CONTENTS

ROBERT'S PROBLEM IS YOUNG GIRLS

I intended to make it a quick trip. Since it was the Wednesday before Thanksgiving, 2000, I knew most people would have stayed home when I made my dreaded weekly visit to the office to show my face to editors, file my expenses, and sort through the postal bins full of promo CDs piled up since my last appearance. The traffic had been dead, so I zoomed down Lake Shore Drive. As I hustled across Wabash Avenue from the parking ramp into the gray, barge-like *Chicago Sun-Times* building overlooking the river, the wind bit ferociously. The temperature hovered in the low twenties, but as Chicagoans say, it's always cooler by the lake. I had only started to thaw out when an editorial assistant grudgingly handed me a fax sent to the main number in the newsroom instead of to the constantly humming machine a few feet from my desk in the features department. A lot of that curly, heat-sensitive fax paper got wasted in the days before everyone used email.

"Dear Mr. DeRogatis," the fax, a one-page, single-spaced letter, began. "I'm sending this to you because I don't know where else to go."

My review of the latest album by singer, songwriter, and producer R. Kelly had run as the lead story in the entertainment section on November 7, the day *TP-2.com* arrived in stores. Like celebrated film critic Roger Ebert, whom I proudly called a colleague, I disliked reductive ratings, stars or thumbs, but our editors demanded them. I thought a line in my critique nailed the dilemma better than the equivocal two out of four stars I'd given the disc. Prince, Marvin Gaye, and Al Green all showed that, under the right circumstances, sex and prayer can be the same thing, I wrote, but Kelly's lyrical shifts from church to boudoir were so jarring, they could give you whiplash.

"You wrote about R. Kelly a couple of weeks ago and compared him to Marvin Gaye," the letter writer continued. "Well, I guess Marvin Gaye had

problems, too, but I don't think they were like Robert's. Robert's problem—
and it's a thing that goes back many years—is young girls."

My stint as the paper's pop-music critic began in 1992, not long after
Kelly rose from busking for change on the city's "L" platforms. I left in 1995,
making a brief foray to *Rolling Stone* in New York. When I returned to the
Sun-Times in 1997, Kelly was firmly ensconced as the dominant voice in
R&B for a generation, well on his way to selling more than a hundred million
records, his own as well as those he crafted for other artists. Both his music
and his story inspired many in his hometown, which embraces local heroes
with a singular devotion.

Boosterism reigns in Chicago. Residents brag that their skyscrapers,
their sports franchises, their entertainers, their crooked politicians, even
their pizzas are bigger and better than those in New York, Los Angeles, or
any other global metropolis you'd care to name. At the same time, Chicago is
perpetually the Second City. Its denizens suffer from a deep-seated inferiority
complex common to the Midwest, but running especially deep in the City
by the Lake, where so many future stars begin their careers, then decamp to
the coasts to become "real" celebrities. This mix of pride and insecurity is
amplified on the South and West Sides, where the black community fights
segregation and pervasive racism. These make black Chicagoans particularly
reluctant to turn on heroes from their streets, especially if they stay once
they've made it. Kelly had made it, and he'd stayed.

I got a lot of angry letters via fax and snail mail in response to my
record and concert reviews. They were especially numerous when I harshly
critiqued aging baby boom favorites like the Rolling Stones, Billy Joel, or Eric
Clapton—I called them "geezers"—and whenever I praised hip-hop. "That's
not music, it's noise!" readers commonly complained. Although the faxed
letter was signed "A Friend," I initially dismissed whoever wrote it as just one
more reactionary jerk trying to disparage a black superstar.

"R. Kelly likes them young" had long been a rumor on the music scene,
almost always whispered in those exact words, by publicists and recording
engineers, radio programmers and concert promoters, fellow critics and fans.
Gossips said he'd married his fifteen-year-old protégé Aaliyah in 1994. That
story seemed strange and unlikely, and both of them had denied it. There

had been little public discussion about what those words actually meant, and I'll confess, I didn't think about them much at first, either.

Although this book and two decades of reporting on the pain R. Kelly has caused dozens of young girls began with that fax, I initially tossed it on the pile of press releases, artists' biographies, and angry letters from aggrieved readers stacked in a wire bin filled to overflowing on the corner of my desk, eventually destined for the trash.

PART I

CHAPTER 1

HE GONNA GROW UP BEING A SHOOTER

In the video for "I Wish," R. Kelly stands atop a Chicago high-rise overlooking the dramatic skyline of the city he calls "the center of my universe." He gazes up at the crisp blue sky. "What does it profit a man to gain the whole world and lose his soul?" asks a disembodied woman's voice. "I want out," the singer replies, removing his shades. "But it's hard. I need answers, Momma." He turns his back. "I need answers."

Almost all of Kelly's albums mix lascivious bedroom jams with soulful prayers or pleas, and "I Wish" is one of the latter, a nostalgic tribute to his late mother and the South Side neighborhoods where he grew up, as well as a bittersweet contemplation of the burdens of fame: "Now you hear my songs the radio is bangin' / Oh, I can't believe my ears / And what everybody's sayin' / Boy, I'll tell you, folks don't know the half."

The 2000 video also portrays Kelly surrounded by friends and family on the wooden porch of a small stucco house near West 107th Street and South Parnell Avenue, one of two homes that loom largest in his childhood memories. A twenty-year-old female extra lovingly braids his hair. Eight years later, she would testify that during a break in filming, she had a threesome with Kelly and an underage girl in his luxurious trailer. Folks don't know the half.

"Rock 'n' roll comes down to myth," my other great critic role model, Lester Bangs, wrote. "There are no 'facts.'" From the beginning, Kelly excelled at building the myth. I have talked to only one of his three half siblings, and aside from scattered quotes another has given to journalists, the primary source about his formative years is *Soulacoaster: The Diary of Me*, Kelly's idiosyncratic 2012 autobiography written with David Ritz, the author of more than three dozen as-told-to celebrity tomes, the best of them about Marvin Gaye. Woefully short on real or full names and specific dates and addresses, the book gets some of those it does mention wrong, citing the corners of streets that don't intersect, referring to buildings that never existed, even misspelling the name of Kelly's younger half brother throughout. Ritz views his role as conveying what his subjects want readers to know.

"I remove all issues of control of the book by giving complete control to them," Ritz said when we appeared on a panel together in 2003, but even Kelly disowns some of his chosen collaborator's work. "He didn't get everything on point," Kelly told Chris Heath of *GQ*, "just like no one ever does. When you say things, you know they'll get them misconstrued. I've read a couple of things in the book that wasn't exactly how I said it."

In addition to *Soulacoaster*, which is not always reliable, and public records, where information often is scarce, my portrait of Kelly's early years draws on sources close to his family, and some of what they told me comes from long conversations with Kelly's mother on her deathbed in 1993. Hundreds of sources talked to me during my time reporting on Kelly, whether on the record, not for attribution, or on background, some for five minutes and some repeatedly over the course of many weeks, months, then years. Every off-the-record agreement I made remains intact in this book, unless the source later gave me permission to name them or went public with the same information.

According to his driver's license and court records, Robert Sylvester Kelly was born on January 8, 1967. A since-deleted section of the Cook County website devoted to "home-grown athletes, celebrities, politicians, and more" reported that his mother, Joann, hailed from the Caribbean island of Guadeloupe. She gave birth to Robert at Chicago Lying-In Hospital, part of the University of Chicago healthcare system, in the Hyde Park neighborhood. County law does not grant access to birth certificates to anyone but the child and the parents, and if a father's name is listed beside his mother's, it remains a mystery.

Joann herself is a ghost in public-records searches, and Kelly has never mentioned her Caribbean roots, if indeed she had them. The county is not immune to screwing up the facts. A friend of the family told me Joann and her mother actually moved to Chicago as part of the Great Migration, when millions of African Americans fled the racism and poverty of the South in search of better opportunities in the cities of the Northeast and Midwest. Chicago, which was 2 percent black in the early 1900s, had become 33 percent black by 1970. Many African Americans relocated to the South and West Sides to neighborhoods like Bronzeville, Pullman, and Austin. There they formed a black belt marred by poorer housing stock and fewer retail businesses, but rich with music venues and churches that served as centers of community, hubs for activism during the Civil Rights movement, and political power bases thereafter.

All four of Joann's children had different fathers. Robert has an older half sister and half brother, Theresa and Bruce, and a younger half brother, Carey. The family called Carey "Killer," after the unseen boyfriend of the flamboyant character Geraldine Jones, portrayed by comedian Flip Wilson in drag on his early seventies TV show. This was a big, complicated family. At times, Robert and his half-siblings lived near or with his maternal grandmother, four uncles, female cousins and aunties, and a man named Lucious, who married Joann and became the stepfather to her four children, around the time Robert turned five. A self-professed mama's boy, Robert resented anyone else vying for Joann's attention, and he disapproved of the marriage, but he grants in his book that Lucious was "a nice man, nice to me, and most times nice to my mother."

Most times. Kelly also recounts several physical fights when his mother and stepfather drank. "That was a very abusive, kind of crazy relationship . . . a lot of fussing and fighting," a friend of the family told me. Carey told Tasha K, YouTube's "Queen of Real Talk," that Lucious worked for one of the airlines. He admitted that Lucious had his flaws, but said he worked hard to provide for the family. For better or worse, Joann remained devoted to him, and the couple stayed together.

Whenever he asked about his own father, Kelly says in *Soulacoaster*, "My mother would just roll her eyes, look away from me, and say, 'Don't say nothing to me about that no-good son of a bitch, because the minute he found out I was pregnant with you, his coward ass left. Disappeared in the wind.'" Describing his mom as a beautiful, heavyset woman, with "flawless brown skin, brown eyes, thick eyebrows," he notes that she "was strong in her faith . . . a praying woman who looked to God for a better way." He also admits she "had her bad habits. She loved her Winston cigarettes and her Miller beer. Sometimes she'd drink too much and get sick."

Talking to ABC's *Primetime Live*, Kelly said he and his mother went to McDonald's together almost every morning: "She'd fix a cup of coffee, she'd wear this cheap lipstick, she'd leave this red lipstick ring around the cup, and I'd turn it around and drink from that part, taste lipstick and coffee at the same time. If I could, I would have married my mom."

Robert and Carey both have said Joann worked at Roseland Community Hospital in the South Side neighborhood of the same name, not far from the house at 107th and Parnell; according to her two sons, she was an EKG technician and a phlebotomist. The hospital, which has long struggled financially, and which has recently been threatened with closing, could not confirm employment records when I inquired.

The family moved a lot during Robert's childhood. In his earliest years, they lived in the Parkway Garden housing project at East 63rd Street and South Martin Luther King Drive. South Siders now call the 6400 block of King Drive "O Block," after a slain gang member. A 2014 series in the *Sun-Times* named it "the most dangerous block in Chicago," with nineteen unsolved shootings in three years, but in the late sixties and early seventies, during the twenty-one-year reign of Chicago's infamous "Boss," Mayor Richard J. Daley, the project ranked among the city's better-maintained and safer low-income housing complexes. Michelle Robinson's family also lived there, when she was a toddler, long before she met and married Barack Obama.

"Back then the projects didn't seem as bad as people make them out to be today," Kelly says in his book. As a kid, he loved watching the sitcom *Good Times*, set in Cabrini-Green, a housing project on the Near North Side. From 1974 to 1980, the show depicted a richer life in public housing, beyond the prejudiced clichés, though some attacked as an insulting caricature the character of the oldest son, J.J., portrayed by breakout star Jimmie Walker. "He can't read or write," Esther Rolle, who played the show's matriarch, complained to Chicago-based *Ebony* magazine. "He doesn't think. Negative images have been slipped in on us."

Around Robert's eighth birthday, Joann moved the family to a home at East 40th Street and South Martin Luther King Drive in Grand Boulevard, a neighborhood that took its name from what had been one of the most bustling commercial strips on the South Side. In the wake of King's assassination in 1968, Chicago, like many other cities across America, rechristened the thoroughfare in his honor. During Kelly's youth, barbershops, nail salons, boutiques, record stores, fried-chicken-and-shrimp joints, storefront churches, and the corner groceries locals call "Food & Liquors" thrived. The neighborhood also retained touches of fading splendor from years past.

Robert and his half brothers frequented the Metropolitan Theatre at 46th and King, a historic vaudeville palace turned movie theater, to watch Bruce Lee films such as *Fist of Fury* and *Enter the Dragon*. Closed in 1979, the theater was demolished by the city in 1997. Joann fondly reminisced about shows at the Regal Theater, an even grander venue built at 47th and Grand Boulevard in 1928, where Aretha Franklin, Al Green, James Brown, the Isley Brothers, and many other greats performed. It closed in 1968 and faced the wrecking ball in 1973. A block off King Drive at 38th Street, Madden Park drew kids from miles around to its Olympic-size swimming pool in the summer, and its basketball courts fostered countless hoop dreams. Both are gone now, too.

Chicago historian Dominic Pacyga, the author of several books about the South Side, says Grand Boulevard during Kelly's formative years was 99.5 percent black, with the lowest average family income in the city, less than $7,000 per year, when the median nationwide topped $10,000. Single mothers headed 70 percent of all households with children under eighteen, and the unemployment rate approached 32 percent, far overshadowing the national rate of 6 percent. Two of Chicago's toughest housing projects, the Robert Taylor Homes and the Ida B. Wells Homes, skewed those numbers, especially by 1970, when gangs such as the Egyptian Cobras, Black P Stones, and Black Disciples began to take hold. Most residents rented in two- or three-flat apartment buildings, but the area also boasted stately old greystones and distinctive brick bungalows like those documented by Lee Bey in *Southern Exposure: The Overlooked Architecture of Chicago's South Side*.

In the early 2010s, some rappers on the city's nihilistic drill scene (and many in the out-of-town media) began calling the South Side "Chiraq," ignoring statistics that don't even place Chicago in the top twenty cities nationally for the murder rate per hundred thousand residents. The numbers were no worse during Kelly's childhood, but numbers don't tell the whole story. On paper, Chicago is one of the most diverse cities in America, equal parts black, white, and Latinx, but its seventy-seven neighborhoods are also heavily segregated. The South and West Sides often seem like different cities from the rest of Chicago. White, brown, and black residents live, work, and play separately. As Natalie Moore argues in *The South Side: A Portrait of Chicago and American Segregation*, that policy of separate and unequal is the root cause of the poverty and crime that prevail in the black community and which sometimes dominate the city's public image.

At the same time, the South Side is "a magical place . . . the heart of black America," Moore writes, with no disrespect to Harlem. Those who don't see the charms are missing big backyard barbecues for extended family and neighbors, daylong church picnics in the parks sponsored by tight-knit congregations that will pay medical bills or rent when a worshipper loses her job, the Bud Billiken Parade back-to-school celebration every August, and the music—everywhere, the music, real-deal electric blues and gospel (not the tourist crap), house and hip-hop, and the deep-cut soul and R&B tracks many call "dusties."

Basketball and music became Kelly's twin passions. He began playing ball at age five and never stopped. At age seventeen, he played on a club team based in the Ida B. Wells Homes in Bronzeville with local legend Ben Wilson. Kelly appeared in ESPN's *30 for 30* documentary *Benji* and recalled playing with his friend. "I always wanted to make people think I'ma shoot the ball," Kelly said, "but then I'd throw this incredible, crazy, magical pass, and Ben used to always love the passes." Tragically, Wilson was shot to death during an altercation in November 1984 near Simeon High School.

"Every kid's dream coming up in the 'hood is to be a pro basketball player," Kelly told Dave Hoekstra of the *Sun-Times* in 1997. That summer, he realized his dream for one season playing with the Atlantic City Seagulls in the short-lived semi-pro United States Basketball League. The USBL's rules allowed each team one spot on its roster for a "celebrity" player. "It wasn't a gimmick. He's a ballplayer. He can play," owner Ken Gross said, but Hoekstra noted that in five games, Kelly played for a total of twenty-four minutes.

Joann first instilled the love of music in Robert with the dusties she spun at home. Some of her favorites became his own, including Stevie Wonder, Al Green, and Donny Hathaway, the smooth-voiced Chicago soul man who died by suicide after "The Ghetto" and "This Christmas" made him a star. (The Rev. Jesse Jackson conducted his funeral.) Joann's singing also captivated her sons, and sometimes Robert and his half brothers, Bruce and Carey, played her Pips while she channeled Gladys Knight.

"Momma Joann could sing her butt off," Robert says in his book. "People said she sounded like Gladys Knight and Aretha Franklin mixed together. Every time she'd open her mouth to sing—whether it was in church, in a club, or outside on the porch—I would watch the people to get their reactions."

At age five, Kelly claims to have been smuggled inside a lounge, hidden in a drum case. He recalls being overwhelmed by "clouds of smoke, swells of laughter, women's sweet perfumes, the strong smell of cigars, and the stink of whiskey," but his mother's performance made the most impact. "She was tearing the roof off that little club, and me, well, I was cherishing every minute. The joy of music was the joy of my mother."

The musical dichotomy between Saturday night and Sunday morning has always been especially striking on the South Side. Legion were the blues and jazz musicians who stumbled out of the clubs at dawn and into church a few hours later, singing along with the choir. Kelly says he loved hearing Joann belt out secular tunes in the lounge as much as he enjoyed hearing her sing "Amazing Grace" at a storefront church, though she frightened him when she shook after "catching spirits." He never names their congregation, or even its denomination, and his relationship with religion is ambiguous. "I love parties, don't get me wrong. I love celebrating. I love kicking it," he told Lou Carlozo of the *Chicago Tribune*. "But I had to take a step toward God, because that's where I come from: that's where we all come from. . . . I'm not afraid to say that God gave me my talent. I'm not afraid to say that God woke me up this morning. . . . I know that God is the head of my life."

From early on, spirituality comforted Kelly at times of stress and loss. In *Soulacoaster*, he recalls Joann consoling him at age eight after the death of a playmate: "Wasn't your fault, baby. You couldn't do anything to save her. Lulu is in heaven now. She's with the Lord, sweetheart, and you're with me." The story of the girl Kelly calls Lulu is one of the most tragic in his book. They played house together in a big cardboard box in the backyard, and he says, "She was my first musical inspiration when it comes to love songs. I can still smell the fragrance of our innocence." He doesn't say how they came to be more than twenty miles from his South Side home, but one day, he and Lulu stood across Concord Drive from Beacon Hill Elementary School near the banks of the rain-swollen Thorn Creek. A tributary of the Little Calumet River in Chicago Heights, the creek is prone to dangerous flooding. Some older kids approached and started shoving them, and Lulu fell into the rushing water.

Helpless, Kelly watched as the fast-moving current carried Lulu away: "I didn't know how to swim, and neither did she. The other kids were running away, and she was screaming. . . . After what felt like forever, some grown-ups arrived. I explained what had happened and followed them downstream until they came upon a big rock. There was Lulu, her head crushed against the rock. She wasn't talking, wasn't moving, but there was a lot of blood coming from her head. . . . Death couldn't be this real."

For years after I first read *Soulacoaster*, I questioned this story—"the fragrance of our innocence" doesn't sound like anything Kelly has ever said— and police and county records held no documentation of the incident. Then, in the archives of the now-long-defunct *Chicago Homewood Flossmoor Star*, I found the obituary of a third-grader one year older than Robert. Louella Simpkins died from drowning in Thorn Creek in July 1974.

I asked one of the foremost developmental and forensic pediatricians in the United States what lingering effects the sudden, violent death of a childhood playmate could have had on an eight-year-old like Robert. "Childhood traumas certainly can cause an individual to develop abnormal thinking and mental health problems that, if not addressed, can contribute to ongoing problems," Dr. Sharon Cooper said. "And if you've had not just one catastrophic event, but also have been exposed to community violence, if you lived in a household where there may have been intimate-partner violence, and where there may have been other types of childhood adversities, then very often we know that individuals can begin to participate in what we refer to as health-risk behaviors: drug use, alcohol, smoking, and promiscuity."

Shy, introspective, and effeminate throughout grade school, according to all my sources, Kelly often turned to his mother for solace or protection when his older half brother, Bruce, or kids in the neighborhood teased and picked on him. "She said he was always the one she worried about," a friend of the family told me. "She had to protect him around other kids, take him in the other room. She couldn't leave him with the other kids."

In 2000, Kelly told dream hampton of *Vibe* that he "worshiped his single mother and considered eavesdropping on his mom, aunt, and sister's kitchen-table talk as important as shooting hoops in the park." Almost two decades later, when hampton served as showrunner for a six-part docu-series on Kelly, Carey told her, "Robert was not cut from the same cloth of being street. He didn't come outside." Added Bruce, who was interviewed while in Cook County Jail, "Robert was shy and very timid. If you stared at him in his face, he would cry." Both of his half brothers are bigger, beefier, and fuller of face than Robert, and they don't resemble him much at all.

Joann also spent more time with Robert because of the problem he calls "something more than dyslexia." In *Soulacoaster*, he says, "When I was a kid, I found out that I couldn't read or write like other kids. I would worry myself sick that something was wrong with me and that my disability would trap me." The Chicago Public Schools (CPS) do not release student records to the public, but all my sources confirmed Kelly's difficulties not only with reading but with basic math. "Literally to shop and get change was a very major problem," a friend of the family told me. Robert tried to hide his struggles from classmates and teachers, but Joann patiently worked with him at night, trying to tutor him and always encouraging him. She built up his self-esteem and fostered the belief that he'd been blessed, in a way no rich white parent in Lincoln Park or the North Shore suburbs could top.

" 'You got genius,' my mother told me after a day at school where kids were laughing at me 'cause I couldn't read," Kelly says. " 'One day you're gonna be famous, baby. . . . I mean famous like Al Green. Famous like Sam Cooke and Marvin Gaye.' " But he also felt deep shame from secrets he didn't share with anyone until years later.

"There were always women in our little house at 40th and King," Kelly says in *Soulacoaster*. "Cousins, aunties, friends of my aunties, all older women. When my mother wasn't home, the women ran a little freer. . . . You could see through their blouses. Sometimes they wore bras, sometimes they didn't. When they walked around in nightgowns or pajamas, you could see their panties and on a few occasions, like on a very hot summer days [*sic*], they wouldn't even wear panties. . . . As I crept up in age . . . and made my way through grammar school, I found myself more curious and sometimes aroused; and I was ashamed of being aroused. . . . Growing up with that shame has haunted me throughout my life."

On a winter afternoon when he came home early from school, Kelly claims to have walked in on a couple having sex. "You can watch, but you better not say shit to nobody about this," the woman said. Stumbling upon another encounter, he says the lovers directed him to take a photo with a Polaroid camera. "They got into positions where I could see their private parts. I snapped the picture. When she showed me how it took only a minute to develop, I was amazed. The photographic technology impressed me more than the sex. She grabbed the photo and kept it for herself. I took the memory of them doing the dirty and stashed it inside my mind's brick box."

The "brick box" is a metaphor Kelly or coauthor David Ritz uses several times in *Soulacoaster*. On yet another evening, after young Robert fell asleep while watching TV on the couch, he claims a woman ten years his senior woke him up by performing oral sex on him. He was eight years old. She also threatened him not to tell—"You better not say shit to no one or else you gonna get a terrible whupping"—and he didn't. "[G]rowing up in the 'hood, the number-one rule was don't snitch. . . . No matter how many times it happened, I knew I could never tell anyone. I was too afraid and too ashamed. All I could do was stash the secret—and hide it in my imaginary brick box."

Kelly claims the sexual contact moved on to intercourse and continued for about six years. In a 2012 interview with Tavis Smiley, who published *Soulacoaster* on his own SmileyBooks imprint, Kelly revealed the abuse came at the hands of "a family member." He repeated that claim in his interview with Chris Heath of *GQ*, as well as in his epic 2018 track "I Admit." In 2019, in two podcast and YouTube interviews, as well as in an interview with me, his half brother Carey named their half sister, Theresa, as both his own and Robert's abuser. "Theresa is the cause of everything happening the way that it did," Carey told me. A week later, Don Russell, the latest of the singer's managers, also named Theresa as Robert's abuser at a press conference. "He was hyper sexual, not because he chose to be, but because of his sister."

A devout Christian and a mother now living in another state under a completely different name, Theresa resembles her mom. She has never spoken publicly about her half brothers, and I failed in many attempts to reach her for comment.

Heath asked Kelly if he realized the relationship was wrong. "At first, I couldn't judge it," he said. "I remember it feeling weird. I remember feeling ashamed. I remember closing my eyes or keeping my hands over my eyes. I remember those things, but couldn't judge it one way or the other fully." After a couple of years, he added, he began "looking forward to it sometimes. You know, acting like I didn't, but did."

Kelly admitted that the sexual abuse at such a young age had a lasting impact. "It teaches you to definitely be sexual earlier than you should have, than you're supposed to. You know, no different than putting a loaded gun in a kid's hand. He gonna grow up being a shooter, probably. I think it affects you tremendously when that happens at an early age, to be more hornier. Your hormones are up more than they would normally be. Mine was."

In his interviews with Heath, Kelly also repeated but did not expand upon another story in his book. One day, around age ten, he says an older man close to the family, whom he calls Mr. Blue, invited him into his apartment. The man gave him a piece of watermelon and disappeared to shower. When he reemerged wearing a robe, he exposed himself and offered Robert five dollars to touch his penis. "Before Mr. Blue could say another word, I was running out the door with his voice trailing after me. He was shouting, 'If you know what's good for you, boy, you won't say nothing to no one. Say a word and I'll cook your goddamn goose!'"

This time, Kelly says he did speak out, after he learned a friend had a similar encounter with the man. Joann called the police. "They showed up at Mr. Blue's door. We never saw the man again." I could find no records of an arrest for exposure or inappropriate sexual contact with a minor in Grand

Boulevard or the areas near either house Kelly mentions during that period. "There was a lot of abuse sexually amongst themselves," a friend of the family told me. "This is out of his mom's mouth, man. Ms. Kelly told me that Robert was abused by a man, either an uncle or a 'play-uncle,' somebody they just called uncle. Robert was very confused regarding it, and I believe very angry with his mom for not protecting him."

Kelly's younger half brother, Carey, told me that "Mr. Henry" exposed himself to all three half brothers, and that he was the one who told their mother. Several of the women who later slept with Kelly told me he'd said he had sexual contact with the man; Carey also said Robert was alone with the man at times, and that he believes things went further between the man and Robert than Robert has publicly admitted. "I want to heal people, because I've been through so much in my life, but Robert took the other route," Carey said. "He started doing what was done to him, but Theresa and Mr. Henry is the person that started that."

Many women who've slept with him have told me Kelly is bisexual and has sex with other cis males. They say he keeps these encounters "on the down low," either because of shame or because it conflicts with the image he projects as the consummate ladies' man on R&B and hip-hop scenes that still are often deeply homophobic. In the clapback track "I Confess," which Carey released in 2018 in response to his half brother's song "I Admit," he raps, "Something ain't right, something smell fishy / What's goin' on? / I confess / What kinda man wanna stay a night at a man's home? / A fuckin' fag, gay as hell."

The mental health professionals I've interviewed say Kelly exhibits many of the common symptoms of childhood victims. Male survivors sometimes struggle with sex addiction, becoming, as Kelly says in his book, "more hornier." They may suffer from insecurity or paranoia. Kelly says he often sleeps in his bedroom closet, and that gives him "a peace of mind." They can be plagued by nightmares. "I've had dreams of being raped by women," Kelly told *GQ*. "I've had dreams about being cornered by things. I have dreams about being chased and shot at all the time." They may fetishize things they've experienced, like voyeurism or documenting their sexual encounters in photos or on video. And some hurt themselves.

Kelly told dream hampton in *Vibe* that at age thirteen, some thugs who wanted his Huffy bicycle shot him in the shoulder. "They could've just pointed at me with their two fingers, like a fake gun, and I would've said, 'Here, man, take it. I live right down the street. I can walk. Y'all have a nice ride.'" In *Soulacoaster*, he claims he caught a stray bullet in the shoulder while riding his bike at age eleven or twelve. I could not find a police report for the incident, and a friend of the family told me a different story: "His mom told me what really happened with Robert; very, very depressed, one day, he shot himself with a revolver that somebody had around the house. He told everybody, his friends and whatnot, that he was shot by some thugs that tried to take his bike. I was stunned when she told me all of this."

Sometimes, mental health experts say, the abused become abusers. "Whether the victim is a young man or a young woman, a couple of things happen," says Dr. Charmaine Jake-Matthews, a visiting professor of psychology at Purdue University. "First of all, the individual's understanding of sexuality is obviously not developed at that age, so they get incorrect messages about what sexuality is and how it is to be expressed. Second, as uncomfortable or inappropriate as those situations are for the victim, such as an eight-year-old boy, they're also arousing, so your sexual arousal becomes associated with the victimization, the discomfort, the abuse. Lastly, what often happens is that the person knows nothing else to do with it except to act out on it towards other people."

To be certain, Dr. Jake-Matthews cautions, "There are many people who have been victimized in that way—more than we would like to know, hear about, or admit—who don't act out like that; people who have taken that pain, that confusion, and either gotten some help with it or channeled it in quite the opposite direction, becoming a champion to make sure it doesn't happen to other people." Jake-Matthews doesn't believe that's the case with Kelly, and she has a unique perspective. As a therapist, she has spent her career counseling troubled black teens in Chicago, including many who've been victims of abuse. She also sang beside Robert in their high school choir.

In the spring of 1984, Robert Kelly stood center stage in Kenwood Academy's expansive auditorium during the annual talent show. Skinny, gangly, and

, six-foot-three with a close-cropped head of nappy hair, he
.e many of his classmates, looking preppy in a white button-down
.iaroon sweater vest, and khaki pants. He masked his nerves with a
of jokey showmanship. Hiding behind a dark pair of sunglasses like the
designer shades Stevie Wonder wore, he had a friend lead him onstage as if
he, too, was blind.

As another classmate accompanied him on piano, Kelly sweetly cooed
the Motown giant's then-current hit, "Ribbon in the Sky," a romantic slow jam
soon to become a ubiquitous wedding song. A decade later, Dave Hoekstra
wrote the first major profile of Kelly in the *Sun-Times*. "That night, it was like
Spider-Man being bit," the singer told Hoekstra. "I discovered this power. I
knew I had something then."

Kenwood Academy, the most expensive school the city had built
when it opened in 1969 at East 50th Street and South Blackstone Avenue,
is roughly two miles equidistant from the house at 40th and King and the
storied campus of the University of Chicago in Hyde Park. CPS intended
for it to serve both less fortunate students from neighborhoods like Grand
Boulevard to the north and west and the children of faculty and staff at
the university to the south. A magnet program drew bright seventh- and
eighth-graders from elementary schools throughout the South Side, and
many went on to take early college courses at the U. of C., but most of
Kenwood's students came from schools in the surrounding neighborhoods.
From the beginning, parents lied and gave the addresses of friends and
relatives so their daughters and sons could go to Kenwood rather than their
neighborhood high school.

Kenwood adhered to tough academic standards, and only four hundred
from the class of seven hundred who enrolled might graduate four years
later. Plenty of poor students fell between the cracks, having been passed
ahead from grammar school despite failing grades, then dropping out before
earning a high school diploma. Since CPS student transcripts are not public
information, I do not know exactly when Kelly ceased to be an official student
there, or if he was ever diagnosed or received special treatment for what he
calls "something more than dyslexia." He simply became one of the three
hundred who didn't make it.

"I got to go there not because I was smart, but because I played basketball," Kelly claims in *Soulacoaster*, but the school's team didn't rank, and the Broncos didn't specifically recruit players. "There was no status from that, the team wasn't producing stars, and if he played, he wasn't going to be the next Michael Jordan or anything," said Dr. Jake-Matthews, who was Charmaine Jake at the time. The girls' swimming and boys' track and field teams won the citywide championships year after year through the eighties, and their members comprised the athletic cliques that garnered most of the glory in the lunchroom, but special status also graced members of the choir led by Lena McLin, whom Kelly calls his "second mom, teacher, and pastor."

McLin was born in Atlanta, but her parents sent her to live in Chicago at age five, when her uncle, the Rev. Thomas A. Dorsey, took over as the music director at Pilgrim Baptist Church in Bronzeville in 1932. The blues and jazz pianist who started performing as Georgia Tom found God when his first wife and son died shortly after childbirth. Leading his new South Side congregation, he became one of the architects of modern gospel music, writing more than five hundred spirituals, including "Precious Lord, Take My Hand" and "Peace in the Valley." He inspired Chicagoans Mahalia Jackson and Albertina Walker, as well as Detroit legend Aretha Franklin. Jackson sang "Precious Lord, Take My Hand" at Rev. Martin Luther King Jr.'s funeral. Dorsey was also an entrepreneur, and he started one of the first black-owned music-publishing companies.

Like her celebrated uncle, McLin became a composer, and she later led a congregation of her own, at Holy Vessel Baptist Church in Hyde Park, in addition to spending a career teaching for CPS, most of it at Kenwood. Heavyset like Joann, with piercing brown eyes and an impressive black bouffant, she headed the music department from 1970 through her retirement, not long before her her uncle died in 1993. The list of performers McLin mentored includes Broadway star Mandy Patinkin, opera singers Jonita Lattimore and Mark Rucker, pop star Jennifer Hudson, gospel singer Calvin Brunson, and R&B great Chaka Khan, who wound up on the teacher's bad side, allegedly because of partying. McLin scowled whenever students mentioned the former Yvette Marie Stevens, but she consistently championed Kelly from the day he initially appeared in Room 126.

"On the first day I met her, Ms. McLin told me, 'You're going to be one of the greatest singers, songwriters, and performers of all time,'" Kelly said in an interview with Maudlyne Ihejirika of the *Sun-Times* in 2015, when he headlined a benefit concert at the Chicago Theatre to raise money to help buy the apartment McLin risked losing as her building went condo.

McLin was a proponent of tough love. Several of her students told me she could be sweet and nurturing as well as a harsh taskmaster, demanding that choir members come to rehearsal early and stay late. She pushed her favorite singers to hit notes they never thought they could reach, and she forced them to drop every other extracurricular activity. She brusquely informed Kelly's basketball coach that he would not be playing on the team. "She didn't like me," said Amy Hundley, whose boyfriend sang in the choir, "and she let me know it. Not in these exact words, but she made it clear she thought I was going to take him down some garden path of sexual vice or whatever. She was a scary lady, in terms of the moral code she was trying to impose on people."

McLin did not tolerate infractions of her rules, such as slouching or chewing gum in class, and she railed at any hint of what she called "minstrelsy." *Pulse: A History of Music,* her 1977 book portraying musical favorites from the baroque era through Stevie Wonder, derides the minstrel shows of the nineteenth century for "making fun of the black man, demeaning and stereotyping him, painting a false picture of a sad people." Confronted with anyone stooping to such tomfoolery, she angrily invoked the star of *Good Times*: "J.J. doesn't speak for all of us!"

The teacher may not have approved of Kelly's blind-man act at the talent show, but she forgave many sins by her favorites. Being chosen as one of her anointed carried the luster of being a champion quarterback at a Texas high school. "Once you became a part of her circle, your experience at school changed to the extent that you could hang around the choir room all day and never go anywhere else," Jake-Matthews said. "Robert was part of that tight circle of people around Ms. McLin. Obviously, he was a soloist, and a lot of the girls thought he was cute. Somebody always had a crush on Robert Kelly." Added Hundley, "For whatever reason, Ms. McLin was in love with him, and he could do no wrong."

Focused and determined, Kelly worked hard to master McLin's lessons about breath control, phrasing, and Italian bel canto singing. He played starring roles in the school productions of *My Fair Lady*, *Carousel*, and *Purlie*, and for years he sang the solo in the song central to Kenwood's annual Christmas pageant, which seems to have been one of McLin's original compositions. In the mid-eighties, the teacher tapped Jake Austen, now an energetic force on Chicago's indie-rock scene as a writer, garage rocker, and public-access television producer, to take the solo.

"Robert and I went into the guitar room next door to the choir room and spent a day of him kind of coaching me on how to sing this song," Austen said. "He didn't actually give me any vocal lessons, he just talked about stage presence, and he said the secret to being onstage is being like Bing Crosby—you have to walk and sing at the same time. Obviously, he'd watched *White Christmas*—he watched everything coming up—and he definitely thought about what people were doing, what it took to be a success." In the end, Kelly wound up taking the solo as usual.

Austen and Jake-Matthews both followed Kelly into Kenwood by two years; they say he should have been a junior when they started their first semester. Kelly claims in *Soulacoaster* that his mentor argued with the principal, who wanted to expel him at the end of his freshman year because of failing grades. "In spite of Ms. McLin's best efforts to keep me in school, I quit—just like that." He does not say that he kept coming back to high school for at least six more years, rehearsing with the choir and performing in its shows, a physically maturing young adult surrounded by awkward, acne-plagued teens.

"This is pre–metal detectors and security, so the fact that he could just walk into the school for years and go to choir, it wasn't really a question," Austen said. Kelly also spent hours in what Austen called the "guitar room," off McLin's classroom. "When I found this secret room at school that everyone seemed to have forgotten about," Kelly says in his book, "it became another . . . safe place. And there was a piano in it."

The aspiring songwriter taught himself to play by ear, an ability he says he first realized a few years earlier, when a neighbor he calls Willie Pearl loaned him a Casiotone 201, the first portable battery-powered keyboard that appeared on the market in 1980. Kelly began picking out rudimentary chords and improvising vocal parts, writing his first songs, including one about his mother: "Hard times, she working night and day / Hard times, just to keep the landlord away / Hard times, she does it all alone / Hard times, her love keeps us strong." He describes it in *Soulacoaster* as "a simple melody in a deep blues bag," while the lyrics seem to crib from the theme song for *Good Times.*

During the years when he continued hanging out at Kenwood, Kelly busked on the streets of downtown Chicago and the Near North Side. When he started earning enough money, he left home and moved into the old YMCA Hotel in the South Loop at East Ninth Street and South Wabash Avenue, close to some of the spots where he performed. Especially lucrative were the bustling "L" stop on Jackson Boulevard in the Loop, servicing both the Red and Blue Lines, and Rush Street, outside the bars catering to middle-age businessmen. He claims he collected as much as $400 a day, accompanying himself on the Casio and mixing songs by Wonder and Hathaway with his originals, including one about the burgers and fries from McDonald's. "He'd sing to people as they exited the Golden Arches," Cheo Hodari Coker wrote in *Vibe,* "hoping they'd leave the restaurant with a smile . . . and leave him some spare change."

Kelly also says in *Soulacoaster* that he worked as a male stripper, singing as part of his act. "Because I had a body—I was ripped real good—women went crazy [and] . . . My voice gave me an advantage over all the other strippers." He provides no other details about what he calls his other "hustle," and no one I've interviewed has ever mentioned it.

Presumably with money he'd saved from both busking and stripping, Kelly eventually boarded a flight to Los Angeles. It was his first airplane trip, and it revealed what would become a growing fear of flying. He spent several months in California in the mid-eighties and claims in his book to have secured a songwriting deal with A&M Records, but it fell apart when he refused to share credit for tunes he'd written on his own. He came back home to Chicago, and once again, Joann consoled him. "The music business is cold-blooded, son. It's testing you. It's saying, 'How bad you want it, boy?'"

After regrouping, Kelly says that he traveled to the West Coast again to make another go of it, "living homeless on the beach" and carrying his clothes in a brown paper bag. This time, he claims in his book, after a few more months of trying to break through, the contract he believed he'd scored with Benny Medina at Warner Bros. Records never materialized. A Motown veteran, Medina became the Vice President of Black Music at Warner Bros. in 1988, but he has never spoken about trying to sign Kelly.

Frustrated with performing at open mics and talent shows, Kelly even failed as a street musician in Venice Beach. He had to compete not only with other street singers, but also with magicians, mimes, comics, and fire-jugglers. He again returned to Chicago in defeat, but he says in *Soulacoaster* that he came up with a new plan.

First, Kelly truncated his first name. " 'Robert' is too ordinary," he told his then-girlfriend, whom he calls Lonneice in his book. " 'R.' sounds more mysterious." Next, seeing that New Edition, the California group the Boys, and Guy (with Teddy Riley) commanded the R&B spotlight, he followed their model. "I decided I was going to get the break I'd been looking for with a group. In 1987, I found three guys who could dance and sing. I put the group together, became the lead singer, and then set to work."

The account Kelly gives in *Soulacoaster* differs from a story in the *Chicago Tribune* about the quartet at the height of its local popularity. Kelly claims he chose the name "R. Kelly and MGM, for Musically Gifted Men," but Karen E. Klages reported that the group had been formed by Vince Walker, Shawn Brooks, and Marc McWilliams six months before Kelly joined, and MGM stood for "Mentally Gifted Men." The acronym "really says a lot," Walker told her. "What it says is that as much as we're musically gifted, we're mentally gifted—keeping drug-free, staying above the average group and going in the positive direction. Definite role models."

MGM dressed in oversize black suede suits with satin collars and rhine-stones fashioned by Chicago designer Barbara Bates, who'd worked with Kool Moe Dee, Bobby Brown, and Whitney Houston. They looked ridiculous, but then a lot of aspiring pop stars did in the late eighties. "Walking around with beepers and with hats turned to the side, you're labeled a gangbanger," Kelly told Klages. "I think it's very important the image you portray. Kids identify with it. Onstage, you have to be careful."

MGM's clean-cut image extended to the lyrics of the songs Kelly wrote for the group. "The music that they do—fast or slow—really has a message," said Eric Payton, the manager who allowed the four to rehearse and practice their dance moves for as many as eight hours a day in his basement whenever the weather made singing on the rocks along the shore of Lake Michigan prohibitive.

Payton was Kelly's second manager. The first, a friend named Chuck Smith, did not last long; he didn't have the connections or the clout Kelly knew he needed. Payton fared better in garnering some attention for Kelly and MGM. "They sing about racial harmony in 'We Are Family' and about the danger of drugs in 'Let's Get It Together,'" Klages wrote. But they also released an indie single and made a self-financed video for the song "Why You Wanna Play Me" that offers a glimpse of the R. Kelly who'd eventually connect with listeners. Over a derivative new jack swing groove that brings a hint of a hip-hop rhythm to the then–au courant boy-band sound, Kelly boasts that he is "not the average guy," and he lashes out at the girlfriend who doesn't respect or love him the way he thinks he deserves.

"Do I look like a doughnut?" Kelly asks. "Then why you wanna glaze me?" The video emphasizes the lyrical couplet he took the most pride in, an attempt to coin a catchphrase with a flash of the gonzo humor that would become a trademark.

Opening for headliners such as En Vogue, Heavy D & the Boyz, and Kool Moe Dee, R. Kelly and MGM began building their own following at the New Regal Theater on East 79th Street and at the Cotton Club on South Michigan Avenue. Though the often-apocryphal "creative differences" percolated—"I felt envy building behind my back," Kelly says in *Soulacoaster*—they became contestants on *The Big Break*, a syndicated TV talent show hosted by Natalie Cole for one season in 1990. They made it through two rounds and won the third and final round to claim the $100,000 grand prize.

In April 1991, shortly after that triumph, the *Tribune* noted that an album on Jive Records would be forthcoming in June. Klages asked Kelly where the foursome would go next. "Farther up," he said. "We don't want to be a fly-by-night group." Indeed, as Klages paraphrased the conversation, MGM would become "the black Beatles."

Things didn't work out that way. "I didn't get a dime of the $100,000 in cash and prizes," Kelly says in his book. "I blamed MGM. I decided that I couldn't deal with them anymore. Our manager decided to stick with the group. I had no choice but to forget MGM—forever." Sources close to the band say that, once again, Kelly's account differs from what they call the facts. They claim MGM actually recorded many of the vocals on what would become Kelly's debut album with a new group, Public Announcement, and that his third manager, Barry Hankerson, had to negotiate the split from Payton after Kelly signed to Jive.

Launched in London in the early eighties, Jive Records scored its first big international success with the oddly coiffed New Wave band A Flock of Seagulls. South African–born label head Clive Calder then partnered with Barry Weiss, a New Yorker who made that city the label's new headquarters. Jive established itself by signing hip-hop artists such as DJ Jazzy Jeff and the Fresh Prince, Too $hort, Schoolly D, A Tribe Called Quest, KRS-One, and E-40. In the late 1990s and 2000s, the label achieved massive success with the Backstreet Boys, *NSYNC, and Britney Spears, but its biggest hits before the teen-pop years came from R. Kelly.

Forever in search of the next big thing, Jive opened a Chicago office in 1990 helmed by A&R rep Wayne Williams. The stepbrother of pioneering deejay Jesse Saunders, another of McLin's star pupils at Kenwood, Williams had worked at Trax Records, a key underground dance label during the heyday of house music in the eighties. He actually enrolled at Chicago's police academy before Jive offered him a job, after he steered a now-long-forgotten soul artist named Adonis to the label. He first saw Kelly by chance, singing at a backyard barbecue on the South Side. "At these parties, the guy singing is generally just doing the recent hits," Williams told Bill Wyman of the *Chicago Reader*. "I heard a song, I didn't know it, but it sounded good. Then I heard another, and that sounded really good, too. I went outside, and I see this guy has it all—choreography, the voice, everything."

By the time Kelly signed to Jive, he had a solid team behind him. Moonlighting from his day job with Tribune Media, attorney Darryl Porter handled legal affairs. The lawyer also worked with brothers Allen and Albert Hughes, and he arranged for the young filmmakers to include a Public Announcement song in the first movie they directed, *Menace II Society*. Porter did not stay with Kelly long, but his other team members did.

Long, lanky, and several years older than Kelly, Demetrius Smith served as his tour manager and personal assistant. He befriended the singer after first hearing him perform an original song called "Strong Enough to Be" during another Kenwood Academy talent show in January 1985, several years after Kelly dropped out. Smith introduced Kelly to his first manager, Chuck Smith (no relation).

Derrel McDavid, an accountant based in Oak Park, a suburb just west of Chicago, initially came on board to balance the books. Husky, biracial, and bespectacled, he compensated for his pale complexion within Kelly's all-black inner circle by adopting a tough-guy persona that seemed to have been cribbed from watching too many gangster movies. McDavid stayed at Kelly's side for two and a half decades, eventually becoming his fourth manager. He appears in countless photos trailing just behind the singer, but Kelly's more camera-shy third manager, Barry Hankerson, was by far the key player early on.

Born in Harlem in 1946, Hankerson grew up Catholic and served as an altar boy. He majored in sociology at Central State University in Ohio and played safety on the football team; he later tried but failed to go pro. Tall, thin, and wiry, Hankerson had an intense demeanor and an afro worthy of *Shaft* that made him seem bigger and more formidable than his actual size. In college, he joined the seventies campus radicals, and after graduating, he went to work as a community organizer. Eventually, he became an assistant to Coleman Young, the first black mayor of Detroit, and there he met and began dating a Motown legend. They married in 1974 and appeared on the cover of Chicago-based *Jet* magazine with the headline "Gladys Knight's New Life with a Pip of a Mate."

Starring together in the 1976 movie *Pipe Dreams*, Hankerson and Knight portrayed a couple struggling to save their marriage in an Alaskan town during construction of the pipeline. The movie, which he co-produced, flopped, leaving the couple $140,000 in debt, and their real marriage ended acrimoniously in 1979, according to *Jet*. The magazine ran another cover story that March, using some of the same photos from its first, glowing profile five years earlier. This one was headlined, "Court Records Tell What Really Broke Up the Marriage of Gladys Knight," and it painted a more troubling portrait of Hankerson.

"The battle behind closed doors now has erupted into Wayne County Circuit Court, Detroit, where records show that bitter struggles over Ms. Knight's business relationship with her background singers and relatives— the Pips—started dissolving the marriage," *Jet* reported in a five-page article that carried no byline. "In his deposition, Hankerson denies beating Ms. Knight, trying to strangle her, shoving her into a closet, and threatening to kill her. . . . He also says he did not try to commit suicide by drinking a household disinfectant."

People are complicated, and divorces are really complicated. In the years after their marriage ended, Hankerson and Knight maintained a relationship that some who knew them called "a deep, real friendship." They shared custody of their son, Shanga Ali Hankerson, saw each other's families, and still appeared together in public. Hankerson even arranged for his ex-wife to meet Kelly's mother, Joann.

In the years after his marriage to Knight ended, Hankerson fared better as an artist's manager and theater producer. In 1987, he brought Ron Milner's gospel musical *Don't Get God Started* to Broadway. The following year, he first heard Kelly sing during auditions for the Chicago production of the show. Kelly claims in his book to have wowed Hankerson with an a cappella rendition of "Amazing Grace." The producer offered him $700 a week to appear in the musical, but Kelly says he told Hankerson he couldn't read or memorize the lines. Instead, he gave Hankerson the demos for several songs, including "If I Could Turn Back the Hands of Time" and "Honey Love," and Hankerson took him on as one of his client artists. Kelly joined a roster led by gospel singers the Winans.

A former colleague of Hankerson's describes part of what he did for Kelly as *Pygmalion* meets Berry Gordy's famous "polishing school" at Motown. "Robert was a big, dumb kid, really immature for his age, and he had a lot of rough edges. I mean, that boy didn't even like to wipe his own ass. Barry worked to smooth them edges out, teach him to carry himself, and not just street, not just ghetto. He wanted to save him, get him to see the quality of life." Hankerson also made connections. "You gotta understand that Barry was extremely hooked up in the black community. *Extremely.* He would come to Chicago and have lunch with Jesse Jackson and dinner with Louis Farrakhan. The man had juice."

Like many people around Kelly, Hankerson could also show flashes of the menacing gangster, and perhaps even act on them. In the mid-2000s, according to lawsuits documented by *Complex* magazine, he bought an ex-girlfriend's hair salon just so he could fire her. She also accused him of trying to blow up her car, charges his lawyers denied. But, one music-industry insider told me, "Barry always had class, and he carried himself more like a politician or a businessman than most of the people around Robert, who could, you know, come off as pretty street."

Recording contract in hand, his crew in place, and Hankerson at the helm, R. Kelly and Public Announcement released *Born into the 90's* on Jive Records in January 1992. Its second single, "Honey Love," reached No. 1 on the Billboard R&B chart, as well as broaching the Top 40 pop chart, if only barely, for two weeks at No. 39. After lurching forward in fits and starts for a decade, at a pace Kelly found excruciatingly slow, the twenty-five-year-old singer and songwriter's career finally started to take flight.

CHAPTER 2

I PROMISE YOU

"Baby, come inside / Now turn down the lights," R. Kelly seductively croons. "'Cause there's something that I want from you right now / Give me that honey love." His first hit is driven by an oozing groove and a lush backing track, and in the video, he literally pours honey over a woman's naked body. The three singers who joined him in Public Announcement—Earl Robinson, Andre Boykins, and Ricky Webster—only appear out of focus, hovering in the background. R. Kelly clearly is the star.

Lacking a truly great voice like Sam Cooke's or Donny Hathaway's, Kelly began to build a reputation through songwriting and crafting memorable images. He talks in every interview about how the songs never stop coming— "I walk around every day with a radio playing constantly in my head," he told Kyle Anderson of *Entertainment Weekly*, "and this radio station plays a lot of hits"—but his output always has evinced as much calculation as inspiration.

"As far back as my first high school performance and my days singing in the subway, my gut told me that I needed a hook," Kelly says in *Soulacoaster*. "Sex and sensuality were going to be my hook." The clean-cut image and messages of MGM became history, and the singer remade himself as a hypersexual "Superfreak," as *Vibe* described him in his first national magazine cover story, as well as the "R&B thug," embracing elements of the street look and attitude he'd scoffed at in the *Chicago Tribune* story about MGM.

"He introduced that hip-hop thing to R&B, that street style, and he knew how to style his vocals that way, too, around the melodies that he wrote," said a record-industry executive who worked with him early on. "Here was this big, strapping guy, not soft at all, with a street image in a natural way, and the direction of his music headed that way, too. *Marketable.*"

Public Announcement toured for much of 1992, even traveling twice to Europe, a challenge because of Kelly's fear of flying. The buzz built, though

Born into the 90's took a year to reach platinum status of a million copies sold, and its sales topped off there. It didn't yield another hit, but Kelly thought he found the key for the follow-up, leaning even more heavily on sex and sensuality. On tour, he developed a skit about a dream of making love to Mary J. Blige, the queen of hip-hop soul. Onstage, he boasted that some men might give her foreplay, but he could deliver three times better; then he enumerated how, in twelve graphic steps. The skit became a song, an album title, and a template.

Leaving Public Announcement behind, the singer took a defiant and aggressive stance on the cover of *12 Play*, the first album credited solely to R. Kelly, and released by Jive Records in November 1993. Open to show off his "ripped" chest, he wears a black vest adorned with random white letters atop baggy black pants. He sports dark shades and a shaven head and brandishes a cane, both a weapon and a Fred Astaire–era prop. His is special, though, and if you don't look closely, you might easily miss the adjustable mirror on a rod at the bottom, intended to look up women's skirts. Novelty stores call it "a dirty-old-man walking stick."

Kelly spent months working on his second album at Chicago Recording Company, which local musicians call CRC. The state-of-the-art studio was spread over three buildings downtown, headquartered on Ohio Street, and top clients paid more than five hundred dollars an hour while the facility catered to their every whim. "They've got a pool table in here and everything for me," Kelly told me with boyish enthusiasm a few years later. He recorded twelve of his raunchiest tracks yet—"Sex Me (Parts I & II)," "Bump N' Grind," and "I Like the Crotch on You"—as well as two sedate soul ballads he could proudly have sung for Lena McLin back at Kenwood Academy. One was an original, "For You." The other was a cover, "Sadie," by the Spinners. It had been one of his mother's favorite songs, and Robert intended it as a tribute to Joann, who died not long before the album's release.

At times, Kelly has claimed he didn't know his mother had cancer, and she banished him from Roseland Hospital when he rushed to her deathbed. "I kept telling her I was sorry, I didn't know," he told Cheo Hodari Coker in *Vibe*. "She begged me to get out, and I did." He said he returned to CRC and sat at the piano, and the call that Joann had died came while he sang "For

You." He repeated this version in *Soulacoaster*, with added detail, but when Kelly talked to Chris Heath of *GQ* years later, he gave a different account.

In that version, Kelly says that when he returned from his second European tour, he immediately joined his mother in the hospital. "She said, 'Please leave, please,'" but he claimed he stayed to bare his soul. "I said, 'First of all, I love you, and I thank you for everything you have done, everything . . . and I'm sorry for every time I've been bad or did something I wasn't supposed to do. And I promise you'—and she died right there on the 'I promise you.' I called the doctor, they came in and they pronounced her dead. I was still holding her hand. But I finished my sentence. I said, 'I promise you, Momma, no matter what, by any means necessary, I will be one of the best singers, songwriters, this world has ever seen.'"

Few people forget the details of their mother's death, and the discrepancies in Kelly's stories bothered journalist Chris Heath. "A good deal of how we come away thinking of R. Kelly must hang on what we think of R. Kelly's relationship with the truth. . . . To not believe him would mean that he is now lying about what happened at his mother's deathbed. And that he is doubling down on the lie to my face." Like many others, Heath wanted to believe. Such is the power of myth.

Several sources told me that once his career began to take off, Kelly actually shunned the mother he claims he worshipped. "Robert cut her off," his half brother Carey said, because Robert didn't approve of Joann's relationship with Lucious. When Kelly got his first big check as an advance from Jive, his crew shamed him for buying himself a new black Mercedes while Joann continued to drive a beater, "a raggedy old Ford" that she had to hot-wire to start. "I should have known there was something wrong," a friend of the family told me. "He was very reluctant to share anything with her. He refused to deal with her medical bills—she checked into the hospital under a false name—although he had the money. I think he was angry with everybody for not protecting him from the abuse, to the point that he got started at the abuse himself. It sparked up something in him."

12 Play left some in the music press cold. "In a year when the big rappers have either repeated tired outrages or outgrown them, Kelly's crude, chartwise new jack swing is black pop's most depressing development," wrote the self-professed dean of American music critics, Robert Christgau. Nevertheless, the album sold more than six million copies in the United States, garnering three Top 20 pop hits with "Bump N' Grind," which made it to No. 1, "Your Body's Callin'," and "Sex Me (Parts I & II)." On the R&B chart, "Bump N' Grind" elbowed aside Whitney Houston's "I Will Always Love You" to claim the top slot. Not surprisingly, its auteur became a sought-after songwriter and producer for other artists, including Hi-Five, Billy Ocean, Toni Braxton, Janet Jackson—and a promising high school student from Detroit named Aaliyah.

Aaliyah Dana Haughton was born in Brooklyn on January 16, 1979, according to her birth certificate. Diane and Michael Haughton chose their second child's name from Jewish and Arabic roots meaning "rising up" or "ascending." She attended Gesu Catholic School in Detroit, where the family resettled so Michael could work in a warehouse owned by Diane's brother, Barry Hankerson. After Aaliyah started singing in church, her proud stage parents paid for years of vocal lessons. She went on to maintain a 4.0 grade-point average at the Detroit High School for the Fine and Performing Arts, focusing on drama, not music. Barely five-foot-one, light-skinned with thick, flowing black hair and hypnotic brown eyes, she always made as much of an impact onstage with her charismatic presence as her vocal abilities.

Host Ed McMahon introduced Aaliyah as a girl with "a big voice and an even bigger dream" when she appeared on the television show *Star Search* at age ten. Looking like a young Whitney Houston in a ruffled pink skirt and jacket with enormous shoulder pads, she confidently sang "My Funny Valentine," building to some vocal flourishes a la Houston or Céline Dion. The next year, at age eleven, she joined her ex-aunt, Gladys Knight, onstage during a five-night stint at Bally's Las Vegas Hotel. Talking to *People* magazine years later, Knight remembered Aaliyah as "brought up in the old school, a sweet, sweet girl. She would walk into a room, and you would feel her light. She'd hug everyone, and she meant it."

At age fourteen, Aaliyah became the first artist signed to Blackground Records, the boutique label her uncle Barry Hankerson started with Jive in 1993. Hankerson introduced the niece he called "the light of my life" to his star client, and she began recording the debut album R. Kelly wrote, produced, and titled for her. Shy and timid by some accounts, Aaliyah was considered "wise beyond her years" and "old for her age" by many people. Released in May 1994, five months after her fifteenth birthday, the cover of *Age Ain't Nothing but a Number* depicts a different girl from the one seen on *Star Search*. Doing her best to look street, Aaliyah poses in a hoodie, leaning against a wall and wearing dark sunglasses under a black skull cap. In the background, the twenty-seven-year-old she thanks in the liner notes as her "mentor, best friend, and producer" peers at her from behind his own dark shades, shirtless and wearing a vest like the one on the cover of *12 Play*.

Kelly and Aaliyah appeared on BET's *Video Soul Gold* in the summer of 1994, dressed in identical hip-hop streetwear. Co-host Sherry Carter started by saying, "Everybody seems to think that y'all are either girlfriend or boyfriend or cousins." Kelly laughed. "I better go get me a white Jeep, uh-oh," he said, presumably referring to the white Bronco O. J. Simpson had recently driven while fleeing police. "Well, no," Aaliyah said. "We're not related at all. No, we're not. We're just very close. He's my best friend." With that, she playfully tapped his arm. "In the whole wide world," Kelly said, completing her thought. Through a wide grin, Aaliyah echoed him in childlike singsong. "In the whole wide world."

The other host, Brett Walker, later asked about the origin of Aaliyah's album title. "She's running around the studio one day with her friends, talking a lot of smack," Kelly said. Aaliyah hung with a posse of three girlfriends everyone called Second Chapter. " 'Tell her age ain't nothing but a number, girl,' " Kelly recalled her telling one of her friends. "I was like, 'So what you trying to say?' So immediately I heard the song, you know, and I called her back fifteen minutes later, told her check this out, and we cut the track right then and there."

Many on the music scene believed Aaliyah was older than the fifteen stated in her record-company bio, so Carter asked, "And for the record you are how old?" Aaliyah smiled, held her finger to her lips, and playfully whispered, "That's a secret. Shhh!"

Kelly's growing Midas touch held as Aaliyah's debut sold two million copies, spawning two Top 10 singles with "Back & Forth" and "At Your Best

(You Are Love)." Six months later, in December 1994, Danyel Smith's cover story on Kelly the "Superfreak" hit the newsstands in *Vibe*, noting for the first time in the national press a rumor about him and Aaliyah. Visiting a black beauty salon at Philadelphia's fading Gallery Mall, Smith described a group of women "discussing R. Kelly because he's headlining at the Spectrum tonight and because, word is, he just married his teenage protégée, Aaliyah. Like the jocks on the radio in New York, Philly, Oakland, and L.A., folks are yammering about Kelly's marriage, making comparisons to Marvin Gaye and Jerry Lee Lewis, joking about jailbait and robbing the cradle."

The illustrations in the four-page magazine spread included a Cook County marriage certificate for Robert S. Kelly and Aaliyah D. Haughton, citing a "religious ceremony" in suburban Rosemont near Chicago's O'Hare Airport on August 31, 1994. It accurately noted Kelly's age, twenty-seven, but listed Aaliyah's as eighteen. Kelly, Aaliyah, and their label reps all declined to comment.

Kelly pulled out of an interview with *Vibe* at the last minute, but Danyel Smith sat in his dressing room backstage at the Spectrum as he nonetheless posed for the photo shoot. Road manager Demetrius Smith warned her not to take notes or ask questions, but two female fans in their early twenties walked in and asked not only about the alleged marriage but about rumors Aaliyah was pregnant. "Don't believe everything you read," Kelly said.

The singer repeated that line often in years to come, whenever he didn't completely avoid the subject of Aaliyah. She is never mentioned in *Soulacoaster*. "In telling my story, certain episodes could not be included for complicated reasons," reads an author's note.

I interviewed Aaliyah by phone for the *Chicago Sun-Times* a week after the publication of the *Vibe* article. My story previewed a Chicago concert supporting her debut album, opening at the UIC Pavilion for Keith Sweat, Silk, and Blackstreet on New Year's Eve, 1994. Smart and sassy in a self-assured but playful way, she told me the phrase that seemed to precede her name in every article didn't bother her. "It's always Aaliyah and R. Kelly, R. Kelly and Aaliyah, but I don't mind being called his protégé, because that's what I am."

Before that interview, I called Cook County Clerk David Orr, and he confirmed that the marriage certificate in *Vibe* was authentic. The officiant it named refused to comment about R. Kelly. "I'm not going to say anything," the Rev. Nathan J. Edmond told me. "If you want to know anything about him, you can ask him."

When we talked, Aaliyah said she had seen the document in *Vibe*, but she didn't have much to say about it. "I saw it, but I don't really comment on that, because I know that's not true. When people ask me, I tell them, 'Hey, don't believe all that mess. We're close and people took it the wrong way.' We're really cool friends. We've known each other for four years, but it's a friendship, and it will continue to be a friendship."

R&B stars' female protégés tend to have short-lived careers, I told Aaliyah. Witness the Mary Jane Girls produced by Rick James, or Vanity 6 produced by Prince. She giggled. "Of course, there's a connection with me and Robert, because he did write the whole album, but as far as the second album, he probably will do some songs, but it won't be a whole project. I do see myself becoming my own artist. If you know your own style and you're sure of yourself, you can definitely overcome the protégé thing."

I made one other call for that story, to Wayne Williams, the Chicago-based A&R rep at Jive for both stars. "I'll tell you this, they ain't married," he said. "You don't see no ring on her finger, right? As far as all that other stuff, I'm sure that's just media hype. Robert has reached a level now where he's going to get a lot of rumors. The more successful he is, the wilder they'll get. I know Robert and Michael Jackson were talking about this. Things get crazy, and they get out of hand after a certain point."

From beginnings even more humble than Kelly's—Jackson and his eight siblings grew up in a 672-square-foot ranch house in Gary, Indiana, thirty miles southeast of Kelly's childhood homes on the South Side—Jackson had become a worldwide superstar, the self-proclaimed King of Pop. While soliciting songs for the album that became *HIStory: Past, Present and Future, Book I*, his managers gave him the demo for a song by Kelly called "You Are Not Alone." Jackson liked it so much, he flew to Chicago to record with Kelly at CRC in November 1994. As much as he longed to work with the King of

Pop, Kelly had come to fear flying to the extent that he didn't want to travel to record at Jackson's Neverland Valley Ranch in Los Olivos, California. The trip testified both to Jackson's fading star and Kelly's ascendant one.

In the summer of 1993, a dentist named Evan Chandler said his thirteen-year-old son Jordan had been sexually abused by Jackson. The star's camp filed suit, claiming a shakedown by the boy's father. In January 1994, prosecutors announced they would not bring extortion charges against Evan Chandler. At the same time, Jackson paid the family a sum of about $25 million; he later claimed his lawyers made the settlement without his consent. Grand jury investigations in Santa Barbara County and Los Angeles continued for several months but ended without the star's indictment.

Released in August 1995, "You Are Not Alone" became Jackson's first No. 1 hit after the child-sex scandal, and the last of thirteen during a solo career that started in 1972 with "Ben." His love song to a rat is only marginally less saccharine than "You Are Not Alone," a leaden ballad. "Another day has gone / I'm still all alone," Jackson sings in the opening, before Kelly joins him on backing vocals a few lines later. "Did you have to go / And leave my world so cold?"

I met Kelly in person once, in January 1995, during an early-morning press conference the Chicago chapter of the National Academy of Recording Arts and Sciences held at a Loop hotel. It took place as nominations for the 1994 Grammy Awards were simultaneously announced in New York, Los Angeles, and Nashville. Given *12 Play*'s phenomenal success, local NARAS members were certain it would garner several nods, and they invited Kelly to the event. They were wrong, and Kelly was shut out.

I approached the singer after the list had been read, while he sat hulking in a chair against a wall, legs splayed wide. Surrounded by handlers, he hid behind his omnipresent shades. We shook hands, and I asked a few dumb questions—Given your success, do prizes even matter?—which prompted only grunts in reply. He seemed pissed-off about being dragged to a stupid press event for nothing. I did not push my luck by asking about Aaliyah.

We talked at length for the only time eight months later, as "You Are Not Alone" sat atop the charts. With a sensibility almost entirely shaped by *USA Today* and the *Today* show, a new editor at the *Sun-Times* couldn't get enough stories about Michael Jackson in the paper, though she always chided me for noting the Jordan Chandler sex scandal, because "it only upsets the readers." My colleague Dave Hoekstra covered Kelly during my first stint at the paper. Hoekstra loved old-school soul and R&B, and that first interview he did with Kelly focused a lot on their mutual appreciation for Donny Hathaway. Since Jackson wasn't talking to anyone, I reached out to Kelly to discuss "You Are Not Alone," but the conversation also touched on the new music he was recording nonstop at CRC, interrupted only by trips to McDonald's or rides in his Mercedes along Lake Shore Drive or on I-94 to the Six Flags Great America amusement park in Gurnee.

The story ran in September 1995, shortly after I left the paper for the first time to become deputy music editor at *Rolling Stone* in New York, and three months before the less imaginatively titled *R. Kelly* album appeared in stores. The Jive publicist who connected us for the phoner warned me not to ask Kelly about Aaliyah, but the singer seemed willing to talk about anything, and he brought up the controversy, albeit obliquely.

"I came up with 'You Are Not Alone' because I was going through some emotional things in my life. I've experienced some shit, maybe not on Michael's level, but on my own level. And you've got to think, 'If I was a nobody, and nobody knew me, nobody could talk about me.'" Kelly compared working with Jackson to playing with Chicago's championship NBA basketball team. "It's like playing with the Bulls; I could sit on the bench and pass out water, and after that I could die. I'm not holding him up, but I feel Michael is special, because despite these things he's going through, he's still trying to get his message across. If you want to get a message across, Michael is the perfect man for the job. I heard they're playing 'You Are Not Alone' in places that don't even exist."

I asked about criticism of the misogyny in Kelly's music, noting that the *Village Voice* had recently said his songs had "the sensitivity of a porno loop." He laughed. "I just do my best and pray to God that people connect with it and try to remember what my mother told me: 'What comes from the heart, touches the heart.' I really love Marvin Gaye, and his albums were pretty sexual. I've read things in old magazines where people had things to say about him, but people are forgetting there's an artist, there's a creative situation, not just this freak. You've got to ask yourself, how can this same guy turn around and write 'You Are Not Alone'?"

As we were wrapping up, Kelly told me he'd enjoyed our conversation, and he wanted to add one more thing. "This is called show business. What I do in my music is what I feel, not necessarily how I am. I don't walk around with my pants down all day saying, 'Gimme a girl!' People need to not judge what they see on the TV. Nobody knows Robert or what he's been through. Not R. Kelly, but Robert. R. Kelly is a thing on TV."

CHAPTER 3

THERE ARE LOTS OF PEOPLE WHO KNOW ABOUT THIS

The Monday after Thanksgiving, 2000, I made a special trip back to the *Sun-Times* offices to take another look at the fax. A few things had bothered me about it over the long holiday weekend, and I cursed myself for not bringing it home. "Robert's problem . . . is young girls." Anyone could have written that, but the letter included a lot of specifics, unusual for mere gossip or rumor, and one passage especially stuck with me: "I'm telling you about it hoping that you or someone at your newspaper will write an article and then Robert will have no choice but to get help and stop hurting the people he's hurting."

I didn't think a random "hater," as his supporters later said, would show that kind of compassion. "If you are not the right person at the newspaper to deal with this, I apologize for bothering you and ask you to pass this letter along to whoever is."

I made a photocopy of the fax and highlighted accusations that jumped out: "A lawsuit was filed by a young girl named Tiffany Hawkins in 1997. . . . Robert's managers and lawyers kept it all quiet, and Robert paid her $250,000 to drop the suit. Since then, there's been five or six young girls like Tiffany." It seemed unlikely the media never reported a lawsuit filed three years earlier against a major star, but that could be checked. (The writer claimed to be sending the letter "along with the first few pages" of the lawsuit, but nothing else had come through. Pages often went astray at the *Sun-Times* fax machines.)

"Right now, he's messing with a thirteen-year-old girl who he tells people is his goddaughter," the fax continued. "This one has been going on for more than two years now, and her parents are turning a blind eye because Robert hired her father, who is a bass player. It makes me sick, which is why I'm sending this to you. The Chicago Police have investigated him, but they never been able to prove anything."

I dug *TP-2.com* out of the bottom right-hand drawer of my desk, where CDs piled up until I took them home and stacked them in more piles there. The credits listed two musicians who contributed guitar and bass, one of them Greg Landfair, and right under "Special thanks to Jaya, Joann, and Drea," who I later learned were Kelly's two children and his wife, came "my goddaughter Reshona, Greg, and Valerie."

"There are lots of people who know about this," the fax said, "but most of them are on Robert's payroll, so they would just deny it all. But you could call Susan Loggins, the lawyer who filed Tiffany's suit." A number followed. I pulled out the Yellow Pages and found a sizable ad for Susan E. Loggans & Associates, Personal Injury Attorneys, same number, different spelling. "Or you could call Robert's brother, Kerry." The liner notes thanked Kelly's half brothers, Bruce and Carey, and his half sister, Theresa, none of whom were names I knew then. "Or you could call Robert's old manager, Barry Hankerson."

That name rang a bell from the Aaliyah controversy, which the letter also mentioned—"The gossip wasn't all wrong"—but I'd never seen Hankerson quoted about whatever happened between his niece and Kelly. "Or you could call Sgt. Chuziki of the Chicago Police. She's the one who was in charge of investigating Robert."

If someone made up a name, I didn't think they'd make up such an odd Polish cop name. I called the main switchboard at CPD and asked for Sergeant Chuziki. The operator couldn't find a listing, and I almost hung up before wondering aloud if any investigator with a similar name worked in sex crimes. The operator groaned and scrolled through what I assumed was a long list of names before connecting me to someone. When a woman picked up—"Chiczewski, Special Investigations"—I introduced myself as a reporter from the *Sun-Times* inquiring about the investigation into R. Kelly. "Oh, I was wondering how long it would take before somebody called about that. I can't talk to you," she said, and hung up.

Fax in hand, I walked across the third floor into the city editor's glass-walled office and told him I might have a story. An unreasonably calm, measured, and paternal presence in the often-chaotic newsroom, Don Hayner had gone to John Marshall Law School in Chicago before the much less lucrative calling of journalism beckoned. He read the letter slowly and carefully—he always read everything slowly and carefully—and agreed. Then I got to work.

How did I get here, a pop music critic assigned to investigate a potentially explosive set of allegations about a hometown hero and one of the biggest names in popular music? At any daily newspaper, critics are first and foremost reporters. If the star tenor had a heart attack onstage midway through the opera, my colleague Wynne Delacoma on the classical music beat would not have written the lede "The performance was lacking last night." Confronted with breaking news, the critic instantly sets opinion aside and as much as possible becomes an objective reporter. Like most journalists, the anonymous letter from someone tipping me to a big story wasn't an anomaly, and I'd had one earlier in my career that led me to another complicated and troubling investigation.

In 1989, I was twenty-five years old and writing a column called Hudson Beat for the *Jersey Journal* when a prisoner in the dangerously overcrowded Hudson County Jail in Jersey City sent me an anonymous letter describing conditions that sounded barbaric, and which he said needed to be exposed. Two broken toilets for every sixty prisoners; piles of garbage and puddles of excrement and vomit left for days; the stench of sweat, urine, and body odor in stifling heat with no ventilation. Built in 1929 to house 280 inmates, the facility held more than 700 at the time, and two prisoners had recently committed suicide. The first column I wrote about the jail prompted more letters and phone calls from other prisoners and their families, as well as whistle-blowers appalled by the county's neglect.

"Why should we care about the scum locked up in there?" one reader wrote in response. County statistics showed that 91 percent of the jail's population was black or Latinx. The majority were male, but two floors also housed female prisoners, quite a few of them pregnant. The reader's question sickened and infuriated me.

I asked Hudson County officials if I could spend twenty-four hours at the jail, something I'd done at a homeless shelter in Hoboken, but the warden vetoed the request. Instead, after showing me an array of ingenious confiscated weaponry, including a toothbrush with a razor blade attached by a strip of adhesive bandage, and a ballpoint pen methodically sharpened into a shiv, he reluctantly granted a two-hour tour. Prisoners spat at, cursed, and insulted me, and I had to dodge plastic cups of urine and feces flung my way. The guard escorting me laughed. "See what we deal with?"

After six columns about the jail, I got a call from the city desk at home in Hoboken one night in December 1989 about some kind of disturbance at the facility, and I rushed to Pavonia Avenue in Jersey City. I worked the crowd for an hour, corralling every cop, fireman, and EMT who'd spare me a second, trying to figure out what was going on inside. I eventually learned that sixty-two prisoners had rushed the guards in the third-floor gymnasium, which served as a makeshift dormitory. Unable to make their way down toward freedom, they ran upstairs and occupied the eighth-floor infirmary. I could hear them yelling and banging on metal pipes from the street, and they occasionally threw burning towels out the barred windows. Then I heard the shot.

I later learned that what prisoners considered a protest (but the warden called a riot) started when jailers delivered a court order allowing a twenty-eight-year-old inmate to attend his mother's funeral, seven hours after the service ended. Preparing for what they called the "Goon Squad," which they knew would rush in with batons swinging, the prisoners wrapped themselves ankles to eyeballs in thin mattresses. According to protocol, the rapid response team should have been armed only with nightsticks and shotguns loaded with "beanbag" rounds; filled with steel pellets, these could knock someone off their feet without killing them. Somehow, one of the guards in the flying wedge of twelve who ran up the stairs three hours after the incident started grabbed a live round. He fired from a distance of six feet at the first prisoner he encountered, aiming at the only part of the man's body left exposed. The inmate's head exploded in a cloud of red gore, just like a scene from the David Cronenberg film *Scanners*, one of the Goon Squad told me.

I ran back to the newsroom to work on the story, and only in the week that followed did I pause to wonder whether the victim had been one of the anonymous sources who'd called or written me. I later felt as if all my reporting hadn't accomplished a thing—the county prosecutor never filed any charges for the disturbance—but six years later, in 1995, the old jail finally closed and demolition began after a new facility opened in Kearny.

I hadn't set out to be a hard-news or investigative reporter. My twin passions were music and writing, and I hoped to combine them, but few journalists start work on the beat they dream of covering. A reporter may aspire to become a foreign correspondent or a member of the White House press corps, but she'll be lucky to begin by reporting about the local sewage authority or school board.

My mother always encouraged my interests. A voracious reader, she instilled the love of writing, but she never shared my obsession with music. She only whistled "Volare" when she cooked or did the laundry. My father worked as an underwriter for the Prudential Insurance Company in Newark until one night in November 1969, when he died from a heart attack in the sixty-nine-year-old wood-frame fixer-upper he and my mom had only recently purchased in Jersey City Heights, just across the Hudson River from Manhattan but part of a different universe. I was five, and my brother was two and a half. Mom sent us to Catholic grammar school at the local parish, Saint Nicholas, scraping by on the Social Security death benefit, payments from my dad's prescient comprehensive coverage, and government cheese.

I discovered music via the small collection of LPs my dad left behind in a wire rack beside the old console stereo, cast recordings from the Broadway musicals *Camelot* and *Oliver!*, *Whipped Cream & Other Delights* by Herb Alpert's Tijuana Brass, and *Hell Bent for Leather!* by Frankie Laine. The first record I bought with money I saved from serving as an altar boy (funerals paid five dollars, but you could earn as much as twenty at a wedding) was *The Beatles/1967–1970*, the greatest-hits collection known to fans as "the Blue Album." My tastes progressed from there thanks to New York radio and records passed down by my older cousins. By high school, I held progressive rockers like Yes, Genesis, and Pink Floyd and punk bands such as the Ramones, the Clash, and the Sex Pistols in equal esteem. Some might say those genres are diametrically opposed, but attempts at transcendence and cathartic venting both seemed like valid responses to life in Jersey City.

In college, New York's nascent hip-hop sounds led me back to R&B, soul, and funk. The first time I heard *Maggot Brain* by Funkadelic blew my young, white, nerdy mind, and though I suspected I wouldn't quite fit in, I wanted to go to *that* party. I had similar reactions to *White Light/White Heat* by the Velvet Underground and *Pink Flag* by Wire. Public Enemy; X-Ray Spex; the Feelies; Hüsker Dü; the Replacements; De La Soul; Patti Smith. The common theme of all the music I devoured, internalized, and loved was, as Robert Christgau wrote of Parliament-Funkadelic, "the forces of life—autonomous intelligence, a childlike openness, sexual energy, and humor—defeat those of death." Hey-ho, let's go!

As essential to me as the music for revealing a bigger, more exciting, and more open-minded world beyond the Heights was the writing that mapped it and put it in context. By seventh grade, the *Village Voice* had become my Bible, thanks to the cutting insights of its music editor, Christgau, and the unbridled passion of his most acclaimed writer, Lester Bangs. But I never just read the alternative weekly's music pages. Media critic Geoffrey Stokes, feminist sex columnist Cynthia Heimel, and investigative reporters William Bastone, Wayne Barrett, and Debbie Nathan inspired me, too, and so did the writers Tom Wolfe compiled in his 1973 anthology, *The New Journalism*. I bought a used copy at the Strand bookstore to read Christgau's piece, and in the bargain discovered Joan Didion, Michael Herr, George Plimpton, Gay Talese, and Wolfe's manifesto that journalism can be literature, but even more powerful, because it is, he said, "true-life."

My Spider-Man moment came on April 14, 1982, toward the end of my senior year at Hudson Catholic Regional School for Boys. The honors students read masterpieces of Western literature, while the wrestlers and football players wound up in journalism. Short sentences, simple words. I took both. I grated on my high school journalism teacher's nerves with never-ending questions about the New Journalism, the difference between criticism and journalism, and investigative reporting in the wake of Woodward and Bernstein and *Rolling Stone*'s exposé about the suspicious death of anti-nuke activist Karen Silkwood. "Look, you've already got your A," he finally said. "You don't have to come to class anymore. Just go interview a hero in your chosen field and write it up."

I picked Lester.

I spent a long afternoon with Bangs in his fifth-floor apartment above Gum Joy Chinese Restaurant, just off Fourteenth Street at the edge of the Village near the Sixth Avenue PATH station. He kept swatting aside the questions I'd scrawled earlier on a yellow legal pad in favor of having a real discussion, asking what I thought, who I was reading, and what I was listening to. I was a fat, nerdy seventeen-year-old with acne from Jersey, and he was America's greatest rock critic. When I left Lester that day in 1982, he signed my copy of his book about Blondie, one of the two quickie fan bios he published in his lifetime. "Now it's your turn." He died two weeks later.

I got to attend New York University on a scholarship, and I majored in journalism and minored in sociology because they seemed like the same thing—the study of people. In my junior year in college, I began writing a music column for the *Hoboken Reporter*. After a few months, the publisher, who'd started a chain of free weeklies in Hudson County to forward his agenda as a real-estate developer, deemed the ungodly sum of $150 a month for music coverage unwarranted. He assigned me to start reporting on city council and planning board meetings, too.

By the start of my last year at NYU, I'd been hired full-time by the 65,000-circulation *Jersey Journal*, covering news stories two nights a week after classes, and writing wedding and church-social announcements the other three days for what were, in 1986, unapologetically still called "the Women's Pages."

The stories never stopped coming during my five years at the paper, first as a reporter covering the Hoboken beat, then digging into county-wide waterfront development. I did a miserable stint as assistant city editor—I hated being stuck in the newsroom, and I missed writing—and finally wound up as a columnist aspiring to some measure of what Jimmy Breslin, Murray Kempton, and Anna Quindlen did across the river. Through it all, I also wrote about music for free for fanzines, photocopied do-it-yourself magazines distributed at rock clubs and record stores such as Maxwell's and Pier Platters in Hoboken. I published my own zine, too, calling it *Reasons for Living*, because that's what music provided. I was nothing if not an earnest young thing.

Like Lester, I saw collecting records, spinning them on college radio, spouting my opinions about them, and making an awful racket myself all as part of the same fanatic impulse. I've always joked that I'm not a musician, but I am a drummer (ba-dum-*bah!*). When I was in my early teens my mom remarried, wedding my former eighth-grade science teacher at Saint Nick's, and my stepfather, Harry Reynolds, gave me the old set of Slingerland drums he'd used to gig in go-go bars up and down the Jersey Shore. I learned to play by bashing along to Ramones records in the basement, and I kept drumming in a series of bands not because I thought any of them would "make it," but because I couldn't imagine *not* doing it. In 1987, my Wire cover band, the Ex-Lion Tamers, opened for Wire itself on a month-long tour of the United States and Canada. During my eighties indie-rock version of *On the Road*, I realized that college friends in cities like Portland, Seattle, Minneapolis, and Montreal all lived better than me. They worked fifteen hours a week running copy machines or making lattes to pay their share of the rent in a big old band house, then devoted the rest of their time to drawing comics, making films, painting or sculpting, and rehearsing in the basement.

Burned out at the *Jersey Journal* after one too many trips to the projects to interview a mother whose son had been shot in the street, I quit, packed what fit in a rented U-Haul trailer—the vinyl albums and drums took priority— and moved to Minneapolis to manage a friend's band and try to make a go of it writing about music.

As luck would have it, I landed a job as assistant editor at a magazine called *Request*, with a free circulation of a million copies monthly at every Musicland and Sam Goody record store in the country. After nearly a decade, I finally got a paycheck for covering my dream beat, and *Request* became my graduate school. That led to my first stint at the *Sun-Times*, from 1992 to 1995, when Chicago enjoyed a brief moment as "the next Seattle" during the alternative-rock explosion, and then to *Rolling Stone*, the big leagues at last—or so I thought. I got canned after eight and a half months for shooting my mouth off when publisher Jann Wenner spiked my negative review of *Fairweather Johnson*, the second album by Hootie & the Blowfish. I wound up back in Minneapolis, freelancing for two years and starting work on a biography of Bangs, until the *Sun-Times* asked in the fall of 1997 if I'd like to return as its pop music critic.

I had never loved any city as much as Chicago. I enjoyed living in Minneapolis, twice, but it truly is a small town, and one where some restaurants at the time thought egg noodles and ketchup were "pasta." By age twenty-two, I'd visited twenty other North American cities on tour with the Ex-Lion Tamers, and eight European burgs when I served as the road manager for a friend's band, but Chicago was special.

Yeah, the racism and segregation in Chicago suck; those suck in New York and Jersey City, Berlin and Paris, too. But Chicago has all the art, energy, and excitement of New York, at a fraction of the cost and aggravation. The cliché about "the city that works" is true, especially in the arts. You can open a gallery or a storefront theater in Chicago, start a restaurant, join an improv troupe, and most of all make music—it's hard to be a garage band in Manhattan, where garages are scarce and absurdly expensive—and you can learn your craft and find a following, or fail with relatively few consequences, then pick yourself up and start again. Residents in the city of Studs Terkel and Nelson Algren, Ethel Payne and Sandra Cisneros, Gene Siskel and Roger Ebert are real people who sneer at pretensions and "people who think who they are." Yet Chicagoans can still talk for hours until last call about politics, philosophy, art, religion, social justice, *and* the forlorn Cubs. The only thing I find lacking is the pizza. There and only there, I'm still New York all the way.

The *Sun-Times* editor I'd clashed with over covering Michael Jackson without mentioning that unpleasantness about sex with boys had left, and a crew of Canadians had taken over, appointed by a new British owner, Lord Conrad Black of Crossharbour. I told the editors who interviewed me that all I wanted in order to return was the deal Ebert had. They rolled their eyes, until I explained I didn't mean money; I'd just like to work at home. And mostly I did for the next thirteen years, except for the weekly visits to pick up the mail and meet with the bosses.

Through the mid-nineties, I continued to follow R. Kelly's burgeoning career with the pride of a hometown journalist and critic who'd been there almost at the start, as well as, I'll admit it, a fan, albeit one with reservations.

Jive Records released the singer's third album, *R. Kelly*, in November 1995, and it sold five million copies. I reviewed it for *Rolling Stone*, giving it three stars on the magazine's five-star scale and summing up his output to date. The knock on his first two solo albums had been that Kelly was a soul man with no real soul, I wrote, just another hot 'n' horny would-be Lothario using his silky-smooth grooves to lure the honeys to his water bed. Coming on the heels of "You Are Not Alone," I found the new album's tonal shifts jarring, but I thought of them as a meta-commentary about the differences between R. the persona and Robert the person. He shamelessly boasted about his success—"Even the Statue of Liberty wants to bump and grind"—but also humbly thanked the Lord. He alternated between the profane and the sacred. "You remind me of my Jeep, I wanna ride it," he sang. "Girl, you look just like my car, I want to wax it." But he could have delivered the spiritual ballads "Religious Love" and "Heaven If You Hear Me" at any church service.

I didn't quite know what to make of "Down Low (Nobody Has to Know)," and I still don't. Despite the title—which became better known as slang for sex between an ostensibly straight man and another man—Kelly's song is an account of sleeping with another man's wife and urging her to keep it a secret. It's just plain weird, especially when the husband, voiced by Ronald Isley, croons in his celebrated falsetto, "How could you go so low?" But I concluded that Kelly had evolved, reaching out to "brothers in the ghetto" in "As I Look into My Life" to follow his example to "love and respect that woman and bring her happiness."

That review would not age well.

In the months that followed the *R. Kelly* album, the singer talked a lot in interviews about finding God. In the spring of 1997, he joined rising gospel star Kirk Franklin onstage in Chicago to announce that he'd been saved. "It amazes me when I look back eight months ago—cars, women, money, the media, I had everyone's attention," Kelly said. "Some may think it's a gimmick, but I tell you, here stands a broken man. Every day I seem to be falling in love with the Lord. . . . I used to be flying in sin. Now, I'm flying in Jesus." Then he sang "I Believe I Can Fly."

Lou Carlozo of the *Chicago Tribune* reported that Franklin, a nondenominational minister from Fort Worth, Texas, helped Kelly find his way to Jesus. Franklin had also counseled Mike Tyson and Tupac Shakur. There was talking of Kelly doing a gospel album.

In November 1998, Kelly's fourth release for Jive significantly expanded his reach from R&B into hip-hop, as well as into mainstream pop. The ambitious double album *R.* sold more than eight million copies, thanks to collaborations with rappers Foxy Brown, Nas, and Jay-Z, as well as an unlikely duet with Céline Dion on "I'm Your Angel," which reached No. 1 on the pop chart. The album also boasted one of Kelly's biggest hits, "I Believe I Can Fly," which first appeared on the soundtrack to *Space Jam* in 1996, and which promptly became a staple at graduation ceremonies and proms. Dave Hoekstra wrote about the song and the film for the *Sun-Times.* Kelly met Michael Jordan on the basketball court at the Athletic Club on the North Side, Hoekstra reported, and their managers worked out the deal for the singer to contribute to the soundtrack of the movie, in which Jordan costarred with Bugs Bunny and the rest of the Looney Tunes crew.

"'I Believe I Can Fly' is the way I think I play," Jordan told Hoekstra. Kelly added that he screened a videotape of the movie several times in his home theater, and that inspired him to write the song. "I loved it. I studied it, and I prayed over it, because I wanted the best thing to come out of it. The film has a lot to do with encouraging kids and making them laugh and smile. That's important to me."

When I returned to the *Sun-Times,* I took over the Kelly beat from Hoekstra, who'd tired of writing about music, preferring more esoteric features and travel stories. In May 1999, I reviewed the first of the singer's two shows supporting *R.* at the United Center. Even at seventy-five dollars apiece, more than double the national average for a concert ticket that year, both Chicago gigs sold out. Fronting a twelve-piece band, Kelly crooned, "I feel like feeling what I feel like feeling right now." The giant video screens showed a woman's hand groping several inches below his big belt buckle, which read "Champ." Pop crossovers and gospel sermons weren't on the set list that night, and the show ended with Kelly pulling a woman from the crowd. He convinced her to strip down to her panties and bra, lured her into a giant red bed, and removed his own clothes. They disappeared beneath the silky sheets, and the stage went dark. There was no encore.

I next wrote about Kelly a little less than a year and a half later, when I reviewed his fifth album, *TP-2.com*. That prompted the fax, and my return to investigative journalism.

CHAPTER 4

SCHOOL AIN'T GONNA MAKE YOU A MILLIONAIRE

"You make some calls to the people mentioned in the fax," *Sun-Times* city editor Don Hayner told me, "and I'll have Abdon Pallasch check Cook County Circuit Court to see if a lawsuit was ever filed. Let's start there." Before Hayner paired us to look into the allegations in the anonymous letter about R. Kelly, I'd only shared the occasional collegial head-nod with Abdon on the battered old escalators leading from the lobby to the third-floor newsroom. A perpetually boyish Irish-Polish leprechaun (he does not object to that description, I should note), Abdon stood out at the *Sun-Times* because he wore suits and ties to work every day, all of them purchased at Irv's discount men's warehouse. "I learned that if I dressed like a lawyer, I could walk past the court clerks into the judges' chambers. It also helped me look like an adult so people would take me seriously."

Two years younger than me, Abdon had taken a path to 401 North Wabash that was just as circuitous as mine. After he earned an undergrad degree in Ireland, he attended Northwestern University's Medill School of Journalism, then did a one-year residency at the larger of Chicago's two daily newspapers, the broadsheet across Michigan Avenue that catered to professionals on the North Side and monied suburban readers. He now scoffed at what he called "*Tribune* arrogance." Abdon spent time as a crime reporter at the independent City News Bureau; traveled to Nicaragua to cover elections for UPI; returned to report on the local legal world for *Chicago Lawyer*; and finally landed at the city-centric, working-class tabloid *Sun-Times*. Whenever he wasn't sitting in state or federal court, he could be found working the phones in the newsroom, one of its aces, at a desk piled high with stacks of legal papers that often spilled onto the floor.

Abdon grew up as a Catholic-school kid with four sisters on Chicago's Northwest Side, and he eventually had five children of his own, including an eldest son living in Ireland. When we started working together, he could sing the first two bars of "I Believe I Can Fly"—"I must have watched that damn movie with my son five hundred times"—but he confessed utter ignorance about the rest of Kelly's catalog, as well as most soul, hip-hop, and R&B. "Who is Curtis Mayfield?" he once asked me. His tastes began and ended with Irish folk-rock, and he knew little about pop culture, as well as some things I assumed anyone would know by age thirty-six. When I included a line in a story about Kelly lewdly singing, "Girl, I'm ready to toss your salad," he asked, "What's so dirty about that?" I said it was slang for anilingus, but the look of puzzlement remained. I told him to look it up.

After we huddled in the newsroom and read the fax together, Abdon jotted down names and dates in his reporter's notebook and set off in search of the case file. Maintained, if you want to be so kind, by political patrons of Cook County Circuit Court Clerk Dorothy Brown, the filing system at Chicago's Daley Center was notorious as the most archaic of any big city in the United States, inaccessible by computer, and with legal papers often going astray, never to be found again. Abdon nevertheless unearthed a file six inches thick for a case initiated by Tiffany Hawkins through her attorney, Susan E. Loggans, three years earlier, in late 1996. Abdon methodically photocopied the 235 pages and brought them back to the newsroom, where we scrutinized them late into the evening, highlighting passages, scrawling questions in the margins, and posting sticky notes next to potential leads.

The lawsuit claimed Kelly "had a propensity to have sexual contact with minors," and that he began a relationship with Tiffany in 1991, when she was fifteen and he was twenty-four. She became a frequent presence at CRC, earning $300 in cash from Kelly when she sang backing vocals on *Born into the 90's*, and a $1,500 check from Barry Hankerson when she performed as a "back-up rapper" on Aaliyah's *Age Ain't Nothing but a Number*. In addition to allegations of underage sex, the lawsuit charged sexual harassment in the workplace, since Kelly had employed Tiffany in the studio. In a subsequent motion deeper in the stack of papers, Kelly's attorneys argued that such allegations must first be aired before the Illinois Department of Human Rights, and Tiffany's attorney dropped that claim.

Tiffany also frequently visited Kelly at home, according to her lawsuit. The first apartment he bought was on the fifteenth floor of Burnham Park Plaza on South Wabash Avenue in the South Loop, a building he'd lived in before, back when it was the YMCA Hotel. The landmark neon sign atop the building had been replaced by a glass pyramid housing a five-level sundeck and an outdoor hot tub, and the rooms he'd once rented while busking had been converted to luxury condo units. Kelly then moved to even fancier digs, a forty-second-floor condo in the Parkshore Tower, on the Lake Michigan waterfront just south of Navy Pier.

In colorless language belying the drama of the story it told, the lawsuit claimed Kelly kicked Tiffany out of the recording studio whenever she didn't want to have sex, and that she agreed to some of the acts he demanded in the studio and at his homes, including threesomes with other underage girls. The suit also claimed she traveled and had sexual contact with Kelly on his tour bus in Ohio, Pennsylvania, Wisconsin, Indiana, and Washington, D.C.

Abdon broke off to check the newsroom's small legal library. The age of consent varies from state to state, and so does the statute of limitations. Illinois prohibits adult men from having sex with girls under seventeen, but prosecutions for statutory rape must be brought within three years. The statute for criminal charges had not expired when Tiffany filed her lawsuit in 1996, but the state's attorney in Illinois generally avoided these cases, Abdon said, because of the difficulty of proving them when it came down to "he said/she said."

The office had pursued one such prosecution six years earlier, however, in a case that would come to reflect and be intertwined with Kelly's life in important ways. In August 1994, a grand jury indicted Rep. Mel Reynolds for sexual assault and criminal sexual abuse in a relationship with a sixteen-year-old volunteer during his successful 1992 campaign for Congress. A rising star in South Side politics, Reynolds was convicted in 1995 and sentenced to five years in prison. He resigned from the House in disgrace, but the state drew harsh criticism for its handling of the case. During the trial, the victim recanted her grand jury testimony, cited her Fifth Amendment right not to incriminate herself, and refused to answer questions on the stand. The judge held her in contempt of court and jailed her. This treatment of an underage victim fueled arguments by the congressman's defenders that the prosecution had been politically motivated to bring down a successful black politician, and the state didn't really care about the victim at all.

Abdon and I returned to the file. The sexual contact between Tiffany and Kelly continued for almost three years, according to the lawsuit, ending four months before her eighteenth birthday, in October 1994. The lawsuit didn't say why it ended but claimed Tiffany was devastated, and two months later, she attempted suicide and spent time at Advocate Trinity Hospital on the South Side. Naming as co-defendants Kelly, Jive Records, and Hankerson's management company, Blackground Enterprises, Tiffany sought $10 million in damages. Her filings included a list of twenty-two witnesses who "presumably will testify" or had already promised to do so, among them Aaliyah, Barry Hankerson, Wayne Williams, members of Public Announcement, staffers at CRC, and Robert's half brother Carey.

Why the hell has none of this been reported? I asked when we came up for air.

Abdon said all the competing reporters who regularly checked the bin of legal filings at the Daley Center were white, and they might not have recognized the name "Robert Sylvester Kelly," or even known who R. Kelly was. Plus, the plaintiff's attorney filed late in the day on December 24. Most reporters went home early for the holidays and didn't return until the new year. We soon learned that Kelly's four lawyers also outflanked their adversary. Tiffany's attorney had notified them of the forthcoming suit on December 5, and hours before her claim was filed on Christmas Eve, Kelly's camp filed a five-page lawsuit of their own. The singer sought damages of $30,000 from Tiffany, charging she had demanded "substantial sums of cash" and a recording contract, or she would "widely publicize the false allegations" that he had fathered her child.

Abdon added a sticky note: "Child? Check."

The hundreds of pages in Tiffany's file made no mention of a paternity claim from her side, and that allegation and the accusation of blackmail never appeared again in any subsequent filing by Kelly's team over the next two years, but his attorneys seemed to want to win a public-relations battle, not a legal fight. Abdon and I got two hits for stories mentioning Kelly and Tiffany in a search of the Nexis news database, both gossip-column items planted by the singer's high-priced New York publicity firm, Dan Klores Associates. The day after Christmas, 1996, columnist Jim Rutenberg reported the Kelly lawsuit in the *Daily News*, quoting Klores: "Many celebrities are constantly being harassed and sued, and more often than not, they decide to settle. Kelly has decided, 'No way.' " The same day, Klores told *Sun-Times* gossip columnist Bill Zwecker, "R. Kelly one-hundred-percent denies that he is the father of this child, one-hundred-percent denies he has had sexual relations with Tiffany Hawkins."

Abdon and I walked across the newsroom to the row of offices occupied by the columnists. We asked our colleague Bill Zwecker if he remembered the story. He vaguely recalled being glad to get a tip from Klores during the notorious holiday news drought, but he didn't know about the more explosive charges in the suit filed by Tiffany. Rutenberg never reported them either. We later learned Tiffany did have a baby after her relationship with Kelly, but the father was a high school boyfriend.

While no other publications picked up the story of the alleged paternity shakedown, Klores and the Kelly team had succeeded in getting in front of a potential scandal. Tiffany's charges were buried, until we found them four years later, thanks to the fax. The voluminous case folder Abdon procured ended with a one-page notice filed on January 23, 1998. The case had been settled out of court.

The next morning, Abdon and I made our first phones calls via speaker-phone from his desk, but they shed little light on the resolution of the claim. "There's a confidentiality agreement, we can't discuss it," said Kim Jones, an assistant to attorney Susan Loggans. Gerald Margolis, a celebrity lawyer in Los Angeles who also represented Courtney Love, Robin Williams, and Mick Jagger, told us, "There was a complaint by Kelly, there was a complaint by her, it was settled, and the settlement is confidential. I have nothing else to say about that case now or ever." Sheila Hawkins, Tiffany's mother, picked up the phone and said the terms of the settlement forbade her or her daughter from talking to the press. A few days later, we visited to see if she'd talk in person, if only on background, but when we rang the bell of a small, neatly kept brick bungalow in the South Side neighborhood of Cottage Grove Heights, the door opened a crack, then a middle-aged woman in a nurse's uniform snapped the deadbolt shut.

Abdon and I thought the story was bigger than the tale of one settled lawsuit, and we spent four weeks digging into every allegation in the anonymous letter. We logged a lot of miles on the South and West Sides, returning to some addresses two or three times, on crisp mornings, sunny fall afternoons, and frigid evenings, trying different times to find anyone at home. We also rang doorbells in the freezing rain in the predominantly black suburbs of Maywood and Bellwood on the West Side, and in the south suburban village of Olympia Fields. None of the addresses were in the projects. Most were homes like the wood-frame fixer-upper with avocado-green aluminum siding where I grew up in Jersey City, or the brick row house in Chicago's Belmont Cragin bungalow belt, where Abdon's parents raised him and four sisters.

As soon as some people realized the awkward, mismatched white duo on the porch weren't cops, social workers, religious proselytizers, or salesmen, they invited us in and shared stories and photos about friends and relatives they said had been wronged by Kelly. Not a single person we spoke with seemed surprised when we asked about him and underage girls. Some proved eager to talk, saying no one had wanted to listen before. We were not part of their community exactly, but we were willing to listen, and it always helped that I could talk with anyone about almost any musical genre. Music, whether Curtis Mayfield or Mavis Staples or Common (all of whom I'd been lucky enough to interview), was often the key to getting the conversations rolling.

One woman I interviewed on my own invited me into the living room of a first-floor apartment in a meticulously well-kept two-flat on the West Side. She offered me tea and alternately cried and raged about how Kelly had treated a family member, who she said couldn't talk. *Judge Judy* played on the TV as we sat on the couch, and a small terrier yipped and ran in circles whenever its owner sobbed or raised her voice. "He needs help," she said, "and he needs to stop hurting people." Abdon and I heard similar comments from almost everyone we interviewed. Few said they hated Kelly. It was always, "Brother needs help. Brother's got to stop."

We hit a lot of dead ends, none more frustrating than the night we pulled up to an address on Devon Avenue in Chicago's Little India neighborhood on the Northwest Side. A source had led us to believe the anonymous fax had come from "an older church lady" who had quit her job in Kelly's office, disgusted by his behavior and frustrated that he refused to address "his problem." We thought we'd found her home during a search of driver's records, but instead arrived at a Mail Boxes Etc. store. The next morning, the manager told us we couldn't leave a note because the box had been closed with no forwarding address. We later heard that the older church lady, who may or may not have been my anonymous correspondent, had left Chicago. We never did succeed in tracking her down. To this day I don't know for certain who sent the fax.

When we weren't driving around together, Abdon and I divided our labors. He ran searches on the database tools in the newsroom and at the courts, looking into every name mentioned in the fax or in Tiffany's lawsuit. He printed out hundreds of pages of background information, phone numbers, and addresses. Given his expertise, Abdon also talked to lawyers, investigators, and court personnel. I called everyone else, starting with the numbers we found for people on Tiffany's witness list, as well as reaching out to everyone I could think of in the music world with a connection to Kelly.

One of my first calls, to a number an organizer of that Grammy press conference insisted did not come from them, started a relationship with a well-placed member of Kelly's inner circle who became an invaluable source for the next seven and a half years, sometimes calling as many as four or five times a week from ever-changing mobile-phone numbers. We agreed I could use any of the information provided in those calls, but not for attribution, and the pact with the former associate stands in this book.

Demetrius Smith became another key source. "Johnny-Boy" to friends and family, Smith grew up in Chicago's Cabrini-Green and Henry Horner Homes housing projects, and he spent thirteen years at Kelly's side, starting in the early days of busking on the "L" platforms. As the singer's career took off, Smith became a personal assistant, road manager, and production overseer, until he found God and quit five years before we first talked in 2000.

We initially spoke off the record, but Smith later went public with much of what he told me, self-publishing a book in 2011. He wrote *The Man Behind the Man: Looking from the Inside Out* while serving sixty-four months in a California prison for shoplifting iPods from Target stores, but he emerged to reconnect with his children and his God. He told me he quit in disgust over Kelly's behavior, though the singer's camp maintains he was fired.

I called Wayne Williams, Kelly's A&R man, who'd earlier told me nothing had happened between Kelly and Aaliyah. He had nothing new to say now and suggested I stick to writing my music columns.

Barry Hankerson, the manager who had started working with Kelly before *Born into the 90's,* only spoke to me on the record a few times, and very briefly. For eight years, he did more than anyone else to make Kelly a star, but he confirmed that he quit in February 2000, five and a half years after Kelly produced *Age Ain't Nothing but a Number* for his niece, Aaliyah. Hankerson would not address that relationship, but he said he resigned as Kelly's manager in a letter to the star's Los Angeles attorney, Gerald Margolis, copying the founder and head of Jive Records, Clive Calder. Hankerson didn't elaborate or share the letter, but he allowed his lawyer to confirm its substance to me, including the key passage that he was leaving because he believed Kelly needed psychiatric help for a compulsion to pursue underage girls.

The Kelly camp maintained that Hankerson was also fired, but sources told me that as a condition of severing their relationship, Hankerson retained a significant share of the artist's royalties for the albums Kelly released during his time as manager. Some said he kept *all* of Kelly's share from those recordings.

Two of Tiffany's close friends, who sometimes called her Tia, spoke to me during lengthy phone calls. One attended Kenwood Academy with her, singing in the choir and sharing the dream of making it in the music business. The other went to a different high school but moved in the same circle as Tiffany and the Kenwood classmate. These sources and four others helped Abdon and I piece together a fuller picture of what allegedly happened between Tiffany and Kelly.

Five-foot-six, with an athletic build and a wide, winning smile, Tiffany enrolled at Kenwood in the fall of 1991. She took the bus most mornings from the South Side neighborhood where she lived with her single mom, who was studying to be a nurse. Like most of the students in Room 126, she seemed starstruck when Kelly came to Lena McLin's class in 1991, returning to the school he continued to visit long after dropping out. A few months before the release of *Born into the 90's*, he stood at the front of the room between the cork bulletin board and the brown chalkboard and launched into song. No one could remember exactly what he sang, but he wowed the students because he sang especially for them.

A few weeks later, Tiffany and a friend saw Kelly cruising in Hyde Park in his luxury SUV. The girls waved him down and gushed about seeing him in Ms. McLin's classroom. Since they were singers, he invited them to CRC to watch him record. Tiffany began hanging out in the studio, and after she contributed to some of Kelly's sessions, she believed he'd make her a star. The Kenwood classmate said she and Tiffany sometimes spent all night at CRC, "until twelve the next noon," and she actually had sexual contact with Kelly before Tiffany did, when she was sixteen and Kelly was twenty-four. The Kenwood classmate never witnessed Kelly having sexual contact with Tiffany, but "I did see him messing with her, playing with her breasts and rubbing on her." Once, she had sexual contact with Kelly while Tiffany watched "and he played with her."

Six years after she last saw Kelly, the Kenwood classmate broke down in tears several times when she talked about him. "I'm gonna be honest with you, I still love R. Kelly's music. I don't hate him. It's a love/hate kind of relationship. He kind of reminds me of like a boyfriend who hurt you that you still love. I'm not trying to down him, because really, honestly, I think it has to be a sickness. The attraction he had to the girls I seen him with—he likes skinny, skinny, malnourished-looking little girls." She paused, sobbing. "Looking at the pictures of how me and Tiffany were when we were freshmen, we were ugly little girls compared to what he could have had."

That statement tore at me, and so did her crying. It took me hours to decompress after that interview, and many of those that followed. I hated making anyone cry, and I tried to be empathetic, but I also had to be a reporter, to keep asking questions, to confirm details, to remain skeptical and "objective," whatever the hell that means. The ideals emphasized in my journalism classes at NYU proved goddamn difficult to maintain with someone emotionally baring intimate and painful details.

Kelly told both teenagers, "I'm gonna make you a star," the Kenwood classmate said, but he added that if they were serious about music, "You gonna have to be at the recording studio and not at school, because school ain't gonna make you a millionaire." Both she and Tiffany dropped out of Kenwood, and when we talked, Tiffany's classmate regretted taking R. Kelly's advice. "That was the biggest hurt to me, and to this day, I feel that I could be something else if I stayed in school."

Sometimes, Kelly gave the girls gifts. "He treated us very well," the Kenwood classmate said. "We got anything we asked for, but we weren't going to ask for much. A pair of Air Jordans or a hundred dollars was a lot of money to us." She said she stopped having sexual contact with Kelly because "I have this jealous thing when I'm sleeping with somebody; if they sleep with somebody else, I kind of get upset." She thought Tiffany's relationship ended for similar reasons. "Tiffany was jealous of other girls, period. Even though Tiffany claimed to be close to her, she was kind of jealous of Aaliyah," whom the two met when Aaliyah was twelve. "Later, I guess Tiffany was trying to be around to cock-block, or whatever you want to call it, because I know Robert was sleeping with Aaliyah. And then Tiffany and Aaliyah fell out."

Sources provided more detail about Tiffany's settlement. The former associate said it came the day after Tiffany gave a seven-and-a-half-hour deposition to Kelly's attorneys, Gerald Margolis and John M. Touhy. The case file did not include a transcript of the deposition. Although it was public record, the deposition had disappeared, and I never have found it. My source said it had been "hair-raising stuff about a predatory relationship based on perverted sexual acts," including threesomes with underage girls. Demetrius Smith, Kelly's longtime road manager and personal assistant, confirmed, "That deposition told the story of their relationship and mentioned other minors," with hours of graphic detail. The sworn testimony stunned everyone in the room.

In exchange for $250,000 (one-fortieth of the $10 million she'd been seeking) Tiffany signed a nondisclosure agreement the next day, barring her from talking about any relationship or settlement with Kelly. Years later, I learned the star actually tried to compel the Hartford insurance company to pay the settlement. In December 1999, Hartford sued him for pressing that claim, "seeking a declaration that it owed no duty to defend or indemnify the insured under a homeowner's policy in an underlying lawsuit asserting claims of negligence and intentional sexual battery." Kelly appealed, and Hartford responded to the appellate court "that the underlying complaint against the insured sufficiently set forth factual allegations of sexual misconduct with a minor to exclude coverage under an 'expected or intended' exclusion."

Hartford won the appeal, and Kelly paid Tiffany himself. A homeowner trying to have his insurer pay for illegal sexual contact with a minor has to stand as one of the strangest cases in the annals of the insurance industry, a business that has seen plenty of strange claims.

The Kenwood classmate believed Tiffany settled with Kelly for so little because "she just got tired of the case," which dragged on for two years. She kept two-thirds of the money after legal fees, and she promptly squandered all of it, my sources said. "Tiffany just jumped once they started talking that money," Smith added. Abdon compared it to Kramer leaping at the offer of free coffee for life in the *Seinfeld* episode about "Java World," but I always wondered if there was more to the story.

Jovante Cunningham also appeared on Tiffany's witness list, and she initially talked to me off the record, and only reluctantly. She, the Kenwood classmate, and Tiffany had been Aaliyah's posse of three teenage girlfriends whom everyone called Second Chapter.

Jovante met Kelly at age fourteen and later worked for him as a dancer and backing vocalist. She knew a lot, she told me, but "if I would tell it, it would be in front of somebody's huge television camera, and they'd have to be paying me a whole bunch of money." Every time I told her the *Sun-Times* did not pay sources, she kept talking anyway. I got a quizzical look when one of the features editors overheard us on the phone. I had to speak especially loudly because my reluctant interview subject seemed to be shopping. "I like those shoes, I'll take those," she said at one point.

"I've seen him do things I can't say," Jovante said of Kelly. "I'm not at liberty to say who, what, where." She did tell me she met Tiffany at a mutual friend's house. "The first thing she said to me was, 'I know R. Kelly!' At the time, he was nobody. His first album hadn't even hit yet. She said, 'Let's go over to his house,' so we went over there. I don't know if she was a recruiter for him or what." She added that she believed Kelly made a mistake by settling with Tiffany—"I thought it would only encourage more girls to come forward"—and she said Kelly should have taken the lawsuit as a wake-up call.

"He should have learned from that and got some help. He definitely has something going on psychologically, and he needs to know there is repercussions. He has no value or respect for people as a whole. The brother got problems. The brother is ill. Robert's thing was a fresh body. I don't think it had anything to do with age. I think he goes for a fresh look, a fresh body, and it turns out to be a young body. There are a lot of different ways you could categorize it, but I'm not a psychologist, I'm just a person who witnessed some things who had her own opinion of it."

Jovante finally got to talk to "somebody's huge television camera" when she appeared nineteen years later in the Lifetime docuseries *Surviving R. Kelly*. In it, she tearfully said she witnessed R. Kelly having sexual contact with sixteen-year-old Tiffany in the studio, as well as with fifteen-year-old Aaliyah on a different occasion aboard his tour bus.

Abdon and I knew we couldn't tell Tiffany's story without one more interview. We had to talk to Lena McLin about Kelly's visits to Kenwood Academy. Several students told us other teachers there warned them the star frequently returned to "cruise" young girls. Abdon reached out to McLin when I told him I didn't have the stomach to pose the questions that needed to be asked of the then-seventy-year-old gospel legend.

"Robert comes back all the time. He considers me his mother and mentor," McLin told Abdon in a scolding tone. "I don't know what he did outside of school, but in the school, there was no hanky-panky. If they were involved in that, the sad thing is, it takes two to tango." She admitted she disliked Kelly's raunchier songs, but she lauded his potential. "He has a very decent moral spirit inside that's dying to come out. It comes out in 'I Believe I Can Fly.' It comes out in the angel song he did with Céline Dion. It will eventually grow. It may be a little baby now, but it will eventually get real big."

As Abdon and I learned more about Tiffany, the question of what really happened with Aaliyah loomed. Tiffany's lawsuit included the marriage certificate that had been published in *Vibe*, as well as a four-page petition filed by an attorney for Aaliyah in Cook County Circuit Court in July 1997 seeking, with legalistic overkill, to "expunge, obliterate, erase, and/or otherwise wholly strike from all public records all marriage documents associated with Plaintiff's August 31, 1994 marriage." Abdon checked, and the marriage certificate was indeed no longer available in the public records. The petition noted that the marriage had "been declared invalid by the Circuit Court of Wayne County, Michigan," but Abdon found that through an order by that court in October 1994, any annulment or divorce in Michigan had also been expunged, obliterated, erased, etcetera.

We thought we'd hit another dead end, until a source provided a copy of a document signed by Kelly, Aaliyah, and her parents, Michael and Diane Haughton, on September 29, 1994, less than a month after the marriage between the then-twenty-seven-year-old producer and his fifteen-year-old protégé. The agreement stipulated that in consideration of payment of $100 by Kelly to Aaliyah—two sources later told me the amount Kelly actually paid "off the books" was $3 million—the two would sever all personal and professional contact and pledge to avoid any public comment about their relationship or the separation agreement, "due to the nature of the music industry and its ability to engender rumors and disseminate personal information, both true and untrue."

In the agreement, Kelly admitted no liability or wrongdoing, and Aaliyah and her parents discharged him from any future legal claims due to "a decline in her ability, reputation, or marketability . . . emotional distress caused by any aspect of her business or personal relationship with Robert . . . [or] physical injury or emotional pain and suffering from any assault or battery perpetrated by Robert against her person." Hankerson and an attorney for

Kelly, Arnold E. Reed, were named as monitors to assure the two complied with the terms of the agreement.

When Abdon and I reviewed these pages with Don Hayner, the law school grad turned city editor, he thought the assault and battery clause could be boilerplate for any divorce agreement. We did not note it in our story. Only years later did the possible significance strike me, after other women began telling me Kelly allegedly physically assaulted them if they broke "his rules."

Unlike many who worked with him, Aaliyah's career thrived after she split with Kelly. She left Jive, the label founded by Clive Calder, and signed with Virgin Records. "In 1994, Hankerson and the Haughtons came to Calder's office," Geoff Edgers of the *Washington Post* reported a quarter-century later. "There was no talk of reprimanding Kelly. Instead, the family demanded that Jive let Aaliyah go. 'And they basically tell me that they want a release from the contract,' Calder said, saying they thought Aaliyah would never get the proper promotion if she was on the same label as Kelly. Calder agreed to let her leave, but only after securing a percentage of her future album sales on a new label."

Aaliyah released her second album, *One in a Million*, on Virgin in August 1996. A radical departure from the slick R&B sounds Kelly crafted for her debut, many of her new, percolating grooves were written and produced by then-rising hip-hop talents Missy Elliott and Timbaland. With them, Aaliyah "helped invent a style that might be called avant-garde R&B," Kelefa Sanneh wrote in the *New York Times*, while in *SPIN*, Jon Caramanica contended these sounds were "the nexus of street-savvy R&B and elegant pop."

The collaboration between Kelly and Aaliyah became history. "Whenever R. Kelly comes up," a Virgin executive told me, "she doesn't even speak his name. When she came over to this label, we were all told on the sly, 'Don't ever bring up R. Kelly's name.' It's just one of those weird topics."

One in a Million eventually sold more than three million copies in the United States, and Aaliyah also started a film career. In March 2000, she costarred in *Romeo Must Die,* a streetwise retelling of Shakespeare's tragic love story. She played the daughter of a gangster in love with kung-fu master Jet Li, an ex-cop investigating the murder of his brother, a member of the Chinese mob. The affair was, of course, star-crossed.

Everyone I interviewed said the affection between Kelly and Aaliyah had been genuine. "He loved Aaliyah," Demetrius Smith said, while he and others described her feelings for Kelly as a teenage crush turned to infatuation. Young, naive, and sheltered by her family, Aaliyah experienced independence for the first time while working on *Age Ain't Nothing but a Number*. All but one of my sources said she and Kelly began having sexual contact during her first recording sessions. Some said he surprised her with the marriage ceremony in a third-floor room at the Sheraton Gateway Suites in suburban Rosemont, and that Aaliyah looked nervous and scared. "She thought it was all an elaborate game," one source said. Another claimed, "She knew she'd regret it—her family wasn't there!—but she just got swept up in the excitement."

Demetrius Smith gave me the most detailed account, later repeated in his book, *The Man Behind the Man*. After a gig in Orlando while on tour with Salt-N-Pepa, Kelly told Smith they had to return to Chicago immediately before the next show in Miami because Aaliyah had run away from home and needed to see him. When they got back to Chicago, Aaliyah told Kelly she was pregnant. Kelly's accountant, Derrel McDavid, and attorney, Gerald Margolis, convinced him he should marry his protégé, Smith claimed. Neither of them would comment. Smith, Kelly, and Aaliyah obtained the Cook County marriage certificate at city hall in suburban Maywood, using fake IDs Smith bought for Aaliyah in what he called "Jewtown," slang for Chicago's famous Maxwell Street Market, which started as a Jewish ghetto but became a hotbed of electric blues and a thriving bazaar where black vendors sold everything from "discount" color television sets and stereos to bootleg CDs and videos.

Aaliyah lied about her age, signing the marriage certificate as an eighteen-year-old, she admitted in the court documents Abdon and I obtained. Several other sources confirmed she told Kelly she was pregnant, but the legal filings made no mention of that.

After the wedding, Smith and Kelly flew back to Florida while Aaliyah stayed at the hotel in Rosemont, but Smith said that within a day, she left and went home to Detroit, telling her parents and uncle Barry Hankerson what had happened. "Aaliyah was a baby. She knew nothing. Aaliyah was just a sweet child, man," Smith said. Others disagreed and said some members of her family knew about the relationship. What is confirmed in the legal documents is that the family immediately set about undoing the marriage and keeping it quiet so as not to damage either star's career.

"We never had any trouble with Aaliyah when that was done," a family member told me. "It was never her trying to see him, call him, or get to him. We didn't want any money. The issue with the family was to move on, and to totally undo what Robert Kelly did. We just thought, 'This guy is stupid. He's like a big, dumb fifteen-year-old hisself.' At that time, we didn't think about pedophilia. It was just, 'How dumb can you be, boy? You're lucky *we* are the family!' We embraced her and she cried and she said she never wanted to see him again. We were apprehensive, and we watched her, but we never took away the freedom of the telephone or the mobility to leave the house. She just never saw him again."

Smith agreed. "Rob made a mistake, that's how the family looked at it." Although Hankerson stayed on as Kelly's manager, "Barry just started backing up after that. He was trying to save his family and his career. Barry is a smart man, and he's compassionate and a good man who realizes that we are all born to sin." The relationship between Kelly and Hankerson was never the same, however, and Derrel McDavid began to play a bigger role in overseeing the singer's career long before Hankerson quit in early 2000.

Instead of Dan Klores Associates, in 2000, Kelly employed as his publicist Regina Daniels, the wife of the owner of the South Side's biggest record store, George's Music Room, which boasted a wall-size mural of Kelly. Midway through our reporting, I called Daniels to ask her about Kelly and Aaliyah. She gave me a statement that exceeded what anyone in the Kelly camp had been authorized to say, and sources told me her employers later chided her for it.

"Rob did date Aaliyah, yes, he did, and he did have a relationship with Aaliyah, yes, he did, and past that, unfortunately, it didn't work out and that was really that. Did they have a relationship? Yes, they did. I'm not gonna sit here and bullshit you or nobody else about it. Yes, they did. Did they get married? Well, there was a marriage certificate, so that pretty much kinda means something happened there. Was I there? No, I wasn't, but there was a relationship. It ended with, 'Maybe we're over our heads, maybe this is too much, maybe we need to go our separate ways. I love you, I always will, I wish you the best, and maybe we just jumped in way too deep into this thing.' And she went her way and he went his."

Daniels chastised me for even asking about the relationship. "Robert has done enough else in his career that if people can't say nothing else other than whether or not he screwed Aaliyah, then they can kiss my ass!" Her tone made it clear she meant me.

According to Smith, the sudden end of Kelly's relationship with Aaliyah crushed him. The singer finished his tour, returned to Chicago, and checked into the Hotel Nikko, where he spent more than a month sleeping in the closet. Whenever Kelly got depressed, Smith said, he tried to get his friend to sing "Hard Times," the song he'd written as a teen about his mom and the early days. When Kelly finally emerged, he wrote a new song called "Trade in My Life" that eventually appeared on the R. Kelly album in November 1995, with backing from a gospel choir led by Kirk Franklin.

"We both know that we made a vow / Said we'd always be together / That our love would endure, yes / But now you're gone and I'm all alone," Kelly croons. The song ends with him posing the same question the heavenly voice asked a few years later in the "I Wish" video: "What does it profit a man to gain the world and lose his soul?"

As Abdon and I continued reporting, we scoured police and court records and found that by late 2000, R. Kelly had had three brushes with the law, the first only nine days after he married Aaliyah. On September 9, 1994, at the end of his tour with Salt-N-Pepa, he headlined the Budweiser Superfest at Madison Square Garden. The singer and his crew stayed at the posh Michelangelo Hotel near Times Square, and the day after the show, police arrested two of his bodyguards in a hotel room on charges of raping and sodomizing a twenty-two-year-old woman. The hotel's guest-services agent confirmed that a rape had been reported, according to New York Newsday, which added that police sought a third suspect.

We could find no resolution of the case, but sources told me the incident actually involved Kelly and an underage girl with a fake ID, who later withdrew her charges when the star paid her a cash settlement. Kelly posted bond for the bodyguards after they spent a night on Rikers Island. Tour manager Demetrius Smith said the pair had rushed to Kelly's room as the girl fled, and they stayed to talk to police while Kelly left the hotel. "He paid them, but then treated them like shit. They took that case for him, but after that, he had no respect for them."

In the summer of 1996, Kelly himself was arrested along with four of his bodyguards after they got into a fight with some local players on the basketball court at a health club in Lafayette, Louisiana, hours before a scheduled performance at the Cajundome. One of the three men who pressed charges had been beaten so badly, he needed 110 stitches on his face, according to police. They charged Kelly with second-degree battery, a felony punishable by up to five years in prison, and he spent the night in jail, missing the concert. In the morning, an attorney posted $11,500 bail. Kelly claimed the men had taunted him and his entourage with racial slurs. The district attorney in Lafayette eventually determined that Kelly had not started the fight, and he reduced the charge to simple battery. The singer drew a sentence of one year of unsupervised probation, and he ended a civil claim by the men with a cash settlement.

Finally, one night in the spring of 1998, Chicago police arrested Kelly for disorderly conduct as he sat in his new Lincoln Navigator blasting loud music outside the Rock 'N' Roll McDonald's on North Clark Street. According to a report in the *Sun-Times*, police said Kelly became loud and abusive when officers asked him to turn down the music. A city ordinance prohibited music so loud it could be heard seventy-five feet from a vehicle. As a crowd gathered to watch, Kelly refused to produce a driver's license, and officers arrested him. He went limp as they carried him to their squad car.

Chicago's black radio stations harshly criticized police for harassing a hometown hero and overreacting by seizing his SUV. A CPD spokesman noted that 4,764 vehicles had been impounded under the ordinance the previous year, and Kelly had been treated no different than any offender. The singer did seem to get special treatment in court, however, which later struck Abdon as unusual. In July 1998, at a hearing that lasted less than a minute, the city dropped its charges.

Kelly's fans applauded, but law enforcement sources told Abdon and me the arrest had never been "only" about the noise. Cops on the beat near the Rock 'N' Roll McDonald's knew the Youth Division of the Special Investigations Unit was looking at Kelly for sexual encounters with underage girls, and they believed he cruised for teens at the garish theme restaurant. Kelly also frequented Evergreen Plaza shopping mall on the South Side, and he loved when girls recognized him there. "We'd go to the shopping mall in every city we visited," Demetrius Smith said. Chicago cops told Abdon and me they "kept an eye out" for Kelly at Evergreen Plaza, too.

A few weeks earlier, before the fax prompted me to check the liner notes for *TP-2.com,* I hadn't realized Kelly had a family. His second wedding, midway between the first with Aaliyah in 1994 and the settlement with Tiffany in 1998, never garnered any mention in the press. Although we couldn't even find the date of the wedding, Abdon and I learned in public-records searches that in 1996, Kelly married twenty-two-year-old Andrea Lee, a dancer from his touring troupe. Sources said they met when she was nineteen. They had two children, Jaya, born earlier that year, and Joann, born in 1998 and named after Kelly's mother.

"He married Andrea to take the attention off of Aaliyah, but he never talks about her," Smith said. Kelly never stopped pursuing other girls, and sources led me to one whose relationship ended a little more than a year before I got the fax, three years after Kelly married Andrea.

A Los Angeles girl told me the singer first tried to seduce her when she visited the set for the video of "If I Could Turn Back the Hands of Time" in the spring of 1999. She was a seventeen-year-old high school senior when one of Kelly's assistants pressed a tiny balled-up piece of paper with a phone number on it into the palm of her hand. "From there we just started talking over the phone." She told him her age. "I don't believe in lying, but he was trying to woo me out there to Chicago despite the fact. Once I brought up the whole thing of, 'Well, I have to ask my mother,' he was like, 'You told your mom? Well, just wait then.'"

The Los Angeles girl told me she continued talking to Kelly, and when they engaged in phone sex, he said they were "soul mates." She believed he loved her, and after he sent her a plane ticket to visit Chicago on her eighteenth birthday, she had sex with him for the first time in August 1999. He never told her he was married, and they started fighting as soon as she found out. "I do believe he does have a problem," she said. "I look back at it now and I think I was stupid; why the hell did I even go out there at all? There are some couples that there is a big age difference, but in this situation, I think that he really does have some kind of sexual problem. . . . He was like, 'You need to act older. There's fifteen-year-old girls who act like they're twenty-one years old.'"

Three weeks into our reporting, Abdon and I felt we had enough for a story, but as we sat in Don Hayner's office reviewing everything we'd learned about R. Kelly and underage girls, the city editor pointed out that all the relationships we could document had taken place in the past. What about the present? "Right now," the fax had said, "he's messing with a thirteen-year-old girl who he tells people is his goddaughter. . . . Robert hired her father, who is a bass player."

Several sources confirmed that the prominent thanks in the liner notes of *TP-2.com* for "my goddaughter Reshona, Greg, and Valerie" referred to Reshona Landfair and her parents, who lived in the village of Oak Park, just west of Chicago. Reshona had recently enrolled at Oak Park and River Forest High School, and four sources told us her sexual contact with Kelly was ongoing. She was now fourteen. We also learned Kelly was allegedly having sexual contact with another girl a year younger, thirteen, from the southwest suburbs, with whom Reshona was close. Abdon and I found the second girl's eighth-grade school photo. We failed to connect with her family or the Landfairs the many times we called, but we made one last, determined push for our story in the *Sun-Times*.

We had learned a lot about the second girl's family, which had a high profile in the black community, unusual for the girls Kelly seemed to pursue. We visited their ostentatious McMansion, newly constructed at a cost of $830,000. The first two times, we didn't get past the gated entry at the end of a long driveway. On our last trip, the gate was open. We parked in the circle in front of the house and rang the bell, but when the girl's father opened the door, he threatened to kick our asses if we didn't leave immediately, an attitude that seemed distinctly at odds with the genteel setting and his profession. It was by far the nastiest reception we got.

That girl's name has never been published, and neither she nor her family members have ever spoken publicly about Kelly. Like most newspapers, the *Sun-Times* did not identify underage crime victims, unless they had been murdered, and it did not name rape victims of any age, unless they made the brave and harrowing decision to go public. This book does not identify any victim unless the woman specifically spoke to me on the record, or her name inescapably became public in court proceedings, like Reshona Landfair, or in legal filings that she initiated, like Tiffany Hawkins.

Abdon and I had no more success when we rang the bell again at the Landfair residence, a quaint, two-story, cream-colored stucco house with white-trimmed windows behind a small patch of lawn from which the last of early December's falling leaves had just been raked. A seven- or eight-year-old station wagon sat in front, parked on the street. When a relative answered the door at the side of the building, before we could even introduce ourselves, she barked, "Ain't we made it clear we ain't talking to you?" But the next day, I did connect with Reshona's aunt, her mother Valerie's sister, Stephanie Edwards.

For a time, Edwards was married to Earl Robinson, who had been a member of Public Announcement with Kelly. She was a singer herself, and she recorded under the name Sparkle. She was Sparkle to everyone, including family, just like Madonna is always Madonna. Sparkle met Kelly in 1989, when he produced Billy Ocean. Three years later, he asked her to come to the studio, where he auditioned her. She sang backing vocals on *Age Ain't Nothing but a Number*, augmenting what she called "Aaliyah's posse . . . They were called Second Chapter, it was three girls," she later told *The Breakfast Club*, a syndicated radio show. She named Jovante Cunningham as one of the three and said, "One of the girls is rapping, you can hear it all through Aaliyah's first album." Sparkle didn't name her, but that was Tiffany Hawkins. The third was Tiffany's Kenwood Academy classmate, who spoke to me off the record, and who's never gone public.

Kelly tried to seduce Sparkle, she and all my sources agreed. Sparkle says she wanted to keep the relationship strictly professional, confining it to sessions at CRC and the occasional meal at Kelly's favorite restaurant, the Rock 'N' Roll McDonald's. She did introduce Kelly to her family, including her brother-in-law, Greg Landfair. The star always needed musicians, and in late 1997, Kelly was also looking for new artists. He had struck a deal with Interscope Records to distribute albums he produced for artists he signed to his new boutique label, Rockland Records.

Interscope had been cofounded in 1990 by the Brooklyn-born record producer Jimmy Iovine, whose credits included albums by John Lennon and Bruce Springsteen. His partner was Chicago native and media entrepreneur Ted Field, the son of Marshall Field IV, a department-store magnate who also owned the *Sun-Times* from 1956 to 1965. Interscope quickly became one of the most successful and edgiest labels in the music business, thanks to a deal with the hard-core hip-hop label Death Row and hit releases by Tupac Shakur, Dr. Dre, and Snoop Dogg. Kelly's Rockland imprint released a handful of albums through Interscope between 1998 and 2001, but the self-titled debut he produced for Sparkle was its only hit. *Sparkle* sold half a million copies and reached No. 3 on the Billboard albums chart in May 1998. Then Kelly's latest protégé split from him.

Sparkle had just released her second album, *Told You So*, on Motown Records when a publicist at her new label connected us for a phone interview. We talked for a couple of minutes about her sophomore disc before I clumsily shifted to the real reason I called, asking Sparkle why she had broken from Kelly. "R. Kelly is a great songwriter, producer, and all of that, but business-wise, he ain't so great. And things happen, a lot of things I can't really touch on." I asked if she meant something happened between Kelly and her niece Reshona Landfair. She did not seem surprised by the question.

Sparkle said she introduced Kelly to Reshona, "my heart," when her niece was twelve. "I introduced them because she is a rapper and I introduced her in hopes that maybe Robert could possibly help her do something. After which she continued to hang out with me and be around me. And after I left the whole situation, to me, I just didn't feel like that was a great situation for her to be around anymore, but I'm not her parents or whatever." Sparkle ended the interview abruptly after those comments.

In December 2000, police told Abdon, they had interviewed Reshona twice over the last eighteen months. "She denied having any type or form of sexual encounter with Robert Kelly," an investigator later told me. They said that when they questioned her parents, Greg and Valerie Landfair, "They looked at me straight in the eye and said, 'We have nothing to say to you.' They were ice-cold." We also learned that the Illinois Division of Children and Family Services had investigated the parents. They "apparently let Kelly take the girl on the road with him and have sexual relations with her, with their full knowledge and consent," according to an email from an anonymous source at the agency. Citing confidentiality, a DCFS spokesperson declined official comment, but a second source confirmed what we learned in the email.

The story Abdon and I began writing on the second weekend in December 2000 made no mention of Reshona or the second girl whose eighth-grade photo I had in a folder on my desk. We were frustrated that we hadn't learned enough to include the information about possible ongoing examples of statutory rape, but we did think we'd confirmed the central allegation in the fax: "Robert's problem—and it's a thing that goes back many years—is young girls."

Abdon always left the writing to me, reading and then tweaking drafts as we kicked the story back and forth. When we had a final draft, we started the long process of answering queries and approving changes requested by Don Hayner and two other editors on the city desk. Once we cleared those hurdles, the story moved to legal vetting by the paper's outside counsel, Damon Dunn, and, given its explosive nature, final reads by the two executives at the top of the masthead, editor Michael Cooke and publisher John Cruickshank.

Cooke was a boisterous Fleet Street veteran imported to run editorial for Lord Conrad Black's American flagship while his fellow but more reserved Canadian John Cruickshank handled the business side, though their duties often overlapped. Reporters in the newsroom called them "Hook and Crook," because of the alliteration, not the securities fraud that eventually landed their boss and the paper's owner behind bars. They slated publication of our article for December 21, the day before Kelly was set to headline the Big

Jam Christmas Concert sponsored by WGCI-FM, the R&B powerhouse of the Midwest.

Early on December 20, I made another call to Kelly's spokeswoman, Regina Daniels. The first time we talked, I'd only asked her about Aaliyah, and she'd rambled on. Now I carefully outlined all the other accusations in our piece, seeking comment from the singer. Daniels said she didn't even need to check with him. "I have no comment to make. There are a lot of people who are very much a player-hater of Robert. All I can go by is the years that I've worked with him and what I've seen. I'm not saying anybody is beyond doing what I don't see, but I'm not looking under the covers with him. All I know is that he has presented himself to me to be a respectable person, and that is what I can go by."

After four weeks of sixteen-hour days, working through weekends and juggling the emotionally draining Kelly reporting with our regular assignments, Abdon and I felt exhausted but wired. We were frustrated by the angles we hadn't nailed, yet confident of a lede we'd spent more time crafting under more scrutinizing eyes than the first paragraph of any other story either of us had ever written.

Chicago singer and songwriter R. Kelly used his position of fame and influence as a pop superstar to meet girls as young as fifteen and have sex with them, according to court records and interviews.

The story continued from there for nearly three thousand words, not counting the timeline sidebar I wrote charting Kelly's career for any readers still unaware of his success. The paper's lawyer, Damon Dunn, had been one of those. He'd never heard of Kelly before he read our story, he wrote in a memo, but concluded Kelly and Aaliyah were public figures, and "I see no basis for actual malice in the story," the key consideration for a libel suit.

Our report started on the bottom of page one as the third of the three biggest stories of the day, but it spread across three full pages inside, an extraordinary amount of space for a tabloid. Abdon and I hovered in the newsroom to read the final page proofs, then headed to the Billy Goat Tavern, the old-time newspaper hangout on the lower level of North Michigan Avenue between the *Tribune* and the *Sun-Times*. I hated the place—it seemed like a cliché out of *The Front Page*, to say nothing of the annoying *Saturday Night Live* "cheezborger, cheezborger" shtick—but Abdon was a regular.

Well aware that we were acting like a couple of j-school novices eager to see their first bylines in the college paper, we emerged after last call to grab the first-offs, the earliest copies of the first edition, which drivers loaded in bundles onto a fleet of idling delivery trucks destined for the suburbs. The rest of the city got the second edition a few hours later with the late sports scores. We were proud of the story. Everyone we'd worked with at the paper was, and we had gotten incredible institutional support. We expected the piece to have real impact the next day. It didn't.

The rival *Chicago Tribune* ignored our story, and the local television news broadcasts made only passing mention in connection with Kelly's Christmas concert. The Associated Press ran a short item stating "the *Sun-Times* has reported . . . ," briefly recapping our work. No other news organization added to what we reported. The Kelly camp issued another one-sentence statement by Daniels—"It saddens me that anyone would write anything like that"— but callers overwhelmed Chicago's black radio stations. "Some were angry at Kelly," Abdon wrote in a follow-up piece. "Others blamed the girls. Some callers and hosts heaped criticism on the *Sun-Times* for reporting the story."

WGCI-FM's popular morning host, "Crazy" Howard McGee, called the Tiffany and Aaliyah legal filings "old news," although the specifics we found had never been reported. He dismissed the charges of sex with underage girls as "only allegations" and urged listeners to "pray for brother Robert." His boss, Elroy Smith, program director for both WGCI and WVAZ, noted that "I Wish" was the most-requested song on the stations' playlists, and he had no intention of removing it.

The *Sun-Times* sent Dave Hoekstra to review the holiday concert, which I happily avoided. In place of the skit on the giant bed, this show ended with Kelly singing "I Believe I Can Fly" with a gospel choir as forty children sat behind him on a white staircase. "Traditionally, an R. Kelly concert is more naughty than nice," Hoekstra wrote in a review that ran on Christmas Eve. "It was a more mellow R. Kelly who headlined WGCI's Big Jam concert before 22,000 adoring fans at the United Center. Part of me believes that

Kelly simply was caught up in the holiday spirit. Another part of me believes Kelly was responding to revelations that he allegedly liked to fool around with teenage girls."

That last line infuriated me, and I was angry with the copy desk for letting it fly. The story Abdon and I had worked on so hard for so long, and which had been so carefully edited and vetted by so many hands at the paper, accused Kelly of criminal behavior that ruined young lives. We'd provided proof for those charges, as well as context to separate them from the usual "celebrity misbehavior." One awkward paragraph our editors insisted we include read, "Kelly is hardly the first celebrity to be accused of taking advantage of underage girls. Gary Glitter, Rob Lowe, Elvis Presley, Jerry Lee Lewis, Roman Polanski, Rolling Stone Bill Wyman and even the legendary Errol Flynn all have been written about in this paper and others for allegedly having trysts with minors." We also mentioned the charges against Michael Jackson. Clearly, we hadn't done enough to make the case that this was more than "fooling around with teenage girls."

I knew pop music history well, and I understood groupie culture. Several of my Gen-X music-critic peers, notably Ann Powers, now saw the celebrated groupies of the sixties and seventies through the prism of postfeminism. They portrayed the GTOs (Girls Together Outrageously) and Chicagoan Cynthia Plaster Caster as teenage girls who'd slept with rock stars as acts of self-empowerment. I was dubious. Pamela Des Barres had become famous for her 1987 memoir, *I'm with the Band: Confessions of a Groupie*, but two of her fellow GTOs died young, one of a drug overdose and another of complications from AIDS. Cynthia, famous for her plaster casts of rock stars' male members, told me and others as many harrowing tales of life on the road as inspiring ones.

On the other hand, I was no prude. I had rejected my Catholic indoctrination as a high school freshman. "Do what thou wilt is the whole of the law, so long as ye shall harm none" stood as my philosophy, derived third-hand from Led Zeppelin via Aleister Crowley, who got it from the Wiccan Rede posited by Doreen Valiente in 1964. Dubious pedigree aside, the last part about harming none is key, and treat others as you'd have them treat you is a cornerstone of most systems of ethical beliefs. Rather than "fooling around," Kelly was destroying lives. Tiffany Hawkins had attempted suicide, according to her lawsuit.

My colleague's use of "teenage girls" bothered me, too. Any parent or teacher can attest that there are enormous differences between thirteen-, fourteen-, or fifteen-year-old girls and young women of eighteen or nineteen. Abdon and I had seen the grammar school photos and high school yearbooks. We'd met some of the girls and their friends and families. They'd shown us evidence of how the victims had been hurt, but we'd apparently failed to make some of our own colleagues see what we'd seen, much less convince many of Kelly's fans.

Our editors also sent *Sun-Times* reporter Sabrina Walters to interview members of Kelly's audience at the holiday concert. Under the headline "Allegations Don't Faze Fans," she quoted an eighteen-year-old girl from suburban Bolingbrook who said, "His personal life doesn't really concern me." A twenty-nine-year-old woman from suburban Glenwood told her, "I know Robert. It's not like him. It's a publicity stunt on the girls' part." By the start of the new year, our attempt to reveal a pattern of predation already a decade old seemed to have been dismissed by many, and ignored or forgotten by most.

CHAPTER 5

NUMEROUS

During our reporting in late 2000 for the first story in the *Chicago Sun-Times* about R. Kelly's pursuit of underage girls, several of my sources told me about "the girl in Miami." Abdon Pallasch and I never succeeded in tracking her down, but she emailed me eighteen years later, and we began a series of long and emotional phone calls during which she spoke publicly for the first time about the sexual contact she says she had with Kelly twenty-three years earlier, when she was seventeen years old. On May 4, 2018, I finally told her story in BuzzFeed News. The girl in Miami was Lizzette Martinez.

After school one evening in the winter of 1995, two years after Tiffany Hawkins ended her relationship with Kelly and a year before she sued him, Lizzette went to the mall in Miami's northern suburb of Aventura. She strolled around, window-shopping, while she waited for her best friend, Michella Powery, to finish her shift at the Merry-Go-Round clothing store. Inseparable since age twelve, the two teenagers were now cheerleaders in their last year at North Miami Beach Senior High School.

A light-skinned Puerto Rican with flowing black hair, almond eyes, and a radiant smile, Lizzette went to church every week and got excellent grades in school, though she and Michella also enjoyed sneaking into the clubs and hitting the dance floor. They chuckled when anyone called them party girls, because neither drank, did drugs, or slept around. Dreaming of a career in the music business, Lizzette sang in a female vocal trio called Sweet Sensations, but the group fell apart because one of her bandmates argued with her boyfriend, who pretended to be their manager.

When Lizzette spotted one of her musical idols strolling through Aventura Mall with a bodyguard, she let out an audible squeal. "I followed music, and I saw him with a really tall guy, maybe seven feet tall, and I said, 'Oh, that's R. Kelly!' I guess he overheard me, and he came over and gave me a hug, and I was kind of stunned."

After Kelly walked away, the bodyguard pressed a tiny balled-up piece of paper with a phone number into her hand and told her she should meet them later by the Sports Authority on Biscayne Boulevard. Lizzette couldn't wait to tell Michella, but her best friend was unimpressed. "She told me that she just met R. Kelly, and I was like, 'Okay, whatever.'" Michella agreed to tag along to Sports Authority anyway, thinking it would be an adventure. "So, we went to go meet him at this parking lot, and he was there with a bunch of other guys. I remember one gentleman's name was Barry, and they took us to Outback."

Barry was Barry Hankerson, Kelly's manager. During dinner at Outback Steakhouse, Lizzette noticed that Hankerson kept looking at her with fatherly concern. "It's like he felt bad, you know, like he wanted to help me." The marriage between Kelly and Hankerson's niece Aaliyah had been annulled only a few months earlier. The age of consent in Florida was eighteen, and Lizzette didn't lie to Kelly. "I said, 'I'm seventeen and I'm in high school,' you know? It just came up at dinner, and Robert was like, 'Oh, okay.'" She also told the star she sang, and he seemed eager to audition her. "You know, he makes it seem like he's the coolest guy in the world, and he's out to help you."

Less shy and more direct than Lizzette, Michella came right out and asked the question many had been posing since the marriage certificate appeared in *Vibe* a year earlier: "Didn't you marry Aaliyah?" Neither teen knew at the time that Hankerson was Aaliyah's uncle, but the question embarrassed Lizzette nonetheless. Her cheeks flushed bright red. "I almost died. Barry was sitting there, and it was just, like, *dead silence.*" Finally, Kelly spoke up. "You can't believe everything you read."

The next day, the girls accepted Kelly's invitation to visit Hit Factory Criteria recording studio, where the singer was holed up recording new material. "I sang for him, and he played the piano," Lizzette said. "He said he wanted to help me and develop me and write songs, and I was really excited about it. I was like, 'Wow, finally, my chance!'" But Kelly never recorded with her. "He would say to me, 'When I get Rockland Records going, I'll have you as an artist,' because he was going to start his own label. I was writing songs myself, but he was always busy, that's what he'd say."

During subsequent visits to the studio, Michella said the towering body-guard pulled her to the side while Kelly took Lizzette into another room. The bodyguard seemed to have eyes for Michella, but she wasn't interested. "That was not my cup of tea." She only went to the studio to look after her friend. "As much as I could, I would try to be around Lizzette when she was with him to make sure that everything was okay." Word spread around school that the girls were hanging out with a superstar. "It was a big thing," Michella said, but Kelly always seemed to make sure that no one outside his inner circle saw him with Lizzette. "It was like he kept me hidden," she said. Soon enough, he pressured her to tell Michella to stop coming around, too.

Lizzette cried a lot when we first talked on the phone, and she sometimes broke down completely. Then she'd take a deep breath—"I'm all right"—and push forward with her story. The sexual contact with the twenty-eight-year-old star started within a month of that dinner at Outback, she said, and it continued for more than three years after he took her virginity. "I had stars in my eyes. I came from a broken home. I didn't have a lot of support from my family, and I wanted to make it, you know? I mean, *seventeen*—I was like really naïve, really innocent."

Michella believes she knows why Kelly chose Lizzette. "He seemed to look for girls who didn't believe in themselves or had dad issues. Lizzette had daddy issues." Another member of Kelly's inner circle at that time put it like this: Night after night, the studio or the green room backstage might fill with twenty beautiful women. Nineteen could be twenty-one-year-olds, but Kelly consistently focused on the self-conscious teen standing alone in the corner, staring at her feet, too shy to talk. "He likes the babies, and that's the sickness," Demetrius Smith confirmed. "He can control her, and she don't know no better."

When Lizzette spent the night with Kelly, she lied and told her parents she stayed with Michella. Eventually, her mother and stepfather learned she was dating an older man. They didn't approve, and Lizzette moved out and stayed with Michella's family. She really spent most of her time with Kelly, at first in the studio or at his hotel in Miami, then in Chicago.

"I was always hotel-hopping," Lizzette said. She sometimes visited Chicago Trax, the new recording studio Kelly co-owned in a warehouse on North Larrabee Street near the Cabrini-Green housing project, but she never went to the home he had recently purchased for $3 million in a converted Baptist church on George Street in the North Side's Lakeview neighborhood. She didn't learn Kelly married Andrea Lee, his former dancer, until a year after their 1996 wedding, but Lizzette knew the singer slept with other women. "I couldn't be with him all the time, because there were a million other women with him all the time."

Despite his wealth, Kelly was a crude man, many sources told me, often going for days without showering, and sometimes wearing the same sweatpants for a week. "I could never understand the women. I'd be like, 'How could you be with him when he stinks like that?' I mean, this boy just left the basketball game and he ain't took a shower," Demetrius Smith said. Music was a huge part of the lure. The girls hoped he would give them a career, as he had Aaliyah, and of course, he played his own music for them. "Robert will sit in front of that piano and play to you and create a song right there in front of you," Smith said. "I've seen Robert make women melt."

Lizzette loved sitting beside Kelly at the piano while he sang. "He would never write anything down, it was just off the top of his head, and I was really impressed by him." Sometimes, she wrote down the lyrics he'd just improvised or sung from memory. He had trouble doing that himself.

The relationship had warning signs, but Lizzette didn't recognize them. "It was very controlled—what I wore, how I spoke, who my friends were, who I could bring around." Kelly made her call him "Daddy." She had to ask for food "like he owned me," and he pressured her to perform some sexual acts against her will, including anal play and threesomes with another girl. "I knew that he was weird sexually, even though he was my first everything. It was just not normal to me. . . . His way of talking me into it was like, 'I don't think it's weird, so *you* shouldn't think it's weird.'" She took a deep breath. "He has a way with people, with women. He's just so controlling, so abusive."

When Lizzette didn't please him, she said Kelly lashed out. She claims the physical abuse started in Miami when she spoke to a driver Kelly sent to pick her up at school. "I couldn't talk to any of them, you know?" When she did, she says she got smacked. Another time, they went to dinner before heading to the studio. "I said hello to someone, and he took me outside and he just smacked me," she said. "I didn't understand why, but basically, the instruction was, 'When you're sitting at the table, you only look at *me* and you only talk to *me*.'"

The worst beating occurred at Swissôtel Chicago, Lizzette said. She saw Kelly's car downstairs, but he didn't come to her room. When he finally appeared, "I asked him, 'Do you have other girls here?' Oh, God, he beat the shit out of me that night. Grabbing me, dragging me in the room. Someone heard, and I guess they called security. He was hiding behind the door when security came, and they asked, 'Are you okay?' Clearly, they knew I wasn't, because . . . *obviously*." Lizzette broke down in tears reliving that moment. "But he was on the side of me, and he was looking, like, 'If you say something, I'm *really* going to kill you.' And I just said, 'I'm fine.'"

Kelly always seemed repentant after he got physical, Lizzette said. "Then, he'd be a nice guy. You know, 'I love you, I'm sorry, you know I'm going to help you. I'm going to do everything for you, but you have to *listen* to me.' It was always I wasn't listening to him, I wasn't doing what he wanted me to do, I wasn't being the way he wanted me to be—a typical domestic-abusive relationship, and this was, like, my first relationship in my life."

Lizzette told her friend Michella about the abuse at the time. "He'd leave her trapped up in a hotel room, and there was a couple of times where she called me and she was stranded and he was nowhere to be found," Michella said. "She mentioned times that he had rough-handed her." The relationship began to unravel when Lizzette grew tired of waiting alone in hotel rooms. Then, a year and a half after they met, when she was eighteen, she said she became pregnant with Kelly's child.

"He wanted me to have an abortion. I came from a very Catholic background, and I didn't believe in abortion. I was so scared. You know, I'm in Chicago by myself, this person is telling me this, and he's never around, and I'm young." One night, while waiting at the Marriott Downtown on Chicago's Magnificent Mile, she miscarried. She tried to call Kelly but couldn't reach him, and she went through the experience alone. "I guess it was for the best. I didn't want to go through that abortion."

The end finally came a year later, a little more than three years into the relationship, after Lizzette caught mononucleosis. "He had mono, and he canceled some shows, and he never told me. After I saw him a week later, I started to feel really sick, and I went to the hospital. They said, 'You have mono. You need to go home.' So I tried calling him, calling him. He wouldn't answer, wouldn't answer. My mono turned into Guillain-Barre, and my body basically shut down. I was almost completely paralyzed. My lungs almost collapsed." She spent almost three weeks in intensive care back in Miami. "My parents called him, and he sent a thousand-dollar check to my mother."

Rosa Villanueva, Lizzette's mom, confirmed that she got a check. "I cannot stand this man," she said, still furious many years later. She cried as we talked, too. "It's not just my daughter; he does this to younger girls. I was devastated. When she came back, she was not the same. Mentally, physically, and emotionally, she was not the same."

"After that, I was done," Lizzette said. "You know, I was really hurt. I was damaged. I didn't want to do music anymore. I kind of gave up on my dreams. I wanted to live a normal life. I was too young to go through those things."

In her early twenties, Lizzette moved on with her life. She reconnected with a high school crush, they married, and she had twins. She initially thought about speaking out after she learned about the first story Abdon Pallasch and I published in December 2000. She thought about it again two years later, when she saw a report on local Miami TV news that mentioned Kelly settling several lawsuits brought by underage girls. She contacted an attorney who told her she could get justice by making Kelly pay, but she decided against it. "I wasn't in it ever for money. I didn't want to go through that. I was hurt by him, but I couldn't rehash it again. It was just too much pain, and I had a new life."

The lawyer Lizzette Martinez called, but never hired, was Susan E. Loggans.

"Chicago lawyer Susan Loggans usually gets what she wants," reads the subhed of a glowing 1994 profile by *Chicago Tribune* business reporter Genevieve Buck. It portrays a maverick attorney with a list of professional and personal accomplishments so long it's hard to believe. At least, I had a hard time believing it, but a quarter of a century later, brushing back her long blond hair as we talked via Skype, Loggans reiterated that in addition to being one of the best personal-injury lawyers in the country, she does indeed raise show horses and is a multi-engine, commercial-rated pilot who used to fly to California just to get her hair cut. "I decided that I wanted to be able to have, like, a pomp hairdo in the evening when I went to the Snuggery"—a bar on Chicago's Gold Coast—"but I had to be able to look like a trial lawyer during the day, and I figured if I went someplace where they did actresses, that they would do that."

"Invariably described as flashy, flamboyant, brash, sultry, and smart," Buck wrote, Loggans told me she doesn't disagree with that description. Born on New Year's Eve, 1949, in the downstate Illinois farming town of Clinton (population 5,945 in 1950), she was raised by a divorced mom who was also a lawyer and who'd served as a lieutenant-commander in the navy. Loggans originally enrolled as a premed student at the University of Arkansas because *Playboy* had named it one of the top party schools. Over the next few years, she transferred to several other colleges, earned several degrees, and passed the bar. "Bottom line: Great grades, but I decided against medicine. I got my master's first in psychology, and I got my PhD after that. I wanted to be a trial lawyer because of the audience factor, because I wanted to do great things and be recognized."

With a $60,000 loan, Loggans opened her own firm in 1977. She quickly made her name by winning big money in malpractice cases, including a $2.75 million settlement for a suit in DuPage County and a $4.5 million judgement in Will County. She loved media attention, kept a thick stack of her clips, and never said no to a television or radio interview. She also had her own call-in radio show for a few years. Not surprisingly, Loggans made enemies. "They call me 'dragon lady' around town," she told Buck in the *Trib*. "I am very tenacious. I consider myself an extremely moral person with the highest of ethics. Within the bounds of doing everything ethical, yes, I'm tough, because I will do whatever it takes within those boundaries to be successful."

Forty-eight years old when Tiffany Hawkins settled in 1998, Loggans turned pursuing cases brought by underage girls against R. Kelly into a specialty for the next two decades. "Word on the street got out after Tiffany that if you want to get money from Kelly, you hire Loggans," one of Kelly's former associates told me. Citing attorney-client confidentiality, she's rarely commented about those cases on the record, and she's never told me exactly how many of his victims she's represented. "Numerous" is all she'd say every time I asked, for eighteen years. I have confirmed the names of six girls who hired her, but sources say the total is about a dozen. I tried again to get Loggans to confirm that in early 2019, asking if I'd be wrong if I reported "twelve." She laughed—she'd seen *All the President's Men*, too—and she just said "numerous" one more time.

Of the numerous claims Loggans has brought against Kelly, most have settled out of court. Her firm has filed only three lawsuits against the star. Sixteen-year-old Tiffany's was the first. Sixteen-year-old Tracy Sampson's was the second, and once again, Abdon and I reported it first in the *Sun-Times*.

Growing up with a single mom in Park Forest, a mostly black suburb southwest of Chicago, Tracy masked her teenage insecurities with the self-confident drive and precocious attitude befitting a rapper. Tall and skinny with a long, pretty face and tightly wound braids, she got excellent grades in high school in neighboring Richton Park, and she graduated a year early. She enrolled in the music-business program at Columbia College Chicago in the South Loop. As a college sophomore, she wrote her own artist's biography under her chosen stage name, Royalty.

> At the age of Nine years old, Tracy "Royalty" Sampson started writing her own songs. By the age of Twelve years old, Tracy discovered she didn't just have a love for writing and arranging her own music, but also for all aspects of the music industry; especially performing and the promotions aspect as well. At the age of Thirteen Tracy decided she would like to pursue a career as a rap artist, but she wanted stage name that defined her true personality. That's

when a friend came up with the name "Royalty" because she said "Tracy only wants the best in life". By the age of Fourteen Tracy had arranged and co-produced her first demo tape. Tracy decided at the age of sixteen she had nothing in common with her peers, so her love for the music industry drove her to graduate from high school early (with honors).

During her first year at Columbia College Chicago, the ambitious sixteen-year-old secured an internship in marketing with the regional office of Epic Records. There, Tracy reported to supervisor Cathy Carroll, a promotions manager who also did some work with R. Kelly, even though he recorded for a competing label. In April 2000, Tracy tagged along with Carroll to an "Expo for Today's Black Woman" sponsored by Chicago radio station V103-FM at the Hyatt Regency Hotel near downtown's Magnificent Mile. Kelly was appearing at the event, and Tracy dragged her friend Kelly W. along, too. They wanted to get the star's autograph for another friend, Harriet, who couldn't come because she couldn't skip school.

Kelly hugged Tracy when Carroll introduced them, and he started to put his phone number under his autograph on a head shot, until Tracy told him the signature was for her friend Harriet. Instead, Kelly scrawled his phone number on a small piece of cardboard and whispered in Tracy's ear, "Call me." Then he hugged her again.

That night, Tracy called from her friend Kelly W.'s house, and Kelly W. listened in as the star invited Tracy to Chicago Trax, according to Tracy's lawsuit and Kelly W.'s sworn affidavit. At the studio, the star played the girls two new songs, "Hold on to Me," which later appeared on the soundtrack to the 2001 film *Ali*, and "True Baller," released the same year as the B-side to the single "Fiesta (Remix)." As they listened, Kelly W. said, "Tracy made suggestions and criticisms that R. Kelly seemed to appreciate." A member of his crew later told me the star couldn't help but laugh. "This mouthy little bitch giving him advice on his mixes was pretty funny." As one of his bodyguards sat chatting with Kelly W., the singer led Tracy by the hand to another room. According to her lawsuit, they kissed, and he asked her to masturbate him. She refused, so he masturbated himself in front of her.

Although Tracy said Kelly scolded her when she arrived with friends, telling her never to bring anyone to the studio without first clearing it with him, she kept returning to Trax. She wanted to learn from the singer, producer, and songwriter, and her lawsuit included a long list of the mentoring lessons he gave her. "Robert Kelly told me about the right and wrong use of other people's work [as samples]. . . . Robert Kelly told me to write the 'hook' of a song first [and] referred me to Jay-Z because he is a genius at hooks. . . . Robert Kelly looked at my demo package and critiqued it." He also advised her against working with Eric Payton, who'd been MGM's manager and who'd shown interest in signing Tracy.

The sexual contact started within the first few weeks, and it lasted from the spring of 2000 until the fall of 2001, according to Tracy's lawsuit. Abdon and I looked at each other in disbelief when we read that. Another affair with an underage girl who could not legally consent, and this one was ongoing even while we were doing the reporting for our first story about Kelly's predatory pursuits.

Tracy claimed in her lawsuit that she lost her virginity to the star at age sixteen. "I was lied to by him. I was coerced into receiving oral sex from a girl I did not want to have sex with. I was often treated as his personal sex object and cast aside. He would tell me to come to his studio and have sex with him, then tell me to go. He often tried to control every aspect of my life, including who I would see and where I would go. During our sexual encounters, he would make me do disgusting things like stick my finger up his butt. As a result of this relationship, I am seeing a counselor. I have increased stress in my life. I am afraid of trusting people. I get headaches whenever I see or hear Robert Kelly. I cry when I think about him and what he made me do."

Tracy later said that during sexual contact, Kelly often told her, "Tell Daddy how old you are."

The threesome especially upset Tracy, her friend Harriet said in her sworn statement. "Tracy was emotionally upset after she stopped seeing R. Kelly as well. She often felt disgusted with herself and would cry all the time." The lawsuit included corroborating records about Tracy's subsequent medical and psychiatric care, as well as dozens of pages of phone logs tracking the star's calls to her. It also included travel records documenting the trip

Tracy took with him to Tampa in January 2001 to attend Super Bowl XXXV. Kelly favored basketball over football, but the NFL invited him to the big game after he sang at the halftime show for that year's NFC Championship two weeks earlier at Giants Stadium in New Jersey's Meadowlands.

Abdon never found notice of a settlement in Tracy's case, but Loggans confirmed to us that several months after filing the lawsuit, Kelly paid her client in exchange for signing a nondisclosure agreement like the one that ended Tiffany's claim. Years later, Geoff Edgers of the *Washington Post* reported that Tracy got the same amount as Tiffany, $250,000, presumably keeping the same two-thirds after Loggans's legal fees and costs. Citing her concern for other girls entangled with Kelly and her frustration with how the star treated her, Tracy spoke to Edgers publicly for the first time. "He makes you feel like he's a wounded puppy, like he's hurt so deeply, that there's good there, he just can't get it all out. Being so much older [now], I see how wrong stuff was and how ultimately gross and pedophile-ish it was, but that's something you have to have your adult brain process."

Tracy also told the *Post* that Cathy Carroll, the supervisor at Epic Records, fired her from her internship. "She told me I was a stupid bitch and I shouldn't have talked to him." Tracy gave up her dream of working in the music business, believing her reputation had been poisoned. Edgers talked to Carroll, who by 2018 had become a senior director of radio promotions and strategy for the gospel label RCA Inspiration. "Rob is really a good person," she said. "I think he's just troubled like a lot of these other artists are." Tracy had been "star-struck," Carroll continued. "A lot of these women who claim stuff, they put themselves out there like that, and then they want to turn around and sue people and sue men. A lot of times, it's not really the men. . . . I just know that people who are artsy are kind of kooky, I guess. Different. But he has got a very good heart."

In their responses to Tracy's legal filings, Kelly's attorneys, Chicagoan John M. Touhy and Los Angeles–based Gerald Margolis, included a para-graph citing the star's many charitable works as evidence of that good heart: "Kelly has visited schools to give talks to students regarding staying in school and other topics; he has participated in charity events to help provide food to children; he has visited hospitals to visit sick children; he has provided

Christmas gifts to sick children; he has participated in religious meetings with children and others."

In the fall of 2001, Kelly also wrote a song called "Soldier's Heart," released as a single and dedicated to "the heroes of September 11." He and Jive Records pledged that all proceeds would benefit the Army Emergency Relief organization and hospitalized veterans in the Chicagoland area. The dull, heavy ballad flopped, peaking at No. 80 on Billboard's Hot 100, but it had a second life in the spring of 2003, during the United States invasion of Iraq.

"Radio stations around the country are playing it around the clock," read a statement from the Kelly camp written by his new publicist, Allan Mayer. A few months later, the star announced a concert at the Bell County Exposition Center in Belton, Texas, near Fort Hood, with all proceeds benefiting the Texas Military Family Foundation. I could find no records or follow-up stories of proceeds from the release of the single or ticket sales from the concert benefiting any military charities. When I asked a Jive Records publicist about how much they had raised, she could not give me a number.

"Man, the only reason he ever gave anyone anything is he seen folks like Michael Jackson and Michael Jordan do it," the former associate told me. "He thought that's what he *had* to do to be big-time—that it would be good for business." So Kelly didn't really care about the troops? I asked. My source laughed. "Shit, man. Robert don't give a shit about nobody but hisself."

In April 2002, Susan Loggans brought her third claim against R. Kelly on behalf of a new client, Patrice Jones, who said she began having sexual contact with the star three years earlier, when she was sixteen. For the first time, the *Sun-Times*, the *Tribune*, and other media outlets in Chicago all reported the lawsuit the day it was filed at Cook County Circuit Court. Kelly's attorneys, John M. Touhy and Gerald Margolis, denied the accusations and vowed they'd never settle. "The cash machine is closed," Margolis said.

Kelly's lawyers paid Patrice in exchange for signing an NDA eight months later, but once again, her lawsuit and interviews with other sources told a harrowing tale.

Patrice's story began at the Rock 'N' Roll McDonald's on the corner of North Clark and West Ontario Streets, in a stretch of downtown catering to tourists. After a long day at the *Sun-Times* in the spring of 2002, I walked seven blocks north and west to the massive, two-story, garishly decorated fast-food franchise. The Rock 'N' Roll McDonald's had been built in 1983, and it once held the distinction of being the chain's busiest outlet in the United States. By 2002, the novelty had long since worn off, and it was notable primarily for higher prices for the same fare sold beneath all the other golden arches. (The chain finally tore down the musically themed restaurant in 2018 and replaced it with a new, supersized "green" one.)

I bought a Diet Coke and intentionally sat at the third table from the left, facing the front door. I took in the smell of French fries and burger grease, the harsh neon lights making the bright yellow and red fixtures and plastic furniture glow, and the cheesy displays of music memorabilia and artifacts from the chain's history—guitars, forty-fives, milkshake mixers, and vintage ads—most dating from the era when Ray Kroc opened his first restaurant in suburban Des Plaines in 1955. The place bustled with the usual mix of suburbanites, out-of-town visitors, down-on-their-luck city-dwellers nursing half-empty cups of coffee, and groups of three or four teenagers, sitting together, laughing, and sometimes singing along to piped-in pop songs blaring on the sound system, including the current hits "Foolish" by Ashanti and "Don't Let Me Get Me" by Pink.

No self-respecting musical superstar would step foot in this place, I thought, but I'd heard for months that R. Kelly came here often. He always sat at the third table from the left, facing the front door, in the spot I'd taken. He didn't materialize that night, and I hadn't hoped he would. I just wanted to see what he saw.

Early in my career at the *Jersey Journal*, editors Pat Martinez and Margaret Schmidt taught me that sometimes you choose your stories, and sometimes they choose you. In either case, you're not a journalist if you don't follow them through to the end. Without visiting the Rock 'N' Roll McDonald's, Kenwood Academy, or Evergreen Plaza and the other shopping malls Kelly frequented, readers might not understand how disturbing it was to think of the star haunting these places, accompanied by bodyguards, looking to pick up girls in their mid-teens. More important, without meeting any of those girls, it may be impossible to feel the same empathy for what they told me about having their dreams crushed, finding themselves separated from friends and family, and sometimes being hurt to the point where they tried to harm themselves. I'd seen the scars—physical and mental.

"I'm telling you about it hoping you will write about it and Robert will stop hurting the people he's hurting," the anonymous fax that started it all had read, but I wasn't trying to "save" anybody. This was a story, and it had chosen me.

According to Patrice's lawsuit, around 11:30 one night in December 1998, Kelly was holding court with two of his bodyguards and a third friend at his usual table when she and her cousin entered the Rock 'N' Roll McDonald's. Patrice wore her hair in an elaborate bun that framed her pretty face, and she sported a full-length white silk dress and a big wrist corsage. She and Shareese, both high school seniors, had just come from their prom. Because their overcrowded CPS high school in the city's South Shore neighborhood had staggered schedules with two graduation ceremonies a year, it held a winter ball at a banquet hall as well as a traditional senior prom in the spring.

While their tuxedoed dates, Kareem and Keyon, waited outside in a rented limousine, Patrice and her cousin got on line and ordered cheeseburgers, fries, and sodas for four. Both fans of Kelly, the girls took a few minutes to recognize the man in the sloppy gym clothes staring at them. When the realization hit, they giggled and waved. R. Kelly smiled and waved back.

One of Kelly's bodyguards approached Patrice and handed her a balled-up napkin with a phone number written on it. The singer wanted her to call him, the man said, but she shouldn't tell anybody. Ignoring those instructions, she and Shareese ran outside and gushed to their dates about who was hanging out at Mickey D's. The boys went in to take a look, and they saw that the girls hadn't been bullshitting. Seeing R. Kelly at the Rock 'N' Roll McDonald's was all anyone could talk about when the limo pulled away, but Patrice's date didn't find the encounter nearly as exciting as the rest of the group. He'd heard stories about Kelly's appetites, and the singer had once tried to pick up his sister.

An aspiring record producer, Patrice hoped to follow in the footsteps of Missy Elliott. A week after the prom, she called the number on the napkin. Kelly invited her to visit Chicago Trax so he could show her how the mixing board and the racks of recording equipment worked. Patrice was devoted to her grandmother Rosie, and they spent a lot of time together. In the months to come, Rosie often picked up the phone when Kelly called the house looking for her granddaughter. She didn't approve when Patrice came home in a cab in the middle of the night, and she worried about what was going on at that studio.

Although Patrice told Kelly she was sixteen, she said the sexual contact began shortly after they met and continued for nine months. When Abdon and I charted the dates on the timeline we'd begun keeping, the sexual contacts with Patrice came after those with Tiffany, Aaliyah, and "the girl in Miami" (who I later learned was Lizzette), but before the sexual contacts with Tracy Sampson. The five girls sometimes overlapped within a five-year period, and there were others still, including Tiffany's Kenwood Academy classmate and the girl in Los Angeles from the video shoot. It was all getting very, very confusing—and overwhelming.

Patrice's lawsuit contained fewer graphic details than the claims Loggans's firm brought for Tiffany and Tracy. It did say Kelly once had sexual contact with Patrice while another woman watched, and that Patrice had sexual contact with the singer at his studio, in several downtown hotels, and on his tour bus when she accompanied him to New York for a concert at the Nassau Coliseum on Long Island. The lawsuit claimed Kelly sometimes gave Patrice gifts or small sums of cash, and once, a woman named Regina took her to Chicago's Magnificent Mile luxury shopping strip along Michigan Avenue. "She is R. Kelly's aunt that took me shopping at R. Kelly's direction to buy clothes," Patrice said. Kelly often called publicist Regina Daniels and her husband "Aunt Regina and Uncle George," though they were not related. Regina was the spokeswoman I'd called for comment in the first story Abdon and I reported, the one who hinted that I should kiss her ass.

In September 1999, at age seventeen, Patrice said she told Kelly she was pregnant. He insisted that she have an abortion, but she did not want to go through with it. The first time the bodyguard who gave her the napkin took her to Concord Medical Group on West Grand Street, she told the doctor she'd changed her mind and left, still allegedly carrying Kelly's child. That night, the singer, a thirty-two-year-old married father with a two-year-old daughter, put Patrice up in a downtown hotel. When he visited, she said he exploded. She cried inconsolably, but he eventually convinced her to have the abortion, "through anger, threats, and then persuasion." He also "began crying, stating that his career would be ruined."

The next day, the same assistant drove Patrice to see another doctor at the Family Planning Associates clinic on West Washington Street. She admitted she lied about her age when filling out the medical consent forms—still only seventeen, she claimed to be older—but she once again tried to avoid having the procedure, fleeing the clinic. The assistant followed, she said, and he dragged her back from a Chicago Red Hots stand a block away. He paid for the abortion with three hundred dollars in cash.

The relationship ended less than three months later, in December 1999, but Patrice was crushed, according to her lawsuit and my other sources. In addition to pledging his love, Kelly promised to help launch her career, but they never recorded together. Once again, Abdon charted the legal proceedings though various motions, countermotions, and notices of depositions, until a sudden settlement in January 2003. The file never specified an amount for damages other than "in excess of fifty thousand dollars" for emotional and physical injuries, "embarrassment, shame, fear, and guilt over having had an abortion."

We never learned the amount Patrice received, but Loggans confirmed the payment had been made in exchange for another NDA.

"I don't like going back into the past," Patrice told Geoff Edgers of the *Washington Post* years later. "I feel like God is the judge. Man is not the judge. Everything that he's doing, he's got to pay for it. He's probably already paying for it."

None of the cases Susan Loggans took led to criminal charges against Kelly, though the statute of limitations had not expired for statutory rape charges in Illinois. The lawsuits also raised the possibility of federal charges, since they claimed Kelly traveled with the underage girls and had sex with them in six other states, as well as in Washington, D.C. In one of the most famous cases of underage sex in pop music history, Chuck Berry had been sentenced to sixty months in federal prison and a $5,000 fine for having sexual contact with a fourteen-year-old after traveling with her across state lines, violating the so-called Mann Act. He served three years in federal prison.

"You can't turn these into criminal cases unless the girls are really dedicated to being witnesses, and they're coming to me as a civil lawyer," Loggans told me in 2002. "They're coming to me saying, 'I have a case against R. Kelly.' They know all I can do is sue for money and damages. I've never done a criminal case in my lifetime."

There are other ways to look at it. The girls Loggans represented were closer to being children than they were to legal drinking age, and they came from black neighborhoods with a long history of good reasons to distrust law enforcement. Word on the street got out after Tiffany, "go to Loggans," and the attorney seemed to get results. She was a star like Kelly, and teenage clients may have been taken with that and quicker to trust her than the police. But after "brother needs help," the phrase I heard more than any other while reporting this story was "I was stupid; I was a kid."

Sponsored by Rep. James Robert Mann, a Republican from Illinois, the United States White-Slave Traffic Act of 1910 was passed by Congress as a tool to crack down on organized prostitution by outlawing the transportation of women for "immoral purposes" across state lines. More commonly called the Mann Act, early opponents attacked the law as overly vague, difficult to enforce, and racially biased. World champion heavyweight boxer Jack Johnson was one of the first men arrested for violating its terms in 1912 because of two separate relationships, one with a white sex worker, and the other with a girlfriend, also white, who later became his wife.

Chuck Berry, a key architect of rock 'n' roll who recorded a string of groundbreaking hits for Chicago's Chess Records starting in 1955, was arrested for violating the Mann Act four years later after he met a fourteen-year-old Native American girl, Janice Norine Escalanti, while she was doing sex work at a bar in Juarez, Mexico. She traveled with his band and, prosecutors said, had sex with Berry as the group toured the United States. Berry claimed Escalanti sold his merchandise when they were on the road, then he gave her "respectable employment" at his St. Louis nightclub. He said she only went to police after he fired her for doing a shoddy job. While he didn't deny that they'd shared a bed while on tour, he said he never knew she was underage.

An all-white jury convicted Berry in March 1960. A federal appeals court overturned the verdict, citing disparaging racial comments by the judge, but federal prosecutors tried and convicted Berry again a year later. He emerged from prison in 1963 and scored several more hits, but his career never fully recovered. The sounds of the British Invasion overshadowed his new music, and his famously bad attitude didn't help. Where he once was playful and easygoing, Berry had become distant, bitter, and mercenary. "Never saw a man so changed," said his fellow rock 'n' roll pioneer Carl Perkins. "I figure it was mostly jail."

The list of pop stars and underage girls never ends. In February 2019, a shaggy-haired, twenty-six-year-old singer and YouTube sensation named Austin Jones, from Chicago's western suburb of Bloomingdale, pleaded guilty to coercing six underage girls to send him sexually explicit videos in which they stripped and performed sex acts to prove they were his "biggest fan." Though U.S. District Judge John Lee has yet to sentence the singer, he faces a minimum of five years in prison.

Before February 2019, R. Kelly had only spent a few hours behind bars before posting bail for charges that were later dropped or of which he was acquitted. When I'm asked how that is possible, one of the reasons I come back to is the attorney who struck "numerous" civil settlements, accepting payments in exchange for NDAs rather than encouraging her clients to press criminal charges. During my nearly two decades of reporting about Kelly, Susan Loggans has given me only two significant interviews on the record. In both of them, I asked her views about the girls she represented.

"There are two aspects to this," Loggans said in 2002. "They don't look at it negatively when it's happening, they look at it as a positive thing, that R. Kelly is their boyfriend. It's not until later when he dumps them and then they try to get a job in the music industry that they realize that they're blackballed. They get older and realize that they screwed up and they fell for it. It's like any young girl feels when she gets dumped by a guy. At that point they start telling people, 'Look at this bad thing that happened to me,' and when they come to us as a civil lawyer, there's no benefit to them to bring a criminal case."

In early 2019, as the #MeToo and Time's Up movements brought newly intense scrutiny to men who abuse their positions of wealth, fame, and power to sexually assault women, I didn't think that comment had aged well. Loggans agreed to speak to me for this book, and I read her that quote and asked if she stood by it. "Yep, that's true," she said. Then she reminded me she had a degree in psychology and wondered why I was still pursuing the R. Kelly story.

"I mean this in the nicest way, Jim, but in one way, your life has been poisoned by this whole R. Kelly experience, because it's occupied an emotional component of your life. . . . I'm sure it traumatized you, even if you've repressed it." I don't feel repressed, nor do I think Loggans is correct about the diagnoses she offered for some of her clients (some of whom she admitted she never even met in person). "Look at *Fifty Shades of Grey*. I really believe there is an inherent desire of a lot of women who are in fatherless homes to have someone who is stronger than they are."

Loggans sees three complicating factors to the Kelly saga. One is that laws about underage sex are "very two-sided. . . . I mean, most of these kids in high school are having sex with one another, and many of them are fifteen. Legally, they're committing a felony." Two, "there's also really a feeling that a lot of these girls lied about their age . . . and the laws are so fucked-up anyway, that why should you, you know, worry about a legal definition?" Finally, Loggans said, regarding legal-age women she said contacted her about Kelly but who she chose not to represent, "The word 'kinky' has a different definition for everybody, okay? Most people I know think that if you're urinating on someone, that's gross, including me. But you know, whether somebody thinks a ménage à trois or with four people or whatever, if they're consulting adults, that's not for me to judge. . . . It's not okay with R. Kelly with adults? I'm bothered by that, even though I've gotten all this money from this guy."

Loggans is concerned about the many legal claims recently filed against powerful men. "It's not going to be long where we're going to see the pendulum swing the other way against the whole #MeToo thing. I feel bad for my legitimate clients, who are eventually going to have a hard time getting a fair jury trial because there's been so much bullshit prosecution out there. And that really bothers me."

Me, I think that just like people have different definitions of "kinky," people are bothered by different things.

CHAPTER 6

TROPHIES

During the fourteen months that followed the first *Chicago Sun-Times* story about R. Kelly in December 2000, no other local or national news organization forwarded the reporting Abdon Pallasch and I had done. Activists in black communities across the country, especially women, protested the singer in many forums, their voices amplified in later years by social media. Some columnists—again, mostly women—frequently and effectively criticized the star, but the only news stories competing reporters ran were items following our revelation of the lawsuit filed by Susan Loggans on behalf of Patrice Jones. Kelly seemed to be Teflon.

Abdon and I were shocked and disappointed, given how many people had talked to us. It wasn't hard to find sources with serious, disturbing stories to tell about the singer, especially in Chicago. In our hometown, Abdon partly blames "*Tribune* arrogance" and the famous rivalry between the *Sun-Times* and its competitor. "It was our scoop, so they ignored it, just like they did with the hired-truck scandal," he says, referring to our paper's investigation revealing that the administration of Mayor Richard M. Daley awarded no-work contracts in return for bribes and campaign contributions. The *Trib* only reluctantly covered that story after the mayor broke down in tears on live television.

My partner also reiterates that almost all of the city's legal affairs and investigative reporters were white, and they didn't understand the black community, much less the music world. But arrogance and ignorance didn't excuse the national media. Conversations with many black colleagues made me think that if Kelly's alleged victims hadn't been black, the story would have gotten much more coverage.

"One white girl in Winnetka and it would have been different," said my friend Mark Anthony Neal, a scholar of African American studies and critic of popular culture at Duke University. A white girl from the wealthy white suburb who was seduced by a man visiting her high school choir class, who had underage sexual contact and was coerced into acts with others at age sixteen, would have been major national news, even without the celebrity angle. (In all my reporting on Kelly before early 2019, I heard of only one relationship with a white partner, in the summer of 2017, when Anna Merlan of Jezebel spoke to a legal-age white woman who had what she called a "very controlling" relationship with the singer.) When eighteen-year-old Natalee Holloway disappeared on a high school trip to Aruba in 2005, it received incessant attention on cable news and in print. Similar examples abounded.

I was particularly saddened that many in the music press continued to review Kelly's albums and concerts without even mentioning the accusations we'd reported. Maybe they didn't consider themselves journalists; maybe they viewed their jobs as critics very narrowly, only writing about the music, or maybe, like that editor who'd chastised me for my columns about Michael Jackson, they didn't want to "upset the readers" by noting charges of underage sex in their music reviews.

Were people actually going to have to catch Kelly in the act of hurting some girl before taking the accusations seriously?

In *Soulacoaster*, R. Kelly talks about his fascination with taking Polaroid photos of a sexual encounter he had watched at age eight. From the start of my reporting, several sources told me he was fascinated with technology, and he always loved to have the latest high-tech video gadget. Two of them said he documented his sexual encounters and carried the tapes in a gym bag he kept with him at all times, only leaving it briefly in his tour bus or on the sidelines of the basketball courts in the high-end health clubs where he played with his crew. "There's about four or five tapes out there, in different cities," the former associate told me. "Literally got to be maybe thirty, forty copies of various tapes circulating."

"When you riding on that bus, he shows certain tapes to people," said Kelly's friend and former road manager, Demetrius Smith. "He might show the 'grown-up' tapes, and then he'll leave it on the bus. . . . He'll underestimate people, and the next thing you know, they done took a couple of tapes."

Another source, the only one who ever mentioned this, claimed Kelly had also recorded his sexual contact with Aaliayh, but those tapes had been destroyed.

Abdon and I interviewed several experts on criminal sexual deviance who told us predators often kept "trophies" to document or remember what they'd done. Several of them used the clinical term "ephebophilia" for the compulsion to have sex with adolescents, reserving "pedophilia" for the sexual attraction to prepubescent children. But Dr. Domeena Renshaw, who agreed to meet with us after she read our work, gave us the most insight into Kelly's alleged crimes, and she used the word "pedophile."

A tiny, grandmotherly professor in the Department of Psychiatry and Behavioral Neurosciences at Loyola University, Renshaw is a South African immigrant who opened one of the first sex clinics in the United States, and she remained a giant in the field for more than forty years, until her retirement in 2009. Several things she said stuck with us. Pedophilia is a "tenacious, severe problem," and while some of her colleagues said men who have sex with teens do so because their partners don't have the experience yet to judge them, she believed no one could say for sure. "It's almost as if the hard-wiring of the brain is wrong, but there's been no technical research because it's been defined in the United States as a crime since 1978." She did say with certainty that pedophiles don't stop, "short of putting them in jail, which is simply containing them. When they come out, they will risk four years back in jail for four minutes with another young girl."

Dr. Renshaw added that she was struck by Kelly's brazen public behavior, a contrast to that of many pedophiles who operated in the shadows. "You might wonder," she said, "whether Kelly wanted to be caught. Maybe it was an unconscious plea to 'stop me.'"

On January 4, 2001, only fourteen days after we published our first story, a FedEx envelope empty except for an unmarked VHS tape arrived in the *Sun-Times* mailroom. Whoever sent it typed my name (missing the capital "R") as both the sender and the recipient. They paid cash at a drop-off center, a FedEx spokesperson told us, and he couldn't say exactly where it originated based on the tracking number, other than "somewhere in Los Angeles."

Abdon and I watched the tape in the paper's closet-size video room, where an editorial assistant recorded the evening newscasts to check for any important local stories the *Sun-Times* might have missed. The video showed a light-skinned black girl or young woman with long black hair kneeling on a pillow. Wearing only a white bra and panties, her bare feet faced the camera as she performed oral sex on Kelly, who seemed bored. At one point, he picked his nose, and he only took off his white sweatshirt midway through the two-and-a-half-minute clip. The singer leaned against a counter set against a wall of rough-hewn, light-colored beams, with a sink and a gold faucet to his right, a microwave to his left, and, just beyond that, a rack of what looked like six VCRs. Eventually, Kelly repositioned his partner with her buttocks facing the camera, apparently preparing to have intercourse, but the tape abruptly ended there.

We had no way of knowing who sent the tape; no immediate way of determining who Kelly's sexual partner was; no time stamp indicating when the recording was made; and no way of telling the age of the girl or young woman.

The two of us watched the tape again a short time later with city editor Don Hayner and editor Michael Cooke in the latter's office. We agreed with our bosses that it was hard to tell the age of Kelly's partner—she may have been underage, or maybe not—and that unless we could determine the girl's identity and prove she was an underage victim, we didn't have a story. We spent twelve days trying to answer those questions.

At first, we thought Kelly's partner might be the girl from the prominent family in the south suburbs who we never mentioned in our first story, but we couldn't be certain when we compared her eighth-grade photo to the video. That family still wouldn't talk to us. Judging by the photos we'd collected from her yearbooks at Oak Park and River Forest High School, we could tell the girl was not Reshona Landfair, the teenager Kelly called his goddaughter, according to the fax and the liner notes of *TP-2.com*. We also knew it wasn't Tiffany Hawkins or Tracy Sampson (nor, we later learned, was it any of the other girls who filed lawsuits against Kelly through Susan Loggans). The *Sun-Times* photo staff pulled a discreet headshot from the video, but none of the dozen sources we showed it to recognized the girl or young woman. We didn't say why we asked.

Frustrated, we sat in a conference room two weeks later with our editors and the paper's outside legal counsel for a conversation with long-ranging ramifications. What should we do with the tape?

Journalists do not get involved in their stories; they observe, and they report to the public. They do not do the work of law enforcement. Every reporter who's ever taken an ethics class in journalism school has heard these ideals presented as absolutes. Abdon and I certainly did at Medill and NYU, respectively. Crystalline in their clarity, like most ethical dictums, they can lead to fascinating debates when you consider specific, thorny examples and ask whether there might be exceptions. Should a reporter witnessing a rape stand there and take notes, or try to help the victim by intervening or calling police? Should a photographer who sees someone fall on the tracks in front of an oncoming train shoot the scene, or try to pull the victim to safety? At what point does professional reserve end and moral obligation begin?

Neither Abdon nor I remember the conversation with our editors being especially lengthy or fraught with disagreement. As a Canadian who'd worked on London's Fleet Street, the paper's top editor, Michael Cooke, had a more activist, British-tabloid view of journalism. He had argued with us when our first story included quotes from sources who said Kelly needed help. "What he needs is to be in jail. He's hurting people!" Having been to law school, Don Hayner represented the opposite pole, favoring caution and demanding fairness and balance, always. Abdon initially opposed any cooperation with law enforcement. "They do their job, we do ours," he said. I presented a hypothetical. If someone left a gun in a manila envelope at the paper's reception desk the day a fatal shooting made headlines, would we keep it or call the police to pick it up?

I did not make the gun analogy lightly. The night after the tape arrived, on January 5, 2001, my now-ex-wife and I sat with friends (who happened to be photojournalists at the *Chicago Tribune*) in the living room of our apartment in Lakeview, equidistant by a mile from Wrigley Field and Kelly's home at the time in the converted Baptist church on George Street. The four of us shared a pizza, then popped a Blockbuster video of the Matthew

McConaughey film *U-571* into the VCR. When we heard a loud crash around 10 p.m., we initially thought the noise was from the movie, but it didn't coincide with any depth charges exploding on-screen. We soon discovered it was something else entirely. Someone had shot out the window beside the front door to our two-flat.

Ashland Avenue always bustled with traffic, but we didn't see any cars or pedestrians. My phone number and address were listed. "It was definitely alarming," one of our friends, *Tribune* photo editor Robin Daughtridge, told Mark Caro of *Chicago* magazine years later. "It was like, 'You've got to be careful, Jim.' They had a young child. It was unnerving, for sure." The *Sun-Times* paid to replace the window, but my editors and I decided not to report the incident to police. We didn't know if there was a connection to our story; we didn't want to become part of that story, and we didn't want to be paranoid or melodramatic. It was also possible that it had been a stray bullet, though we lived in a safe, yuppie neighborhood where no one ever heard of errant gunfire.

This was not long after the mid-nineties shooting deaths of hip-hop superstars Tupac Shakur and Biggie Smalls. Many rappers and R&B singers *posed* as gangsters. I had talked to dozens of people close to Kelly, and to varying degrees, they all *talked* tough, reflections of the "R&B thug." But were they really, or was it all fronting? I had never been eager to find out. The Kelly associate who rattled me most was, ironically, the beefy but bespectacled light-skinned accountant, Derrel McDavid.

When we discussed what we should do with the FedEx tape, Cooke advocated giving it to police from the start. Publisher John Cruickshank agreed. My gun analogy convinced Abdon, and he echoed it often in the years to come. Though Hayner still expressed doubts, he ultimately agreed, too, and so did the paper's media attorney, Damon Dunn, and the head of the editorial board, Steve Huntley, its institutional conscience. CPD and the state's child protective services had been investigating Kelly for several years, and the tape presented possible evidence of a felony. Most important, the female subject of the tape could be in harm's way. As much as we didn't want to become part of the story or cross an ethical boundary, we agreed this was the one-in-a-million exception.

Abdon called the Youth Division of the Special Investigations Unit at CPD. He handed Det. Dan Everett the original tape in its FedEx envelope when the investigator came to the newsroom. "You should have this," Abdon said. He didn't say anything more. We didn't know any more about that tape, but Abdon wouldn't have given him additional information even if we did. While the cops set off to do their job, we continued to do ours, but the *Sun-Times* did not report the first video until thirteen months later, in April 2002.

Through the first decade of a career in which he consistently topped the pop and R&B charts, the only association many fans made between Kelly and the word "video" was the slicky produced clips he crafted for his hit singles. It wasn't until early 2002 that a different sort of Kelly video began to proliferate, via bootlegs sold on street corners across the country, as well as in some major record-store chains.

The most famous sex tape before then had been stolen in 1996 from the home of *Baywatch* star Pamela Anderson and her husband, Mötley Crüe drummer Tommy Lee. After a private detective hired by the celebrity couple failed to recover the video, and it began to be appear as a bootleg, Anderson and Lee sold the copyright to a website called Club Love and chose a company for an official release on DVD. "It made an estimated $77 million in less than twelve months," *Rolling Stone* reported, "and that's just on legitimate sales."

A little more than a year after the first Kelly videotape arrived at the *Sun-Times* via FedEx, Abdon bought a video called *R. Kelly Triple-X Sex Tape* on VHS for $10 on a street corner in the Loop. A few days later, I purchased a video called *R. Kelly: Bump & Grind "You Be the Judge"* on DVD for $14.99 at Tower Records on North Clark Street in Lincoln Park. Both of us expensed the *Sun-Times*.

The front cover of the DVD I bought carried a "Parental Advisory Explicit Content" notice like the ones the music industry had begun to place on CDs with explicit lyrics a little more than a decade earlier. It featured a picture of Kelly, bare-chested except for a thick gold chain, with his head bowed in prayer. The back cover noted "©2002 Underground Entertainment." The company, the copyright, and the South Loop post office box it listed all seemed to be fake when I checked into them. Along with four more photos of Kelly, the back cover also included some teaser marketing copy. "You heard about it on the news and everywhere in the streets. Now see it for yourself. R. Kelly's Bump & Grind (and this AIN'T the music video). To say he's a 'Super Freak' would be an understatement. Check out the multi-platinum R&B superstar live, raw, and in the flesh!"

Despite the different titles, the videos Abdon and I bought were identical, interspersing two different scenes of Kelly with two different women. The first was the brief scene from the first video we'd received at the paper. The second depicted someone we only identified after she became the fourth woman to file a lawsuit against Kelly, in May 2002.

Local attorney Donna Makowski sued Kelly on behalf of Montina Woods, a thirty-three-year-old Chicago model, actress, and dancer. It was the first lawsuit by a legal-age woman, and the first from an attorney other than Susan Loggans. In it, Woods claimed that during the summer of 1999, Kelly illegally and surreptitiously recorded her having sex with him in an office at his recording studio, Chicago Trax. She sought damages "in excess of $50,000" for intentional infliction of emotional distress and invasion of privacy. In addition to the singer, she named as defendants Trax studio, Jive Records, and Kelly's accountant, Derrel McDavid, citing all of them for negligence in having "knowledge of the performer's sexual misconduct and failing to act to prevent further harm to the public sector in securing any type of treatment for R. Kelly, who generated income on their behalf."

Age thirty in 1999, Woods danced in Kelly's stage shows, portraying the woman on the giant bed at the end of the concerts on the Get Up on a Room tour. She also toured as a dancer with his friend Ronald Isley, whom Kelly christened "Mr. Biggs." By the early 2000s, the legendary leader of the Isley Brothers was the rarest of pop, rock, R&B, and soul superstars, having scored major hits in almost every decade—the fifties ("Shout"), sixties ("Who's That Lady"), seventies ("Fight the Power"), and nineties, the latter courtesy of Kelly. Isley had guested on Kelly's 1996 single "Down Low (Nobody Has to Know)," and Kelly had contributed to the Isley Brothers' twenty-seventh studio album, *Mission to Please*. On that disc and in its videos, Ronald, then fifty-five, relished playing the role of Mr. Biggs, updating the gangster characters seen in vintage Blaxploitation movies for the hip-hop era.

Attorney Donna Makowski would not talk to Abdon about her client's case, but he later learned that Montina Woods also settled out of court for an undisclosed sum in exchange for signing an NDA. Her lawsuit noted that the scene of her having sex with Kelly had been included on a video sold in Chicago, Atlanta, Los Angeles, Detroit, and New York called *R. Kelly Triple-X Sex Tape*—the same one Abdon had purchased.

The identity of the other girl or woman in those bootleg videos remains a mystery, at least to me. The police proved no more successful in identifying her than we had, though Abdon and I marveled at a curious fact an investigator later shared with us. An FBI expert had determined Kelly's partner almost certainly was in her mid-teens, the investigator said, based on examining the images of the soles of her feet. We remain puzzled about how that worked, and we never connected with anyone who could enlighten us about that particular forensic specialty. Two sources later told me the girl was *not* underage, and that she was "in your line of work," as one said, a member of the media in another Midwestern city.

Woods accepted a settlement, and the other girl or woman may have, too, one of those sources suggested. If she was of legal age, the only crime may have been an unreasonable invasion of privacy. The scenes themselves were ultimately no more disturbing (or titillating) than most of the amateur porn clips that had begun to take up a lot of bandwidth in the early days of streaming video on the Net. But the video the *Sun-Times* received via FedEx set a precedent that held when we received a second, much more troubling and ultimately notorious tape.

PART II

CHAPTER 7

GO TO YOUR MAILBOX

The first Friday in February 2002, I planned to spend a long day working at home. Powering through on four cups of coffee after taking my five-year-old daughter to preschool, I spent the morning transcribing a phone interview with neo-soul singer Alicia Keys, who was returning to Chicago on a tour stop supporting her phenomenally successful debut, *Songs in A Minor*. "There's always those two sides," Keys said when I asked about the mix of praise and criticism she'd gotten for talking about how hip-hop sometimes disrespects women. "I just feel it's time to show people how beautiful a woman is and how much she's worth and how much she should be respected. There's so much more than what's kind of become the cliché of women in music."

As the pop music critic at the *Chicago Sun-Times*, I spent a lot of my time writing feature previews of artists coming to town, as well as reviewing their shows. For important national or high-profile local artists, I wrote longer features for the Sunday paper, as well as reviewing albums every Sunday, and sometimes on Tuesdays when an especially anticipated release arrived in stores. I wrote obituaries of the greats on deadline—James Brown delayed my daughter opening her presents for a few hours on Christmas morning, 2006—and I reported or wrote commentary on news stories on my beat, from a stampede at the E2 nightclub on the South Side that left twenty-one people dead in 2003, to the corporate merger of Ticketmaster and concert promoters Live Nation, which sent the price of tickets soaring. Investigative stories about R. Kelly added to the usual workload for both legal affairs reporter Abdon Pallasch and me—rare was the week when each of us didn't have half a dozen bylines on our respective beats—but sometimes you choose your stories, and sometimes they choose you.

After I transcribed the Keys interview, I wrote and filed the feature to run before her show at the South Side's Arie Crown Theater. Then I dove into transcribing another phoner with Scotty Moore, the guitarist who'd been a sideman on the best recordings by Elvis Presley. My job was nothing if not musically diverse. I planned to get a jump on the deadline for writing that column when the phone rang. Annoyed and eager to be done for the day, I answered in practiced harried-journalist dudgeon. "Jim DeRogatis."

"Go to your mailbox," a gruff baritone commanded, then hung up.

I already expected—and dreaded—what I'd find.

Frustrated that we hadn't been able to nail all the facts about R. Kelly and the girl he called his goddaughter, Reshona Landfair, the first story Abdon Pallasch and I published in the *Sun-Times* a few days before Christmas 2000 made no mention of that relationship. Only one sentence even hinted at its existence. "Chicago police twice have investigated allegations that Kelly was having sex with an underage female but dropped the investigations because the girl would not cooperate."

Six weeks after the first story ran, Abdon and I each got a letter, cc'd to editor Michael Cooke as well as the paper's media attorney, Damon Dunn. Writing on behalf of his clients, Greg and Valerie Landfair, and their daughter, Reshona, Chicago lawyer Daniel H. Touhy cited that one sentence: "The natural and obvious implications are false and defamatory. The fact that the Landfairs are not identified by name in your article makes no difference. It is well-known in their community that Robert Kelly is a close friend. Demand is hereby made upon you to immediately cease and desist."

The letter mentioned Reshona's name four times, and misspelled it twice.

Rather than worrying anyone at the paper, we thought the letter confirmed we'd been on to something. Kelly himself never threatened to sue the paper for any story Abdon and I wrote—ultimately, we would share thirty-three bylines between 2000 and 2008—and his camp never even demanded a correction or a clarification. We didn't learn anything else about Kelly's relationship with Reshona until shortly before the next Christmas, on December 19, 2001. (The Kelly story had a way of ruining my holidays.) Sparkle called *me* this time, her voice shaking and fraught with emotion.

"When you talked to me last year, I couldn't say anything, but I've since gotten proof. This is not a rumor, this is something that I totally seen with my eyes. I got a phone call on Friday stating that there was a tape surfacing with my niece, and I know you can't publish minors' names, but I was just like, okay, is it true, is it true, is it true? So, two of my friends actually viewed the tape and know my family personally, so they knew it was my niece."

During my reporting a year earlier, Sparkle hadn't said much when I connected with her through a Motown Records publicist and asked about the relationship between Kelly and her niece Reshona. "I'm not her parents or whatever." Now, she continued, a man had come to her apartment claiming to represent a Chicago attorney named Buddy Meyers. He gave her the lawyer's card, and then he showed her a videotape. What she saw left her disgusted, horrified, and enraged. She said the man left with the tape, and she didn't hear from him again, but she began making phone calls, telling people what she'd seen. She asked her brother to call their sister. Sparkle had been estranged from Valerie and Greg Landfair since she'd told them to keep their daughter away from the star after she split with him.

Next, Sparkle called the Illinois state's attorney's office. She didn't know exactly who to ask for, and wound up talking to the deputy supervisor of felony review. She took notes during these calls, and she carefully spelled the name of the man, Robert Heilingoetter. Years later, I talked to Heilingoetter, now retired. "I worked murder cases, not sex crimes, but I took Sparkle's cold call. I remember she was speaking very cryptically. 'Well, what if I had this, and what if I had that, and can't you do something without?' And I'm like, 'Well, if what you're saying is true, you have to come forward. And we'd have to see this tape.' "

Next, Sparkle called the Illinois Department of Children and Family Services, where she spoke to a woman named Kim. She didn't catch her last name. Kim told Sparkle the same thing. The office could only act if it had a copy of the tape.

Finally, Sparkle called me. At first, I thought she might have seen the first tape that had been sent to the *Sun-Times* via FedEx eleven months earlier, but she described a much longer and more disturbing video. She believed her now-seventeen-year-old niece Reshona appeared in the scene with Kelly when she was fourteen, based on her hairstyle at the time. "The horrible thing about this tape is he's doing some things to her that I know it had to have been going on for a long time. The most demeaning thing on the tape is that he's pissing in her mouth and, excuse my language, nutting in her mouth. Telling her to pucker up her lips. She's a young girl, so he's just brainwashed her to death. Something needs to be done."

I called William "Buddy" Meyers first thing the next morning. "I have no idea why they threw my name around. I'm not involved with R. Kelly right now or anybody connected with R. Kelly right now." The attorney kept a low public profile, Abdon said, though Meyers also had been one of the owners of the Chicago Wolves American Hockey League team since its inception. Sparkle told me she believed that whether or not the man who showed her the tape was connected to Meyers, he did it to confirm the girl was Reshona and that she'd been underage in the clip, probably so he could blackmail Kelly. The way Meyers said those last two words, *right now*, prompted me to keep questioning. Have you *ever* represented anyone connected to Kelly? *Will* you? Do you have a videotape of Kelly in your office? Have you seen one?

"I don't have a videotape. I've got some people I've talked to briefly, but nothing further. Right now, my firm has not been engaged with anybody having anything to do with R. Kelly. I've heard some scuttlebutt, but that's all I'm at liberty to say right now."

Through the holidays and into the new year, Abdon and I called all the sources we'd developed. As of the first week of January 2002, none of them had yet seen a tape with Reshona, though several had heard about "a new video on the streets." We agreed with city editor Don Hayner: We didn't have a story yet because we didn't have a tape, but we kept making calls. Then, a month later, somebody called me.

"Go to your mailbox."

I went to the mailbox beside the front door of the house I'd only recently purchased on Grace Street on Chicago's Northwest Side and found an unmarked VHS cassette in a blank manila envelope. You have to be accessible if you're a journalist, and even after the bullet through the window on

Ashland Avenue, I'd made sure my home-office number and address were listed. I ran upstairs to my daughter's bedroom, popped *Toy Story 2* out of the VCR, put the unmarked tape in, tossed her beloved Jessie doll aside so I could sit on the edge of what she called her "big-girl bed," and hit play.

The twenty-six-minute, thirty-nine-second video seemed to have been shot in the same location as the first short tape we'd received, in the room with the rough-hewn, light-colored beams. Abdon and I had since learned that some members of Kelly's crew called it "the Colorado room," though most referred to it as the "log-cabin playroom." It was located in the converted Baptist church he owned on George Street. More of the room could be seen in this new tape, including a huge pine-paneled hot tub. The video lacked a time stamp, but we later concluded it was made sometime in late 1998 or early 1999, possibly around the holidays. An unseen television played in the background, tuned to a new-music video program. "Let's Have a Party Tonight" by the Backstreet Boys and "Too Much" by the Spice Girls could be heard, both big hits at the time, and the station aired a commercial for the Money Store, a lender specializing in sub-prime home-equity loans that had stopped using that name about six months after its sale in June 1998.

Much clearer and longer than the tape from FedEx or the bootlegged clip with the legal-age dancer, Montina Woods, this video started with a man I immediately recognized as Kelly sitting on a cushioned bench beside the hot tub, dressed in red sweat pants and a white T-shirt, seemingly checking the angle of an unseen camera. The tape cut out for a second, then returned as the man handed something—I couldn't initially see what—to a fully dressed, big-breasted, short-haired girl with round chipmunk cheeks. I thought I recognized her, too, from the Oak Park and River Forest High School yearbook pictures Abdon had photocopied more than a year earlier. It was Reshona Landfair.

"Thank you," she muttered, before she performed fellatio on Kelly, occasionally shooting glances at the camera. The video cut out again, then came back as she danced for him in and atop the ledge of the hot tub, following his directions—"Dance faster, baby"—now naked except for a big silver cross around her neck. At his prompting, she urinated on the floor outside the hot tub, then straddled him as he sat on the bench and they had intercourse. Seemingly double her size, he called her "Shona," and she called him "Daddy."

"Daddy fuck you?" he asked. "Yes, Daddy," she said. The girl's eyes had a vacant, disembodied look as she robotically followed Kelly's commands, and her expression showed no signs of pleasure, or any emotion at all.

The tape cut out again before it returned with the girl lying on the bench next to the hot tub, performing fellatio again, then opening her mouth as Kelly urinated in it and over her breasts and stomach before fondling himself and ejaculating. There the video ended.

I hit eject, immediately got in my car, and drove the nine miles to the gray, barge-like *Sun-Times* building, walking straight into city editor Don Hayner's office. He told me Abdon had just left. I caught my partner on his cell phone as he rode the Orange Line to Midway Airport for a flight to Denver and the rare splurge of a snowboarding weekend with college buddies and his then-fifteen-year-old son. "No shit," Abdon repeated several times as I told him about what I'd seen. "No shit." I watched the tape for a second time within ninety minutes with Hayner and my immediate boss, entertainment editor John Barron, in the paper's closet-size video room full of VCRs and television sets. Hayner and I watched it again half an hour later with the top news executive, Michael Cooke, this time on the VCR and much larger TV in his spacious office with windows overlooking the Chicago River.

The *Sun-Times* had set a precedent—or crossed an ethical Rubicon, if you sided with those who criticized us—by giving the first tape to police, and we didn't debate what to do now. Cooke and Hayner called Damon Dunn to inform him of what we'd gotten. Someone in the newsroom—I think it was Hayner, but he doesn't recall—called the Special Investigations Unit at CPD and asked them to come to the office. I went outside and had a smoke, a nasty habit I'd idiotically picked up in the past year, at age thirty-seven.

Less than four hours passed between the time I found the tape in my mailbox and when Det. Dan Everett, Sgt. Debbie Chiczewski, and a third member of their squad buzzed the intercom at the glass doors between the elevators and the newsroom. John Barron and I met them in the hall and gave them the tape in the manila envelope, barely saying a word. The investigators left, then came back and buzzed again a few minutes later. "Was there a note?" Sergeant Chiczewski asked. "And is this the original tape you got?" We assured the officers there wasn't, and it was.

A few months later, the Ethics Corner column of the journalism trade magazine *Editor & Publisher* harshly criticized us for these actions. Columnist Allan Wolper excoriated us and our editors, saying we "had forgotten for a moment that newspapers report to the public, not to the police." Steve Rhodes also questioned the paper's decision in his media column in *Chicago* magazine: "Several experts in media ethics say the action by the *Sun-Times* is dangerous, that there is a risk in a news organization's becoming, to use a commonly invoked phrase, 'an arm of law enforcement,' jeopardizing its independence and throwing in with the prosecution."

The *Sun-Times* responded in a column written by Michael Cooke and editorial page editor Steve Huntley, unanimously approved by the rest of the editorial board.

> We think Rhodes and the critics are missing a few obvious and important points. First, no one subpoenaed or pressured the *Sun-Times* to give police the video. It was our idea. We did it voluntarily because while sources must be protected—otherwise no one would take their stories to a newspaper—the videotape was not a source; it was a piece of evidence in a criminal investigation that up to that point had been stalled. Second, we do not view crime indifferently. The video showed an adult sexually exploiting a teenage girl and urinating on her. Perhaps Rhodes and company should talk to a few parents to get a sense of this crime. . . . We agree that we are not a law enforcement agency. But we are citizens—not of some journalistic utopia, but of Chicago—and as such we try to both publish news and do our civic duty.

I never thought we did the wrong thing by handing the tape to police. Neither did Abdon, who was as sickened by the video as I was when he saw it on Monday. Hayner tried to clear the decks for both of us to spend as much time as necessary on the required reporting before we could write about the tape, but we needed to move fast. We didn't know if any other news organization had it; we didn't know how quickly the police would act, and most important, we didn't know if the actions it depicted were ongoing with Reshona or any other young girl, although we certainly feared the worst.

Before the police arrived that Friday evening and entertainment editor John Barron and I gave them the tape, I made a copy in the paper's video closet. *Sun-Times* lawyer Damon Dunn will groan when he reads that sentence, but it's a fact. We had to do our job, to verify and report. After the cops left, I called Sparkle. Hayner had confirmed what I'd already known, that I had to show her the tape to determine if it was the one she'd seen and if the girl was her niece Reshona. Sparkle couldn't come into the office until Monday.

That weekend was one of the longest of my life. I rehearsed as usual on Saturday at noon, playing drums with my punk band, Vortis, then took my daughter to the movies early that evening to see *Monsters, Inc.* I went grocery shopping on Sunday morning, then watched Super Bowl XXXVI, but only because I had to review the halftime show on deadline. (I hate sports.) U2 performed with a melodramatic and bombastic tribute to the victims of 9/11. Commenting on the televised music in broadcast spectacles like the Super Bowl and the Grammys ranked among my least-favorite tasks as pop music critic. Watching the video with Sparkle the next day stands as the hardest thing I've ever done as a journalist.

Early Monday morning, Sparkle walked off the elevator on the third floor of the *Sun-Times* a full-on diva, wearing a white fur coat over a glittery purple dress, sporting dark blue eyeshadow and bright lavender lipstick, her long blond hair flowing down her back. Uncertain about where to find me, the business reporter she met in the elevator led her to the desk I rarely used in the features department. Pop stars didn't often come into the office, and certainly not dressed as a cutthroat femme fatale. "Somebody's here to see you, DeRo," my colleague said. As we headed to the video closet, he silently mouthed, "*Wow.*"

While we watched the tape, which was indeed the same one the man who came to her apartment had shown her, Sparkle wasn't a pop star or a diva. She was a worried and sickened twenty-six-year-old named Stephanie Edwards, who grew up singing in the church, and who'd seen her dream of a musical career recast as a nightmare. She trembled at times as she spoke. There were no tissues in the video closet, so when she began to cry, I pulled the handkerchief out of my left pants pocket and handed it to her. She laughed. It seemed like a very old-fashioned thing to do, but my stepdad always carried a handkerchief, and since I emulated him in many ways, so did I.

I'd had a woman close to me share her story of sexual assault before, in college. Then, I just listened. Now, I had to ask questions—it was my job—in a claustrophobic space, while the worst video I've ever seen played for us. I don't think any actress could fake the emotion Sparkle showed about what she saw happening to "my heart," her niece, or about the way it had torn her family apart. "I mean, the most horrible thing about the tape is when he's relieving himself in her mouth and it's . . . I can't even fathom."

Sparkle had introduced Reshona to Kelly when her niece was twelve, she reminded me, hoping he'd help her musical career. She clearly felt incredible guilt for that. She repeated that Reshona looked to be fourteen on the tape. Kelly was just shy of or had just turned thirty-two. "She doesn't have her hair like that now. She wears braids now. And by this tape, it looks like she's been doing it longer than fourteen. It's definitely a plan, a script, she's used to it, she's like, 'Now I have to do *this*.'"

Sparkle grew most emotional when talking about how Kelly handed Reshona money. "She is not a fucking whore!" I hadn't noticed what Kelly gave her when I'd watched before, only that something changed hands. Sparkle asked me to rewind and pointed to the screen. Now I saw the cash. "You see that? He's paying her money!" That thought made her furious, and she broke down, racked by sobs.

"He has to stop," Sparkle said when she caught her breath. "There have been too many to count. They definitely had to be young. His whole MO, he stated this to me long ago, he likes them when they are ripe and young because he can mold them into what he wants them to be, and control their minds and make them do what women 'should' do. That's what he thinks, you know, be a servant, be the 'yes.' She's on there calling him Daddy! What kind of daddy would do this to their daughter?"

Of course I asked Sparkle who she thought brought me the videotape. She said she didn't know. Journalists often say or ask something because they're fishing for a reaction, or floating a trial balloon, if you prefer that metaphor. I said I thought Kelly's ex-manager Barry Hankerson had to be angry about what Kelly had done to his niece Aaliyah. He was also disgusted by his former client's compulsion to pursue underage girls; he'd asked his lawyer to confirm to me that he'd made that claim in his resignation letter. Did he steer the tape to me? "I don't know," Sparkle said. "I'm sure he would tell you. He'd have no problem telling you." Hankerson never did.

After Sparkle left on Monday, I called John M. Touhy, Kelly's Chicago-based attorney. As Hayner and Damon Dunn instructed, I told Touhy the paper had received a videotape apparently showing Kelly having sexual contact with an underage girl, and the attorney could come to the office to view it and comment. He declined. It was, Touhy later wrote, "an invitation that I was unable to accept at that time."

On Tuesday, Abdon and I returned to the modest cream-colored stucco house that we'd first visited thirteen months earlier in Oak Park. A "village" of fifty-two thousand people, Oak Park is actually the twenty-ninth biggest city in Illinois, one of quaint storefronts and beautiful turn-of-the-century houses, including twenty-five designed by Frank Lloyd Wright, whose home and studio were there. It all provides a stark contrast to Chicago's neighboring West Side, immediately across Austin Boulevard. Many of the stores that burned there during the 1968 riot still haven't reopened, half a century later. Driving away from Lake Michigan through the West Side to Oak Park can feel at times like traveling from a postapocalyptic landscape to Main Street, U.S.A. in Disney World.

No one answered the door at the Landfair home on that trip or during our next two visits, the first on a relatively balmy thirty-degree afternoon, and the second that evening when the temperature had plummeted and we stood shivering on the doorstep. The family seemed to have left town. We later learned they'd gone to Europe, ostensibly for a tour by 4 the Cause, an R&B group comprised of Reshona and three of her cousins, but they stayed for several months. Reshona's parents, Greg and Valerie, did not return our calls. They weren't returning calls from family members, either, Sparkle said.

While racially and economically diverse, the student body at Oak Park and River Forest High School ultimately was as stratified as the neighboring communities. On Wednesday, I interviewed several of Reshona's classmates, feeling decidedly creepy as I approached groups of girls carrying their backpacks and giggling when school let out. I found a trio who said they knew Reshona. She bragged about her friendship with R. Kelly, they said, and the student newspaper had published a photo of Kelly sitting in the bleachers watching her play basketball. The girls had heard about a video "on the streets." They and other classmates I later talked to told me more about Reshona, a bubbly teen known for stopping and hugging friends in the halls between classes. She had as many white as black friends, and she was a good though not great student. She loved to listen to all kinds of music, shoot hoops, and hit North Riverside Park Mall after class, especially when the new Air Jordans arrived, so she could be first to wear them to school the next day.

Meanwhile, Abdon called a video expert. "Slim to none," he said when Abdon asked about the possibility of fabricating such a tape. "Twenty-six minutes of putting someone else's head on someone's body, you're talking about hundreds of thousands of hours of frame-by-frame manipulation to make that work." (Digital video didn't start to take off until the mid-1990s, and the ability to edit it on home computers only became widely available in the mid-2000s.)

On Thursday morning, I called Gerald Margolis, Kelly's celebrity attorney in Los Angeles, and left a message that the *Sun-Times* sought comment for a story about his star client, an underage girl, and a videotape. John Touhy called me. "Any tape you have is a fake, and we find the timing of these events to be extremely suspicious," Touhy said of the video he had declined to watch. Asked about the investigation, Touhy said, "I would imagine that the police will do their job." Questioned whether he knew if Kelly videotaped his sexual encounters, he snapped at me, "I don't think it's any of your business."

(After the *Sun-Times* published its first story about the tape, Margolis asked to see it, but the paper's editors and attorneys said it had been a one-time invitation. In a letter dated March 1, Touhy wrote that that decision was "grossly unfair." He also noted, "A videotape similar to the one described in the *Sun-Times* article has been available on an Internet site. The owner of that site . . . has been widely quoted in the press, and also personally stated to us, that the videotape he placed on the Internet is a 'fake' and that he put it on the Internet to demonstrate it is not Mr. Kelly." Abdon and I watched that scene, and indeed, it was not R. Kelly. It also was not the video we'd received.)

By Thursday evening, Abdon and I had written the final draft of our story. It had been read by Hayner and the copy desk, vetted by Dunn, and laid out by the designers. Abdon, Barron, Hayner, and I gathered in a conference room with Hook and Crook, editor Michael Cooke and publisher John Cruickshank, and the top bosses read the page proofs. The story did not name Reshona or Sparkle; Sparkle had talked on the record, but identifying her would mean effectively identifying her niece, an underage rape victim. The story did reveal for the first time that we had received another video a year earlier, the one that came via FedEx. "It appeared to show Kelly having sex with a different woman, whose age and identity have not been determined." Based on what police told him that morning about the new tape, Abdon wrote, "Now, with the video, authorities tell the *Sun-Times* they are more optimistic about building a case against Kelly."

At one point, Cooke stopped reading and pounded the conference table with the palm of his hand. "People do not want to read about urination in their morning paper!" The language had become more discreet and less specific with each draft, but I argued that we had to include the specific act. We have to let people know this is not a good-time, Tommy Lee and Pamela Anderson sex tape, I said. This is different.

Cooke conceded, but the sentence "The sex acts include intercourse, fellatio, and urination" only appeared in the thirtieth of thirty-six paragraphs when the story ran as the smaller of two on the front page on February 8, 2002, a week after I received the tape.

Chicago police are investigating whether R&B superstar R. Kelly—part of today's opening act at the Winter Olympics in Salt Lake City—had sex with an underage girl and videotaped the illegal act.

A twenty-six-minute, thirty-nine-second videotape, which was sent anonymously to the *Sun-Times* last week, shows the singer-songwriter performing various sex acts with the underage girl.

"I'm that little bit of hope / When my back's against the ropes / I can feel it / I'm the world's greatest," Kelly sang at the Olympics that day. The opening ceremony received the highest Nielsen ratings of any to that point, reaching an estimated seventy-two million viewers, according to the *New York Times.* Kelly belted out his new single from the movie *Ali*, another attempt at a rousing anthem like "I Believe I Can Fly," complete with a gospel choir. The Olympics were a hell of a news peg, but the timing was accidental. The story was a complicated one, and it hadn't been ready to publish a minute earlier.

Kelly spoke to Chicago's NBC affiliate, WMAQ, before he took the stage in Utah. "It's not true," the thirty-five-year-old singer said. "All I know is this: I have a few people in the past that I've fired . . . people that I've thought were my friends that's not my friends. It's crap, and that's how we're going to treat it. The reason these things are happening, I really do believe, is because of the fact that I didn't fall back as far as blackmail was concerned. I didn't give them any money. The world is getting ready to watch me sing a song called 'The World's Greatest,' and you've got a tape out there trying to ruin my career. I feel like I owe my fans."

The videotape story got much more attention than anything Abdon and I had reported about Kelly before. Once again, the Associated Press picked it up as "The *Chicago Sun-Times* is reporting . . . ," recapping that police were investigating a tape with an underage girl, and prominently quoting Kelly's denial. No other news organization locally or nationally forwarded our work or added to the accusations in the weeks that followed, but this time, ministers and community activists in Chicago, Philadelphia, New York, Atlanta, and Los Angeles decried the star's behavior. Many black women urged boycotts of stores selling Kelly's music and radio stations playing his songs. Few of those businesses complied.

The singer's record label promptly released a one-sentence statement defending one of its biggest hit-makers: "R. Kelly has been with Jive Records for eleven years, and we fully support him and his music."

On March 19, 2002, Kelly released his next album, a collaboration with rapper Jay-Z, *The Best of Both Worlds.* The disc had the combined marketing muscle of four record companies: Jay-Z's boutique label Roc-A-Fella and

Kelly's Rockland Records, and the larger labels for which the artists recorded, Def Jam and Jive. Sales proved disappointing for a joint effort pairing the biggest stars in hip-hop and R&B. The disc sold only 285,000 copies in its first week, at a time when superstar product still regularly moved a million units or more upon release. Although he didn't comment on the video story, Jay-Z distanced himself from Kelly, canceling the planned tour supporting the album.

This time, a few of Kelly's peers weighed in, dissing Kelly. Rapper Nas told a concert audience, "We're not up here molesting children. We're not 'The Best of Both Worlds.'" Sisqo, who'd scored a hit with the Kelly-like "Thong Song," released a new track with the call-out, "The world's greatest? Whatever / Ain't nothing but a child molester." And multiplatinum producer Dr. Dre shelved a single by his own latest protégé, R&B singer Truth Hurts, because it featured a cameo by Kelly. As a member of pioneering gangster-rappers N.W.A, Dr. Dre had a hand in crafting vilely misogynistic tracks such as "Findum, Fuckum & Flee," "One Less Bitch," and "I'd Rather Fuck You." He also had beaten journalist Dee Barnes and tried to throw her down a flight of stairs, according to *Rolling Stone*. But even he had limits.

"I haven't seen the video," Dr. Dre told MTV, "nor do I want to see it, because there's a kid involved. That's where I draw the line."

Abdon and I continued following every development on the R. Kelly front through the winter and into the spring. In April 2002, Kelly sold his home in the converted Baptist church on George Street. He'd purchased it in the fall of 1994, and we believed it was the scene of both videos we'd received. The singer had recently bought a sprawling, twenty-two-thousand-square-foot stone mansion in south-suburban Olympia Fields for $5 million. He'd always been impressed by the place when he drove by with his friends, he says in *Soulacoaster*, all the more so after he learned it had been built by an executive of his favorite restaurant chain, McDonald's.

Abdon made an appointment and toured the now-empty home on George Street while it was on the market. I laughed when I thought about him in his suit from Irv's discount men's warehouse, viewing the place with a real estate agent, as if he was a buyer who could afford a $3 million property. I know I couldn't have pulled that off.

The listing agent from Coldwell Banker pitched the redbrick building in the *Chicago Tribune* as "a very specialized property that would appeal only to a very narrow segment of the population." The house boasted an indoor lap pool, a wall-size shark tank, a home movie theater, and a basketball court adorned with a *Space Jam*–inspired mural. It depicted Kelly shooting hoops with the Tasmanian Devil, Michael Jordan refereeing, and Yosemite Sam and Elmer Fudd sitting in the stands. Foghorn Leghorn also appeared, holding a sign reading, "Go R. Kelly!"

The log-cabin playroom interested Abdon the most, and he noted that it came complete with video cameras mounted on a wall and on the ceiling above the hot tub. My sources said Kelly had already built an identical room in his new mansion. Investigators told us they'd toured and scrutinized every inch of the house on George Street, but they were frustrated that Mark Cavins, supervisor of the child sex abuse unit for the Cook County state's attorney's office, refused to request a warrant for them to do the same at the Olympia Fields mansion. They had hoped to find the clothes Kelly wore in the video. Some thought the state showed too much concern about possible criticism for harassing a black male superstar and not enough consideration of the young black girl he had victimized.

The Landfairs still were not cooperating with law enforcement, and they weren't letting investigators near Reshona. One of them who'd earlier told me that Greg and Valerie Landfair "were ice-cold" during their initial interviews in 1999 and 2000 said that during the new interviews about the videotape, they thought Greg was on the verge of talking. "We kept saying to him, 'Man, this is your daughter, you're a father, how can you watch this and not be furious?' But his wife, realizing we were in there with him alone, burst into the room and said, 'This conversation is over,' and she dragged him out."

I continued talking to all the sources I'd developed, and by late April, three months after the *Sun-Times* revealed the existence of the video, some of them had received subpoenas to appear before a grand jury. The star's handlers fully expected an indictment, and in an attempt to get in front of it, they arranged for Kelly to give a long interview to journalist Ed Gordon for *BET Tonight*. They intended the conversation to be the opening salvo of an aggressive campaign to minimize the damage to an incredibly lucrative career. By 2019, Kelly would prove to have earned nearly $250 million for himself and a full $1 billion for Jive Records, according to a source who knew the finances.

Derrel McDavid, Kelly's accountant-turned-manager, followed the advice of Los Angeles attorney Gerald Margolis and executives at Jive not only to retain a top-flight criminal defense attorney in Chicago, but to hire publicist Allan Mayer, as well. The public-relations battle would be as important as the legal fight, and *Variety* described Mayer as "Hollywood's most prominent crisis specialist." He had even coauthored a book on how to handle celebrity scandals, *Spin: How to Turn the Power of the Press to Your Advantage.* In his first big job for Kelly, he prepped the singer for the interview with Gordon, who'd been chosen for the exclusive because he'd be tough but fair. Kelly had trouble reading the notes Mayer prepared for him, so he walked the singer through them verbally. "Like a lot of people with a disability, they compensate in other ways," Mayer told me. "He had an amazing memory."

During the interview, which first aired on May 8, 2002, Kelly sat across from Gordon in a luxurious suite in a downtown Chicago hotel. Hair neatly braided, beard trimmed, and eyes clear and sharp, Kelly wore a striped charcoal suit jacket over a black sweater vest and a white T-shirt. He looked unnaturally cool for a man risking fifteen years in prison and the destruction of everything he'd spent many of his thirty-five years building.

For part of the interview, the Rev. James Meeks joined Gordon and Kelly. Introduced as the singer's "spiritual advisor," Meeks served as pastor of Salem Baptist Church in the South Side's Pullman neighborhood. He was also second in command to the Rev. Jesse Jackson in the black community's activist Rainbow/PUSH Coalition. "In America, we're innocent until proven guilty," Meeks said. "Rob hasn't been convicted of anything, Rob hasn't been charged of anything. . . . But, Ed, I would want the record to read that if he *had* been convicted and charged, God still has an umbrella big enough for all of us to fit under."

Kelly said Meeks supported him while he sought help for a problem he never specified. "I've done a lot of things in my life right now that I'm trying to get help for." Two of his handlers told me they forced him to take medication to curb his sex drive (his attorney Ed Genson later confirmed that, saying, "I had him go to a doctor to get shots, libido-killing shots") and he talked to a professional about his sexual addiction and compulsion to pursue young girls. Kelly saw Dr. Carl Bell, director of public and community psychiatry at the University of Illinois, and one of the most respected therapists in Chicago's black community. Not surprising, given patient confidentiality, Dr. Bell declined to speak to me.

Kelly perfectly parroted Mayer's talking points for most of the interview. The singer said he was no angel, "but I'm not a monster." He asked fans to have faith in him and to "focus on my music." Yes, he admitted, he had been thinking a lot about the impact of all this on his family. "I'm very concerned about my career, but most of all, I'm concerned about my life. I'm trying to protect my life right now." Then Gordon asked about Aaliyah.

"It has nothing to do with this," Kelly said, his face registering pain and loss. He seemed on the verge of tears. "I really don't think it's fair to say anything about Aaliyah."

Aaliyah had released her third album in July 2001, a self-titled disc that found her once again working with Timbaland, as well as several new producers. That August, she had traveled to the Bahamas to shoot a video for the single "Rock the Boat." The morning after completing her scenes, she boarded a chartered Cessna 402 with six members of the video crew and the pilot for the return trip to Florida. The plane crashed shortly after takeoff, killing everyone onboard. Aaliyah was twenty-two.

Only a few months after the accident, I had a short but emotional conversation with her mother, Diane Haughton. I gave her my condolences, and she thanked me for the reporting I'd done about Kelly, even though it included revelations about his relationship with her daughter. "Everything that went wrong in her life began then," Haughton said, crying. She did not say anything more.

The third and final album by Kelly's former protégé shot to No. 1 on the Billboard pop albums chart and ultimately sold more than two million copies. Aaliyah had also made a second film, *Queen of the Damned*, starring as Anne Rice's vampire queen Akasha. It opened six months after her death, and although it received lukewarm reviews, it became a cult classic.

Kelly's handlers couldn't have been happier with the way he fielded the Aaliyah question. You're too hurt to talk about her and too respectful of her family to get into all that again, they'd advised, but another tactic backfired. When Abdon and I first broke news of the tape, they began suggesting to anyone who'd listen that their client's former manager, Barry Hankerson, and an artist who'd split from him, Sparkle, were using it to blackmail him. At the Olympics, Kelly himself had blamed the tape on "people in the past that I've fired." His handlers suggested that Hankerson and Sparkle were angry they wouldn't be making any more money with Kelly. The star having sexual contact with the nieces they loved (and other underage girls) couldn't possibly have been a motive to make the tape public. Instead it was all about money.

"The operative theory by the people around Rob," one of Kelly's handlers told me years later, "was that Rob and Barry had a bad falling-out over Aaliyah. But what really pushed Barry over the edge about really wanting to destroy Rob was that Aaliyah died, and the guilt he felt. Even though Rob had nothing to do with that, obviously, Barry had a lot of guilt about that whole thing, because he had pushed the two of them together initially. He may not have been expecting the way that it turned out, but he knew Rob pretty well. As screwed up as Rob was, and as Byzantine as all that psychology was, I think Barry's psychology is equally Byzantine. . . . He knew that Rob was enormously talented and that he was a real meal ticket, and he had sense that Aaliyah had it, too. He put them together, and yeah, don't worry about the other stuff."

When the BET interview touched on this alleged conspiracy to blackmail and bring him down, Kelly shifted uneasily in his chair, caught off guard and unprepared. "You had said that you believe that there is a smear campaign out against you," Gordon began, "that you think people are out to get you. Who is 'they'?"

"Well, I'm gonna be very honest." Now Kelly talked quickly and stumbled over his words. "I know a lot of things that, uh, unfortunately, I just can't discuss, 'cause, uh, I can't get on TV claiming this person or that person. I just can't say names and who's doin' this to me."

"You have in the past mentioned your former agent, though," Gordon said, referring to Hankerson, Kelly's ex-manager. "Yes, I have," Kelly said. He began fidgeting nervously with his hands and blinking a lot. Gordon named him. "Barry Hankerson. And your suggestion is that he was behind some of this. Do you believe that he is behind any of this smear campaign?"

"Well, you know what, that's something I have to let my lawyers handle," Kelly said. He looked frightened. "My lawyers are handling that, you know? And, and, looking into that, and, unfortunately, man, like I say, I'm, I'm biting my teeth here. I wish that I could say a lot of things. Because I owe it to my fans. That's why I'm here. I owe it to people. I owe it to my family and myself. To be here. And I'm makin' a big step to be here and talk about this. It's just that I'm doin' it with a hand behind my back. I can't say a lot of things, unfortunately. And I apologize for that. But you know, I hope that people understand how the legal thing goes. Especially when you're a celebrity, the first thing they do is tell you, you can't say anything. I'm not even supposed to be here talkin' about it. But I, I just feel I have to say something."

Gordon didn't stop. "I mention Barry Hankerson only in the sense that you had mentioned him publicly before. There's been word that an old protégé—" The interviewer was about to name Sparkle when Kelly nervously interjected. "I never said Barry Hankerson."

"You tell me if you said this," Gordon said. He proceeded to read part of a quote from a radio interview Kelly had given, which actually didn't name Hankerson. Gordon, quoting from Kelly's own interview, read, "I've got an ex-manager on my back. People are trying to make money off my music and my name in a very, very negative way. I've been blackmailed for the last four years. I didn't give in. I'm still not going to give in. A lot of people are very jealous of me and they're trying to destroy me." Gordon looked up from the transcript he'd just read and stared at Kelly. "Did you not mean Barry Hankerson there?"

"Well, like I say, because of the legal thing, I can't just name names," Kelly said. He had started to sweat. "I've had a lot of managers in the past, but right now I can't, I can't say this man's name. I wish that I could. Believe me, I wish that I could. The human, just the regular guy, Robert, wants to.

But if I'm payin' lawyers to clear this and make sure I'm okay and all that, then I have to follow some advice."

Less than a month later, on the afternoon of June 4, State's Attorney Dick Devine told *Sun-Times* editor Michael Cooke that indictments against Kelly would be announced the following day. Abdon and I broke the scoop that morning, scoring for the first time the prime place on page one, or "the wood," in newspaper jargon antiquated even then. The indictment charged Kelly with twenty-one counts of making child pornography: seven counts of videotaping each specific sex act, seven counts of producing the video for each specific sex act, and seven counts of soliciting an underage partner for each specific sex act. He faced a prison term of up to fifteen years and a fine of $100,000 if convicted.

"While police and other family members who were cooperating with the investigation grew impatient for prosecutors to charge Kelly, the Cook County State's Attorney's office took months, it said, trying to make sure it had an ironclad case," Abdon wrote. "Prosecutors were haunted by a case fourteen years ago, when they had a similarly uncooperative witness who had been taped having sex with a man when she was underage." (This was before the Mel Reynolds case.) "Prosecutors charged him anyway, and he was acquitted."

Abdon and I attended the standing-room-only press conference on the afternoon of June 5 at CPD headquarters, 3510 South Michigan Avenue. Top city and state law enforcement officials crowded the podium, and after Chicago Police Supt. Terry Hillard introduced them all, he said he wanted to provide some background. "We're here today to announce the indictment of Chicago-based singer Robert Kelly. Back in February, the *Chicago Sun-Times* contacted the Chicago Police Department to tell us of a tape they received that features R. Kelly performing sex acts with a minor. The *Sun-Times* provided a copy of the tape to us."

Sitting at the left end of the fourth row, Abdon and I winced. We'd been hoping the lede would be that a video provided evidence leading to an indictment after a long police investigation of Kelly's sexual contact with underage girls. "Fuck!" Abdon whispered. "They're making this about us!"

They also were making it all about one teenage girl on one videotape, with nothing about the pattern of behavior we'd reported.

"It's unfortunate to see Mr. Kelly's talents go to waste, but make no mistake, these acts are serious crimes," Superintendent Hillard said. "[A]nyone who is selling this tape, as well as anyone who has purchased it, is now in possession of child pornography. It would be my advice to dispose of these tapes." Like the earlier videotapes, bootlegged copies of the one with Reshona had begun to appear for sale on the streets.

State's Attorney Dick Devine said the tape had been authenticated by the FBI Crime Lab in Quantico, Virginia, and experts there concluded it was not a forgery. "Sexual predators are a scourge on society. This indictment should send a clear message that illicit acts with minor children will not be tolerated in the community."

At the start of the press conference, an aide from Devine's office had handed a two-page press release and a copy of the twenty-four-page indictment to every reporter. Abdon and I couldn't believe it, but Reshona Landfair's name had not been redacted. The names of underage victims and rape victims of any age almost always are withheld by law enforcement. Another reporter pointed out the error, and the panicked aide collected all the documents she'd just distributed, then rushed to make new copies with Reshona's name crossed out with a black marker. I wondered if that would have happened with the name of a white girl from Lakeview or the North Shore suburbs.

"As soon as we see Mr. Kelly, he'll be placed in handcuffs. We're not going to treat R. Kelly any different than anybody else," Chicago Chief of Detectives Phil Cline said. He announced that a warrant had been issued that morning for the star's arrest. Then the officials took questions, most of them fielded by Lieutenant Robert Hargesheimer, head of the Special Investigations Unit.

Many of the questions from our fellow journalists—who hadn't seen the tape—centered on what it showed. "We're not going to comment on that," came the reply again and again. The same response greeted queries about whether the fourteen-year-old victim was cooperating in the investigation. After ten minutes, I couldn't keep quiet, though Abdon elbowed me that I shouldn't say anything to tip off our competitors. "We can ask later!"

Ignoring him, and with my Sony Pressman cassette recorder rolling, I asked if anyone at the podium knew whether the girl and her family had signed a nondisclosure agreement with Kelly. "I am not aware of that," Lieutenant Hargesheimer said. I said the *Sun-Times* had reported that Kelly was accused of statutory rape in three civil lawsuits by underage girls, that he'd settled those claims by paying the girls in exchange for nondisclosure agreements, and that he'd married Aaliyah under a falsified Cook County marriage certificate when she was underage. Was the state looking into the possibility of charges in those cases? "Our investigation, what we're talking about today, deals with the tape," Hargesheimer said.

Now Abdon piped up. "In the general law, is it harder to prove a sex-crimes charge than a child-pornography charge?" State's Attorney Devine replied that "it depends on the evidence that we have. We take each case as it comes."

I posed the last question before the press conference ended. Given that the tape was widely available for sale across the country, did Kelly face federal charges? I asked. Devine grinned and said, "You'd have to ask the U.S. attorney about that." Abdon did, several times in the coming weeks, and a spokesperson for U.S. Attorney Patrick Fitzgerald declined to comment. In the years since, I have heard that federal authorities wanted to take over the case, but Illinois prosecutors did not want to cede it to them.

Abdon and I rushed back to the newsroom, where Don Hayner already had three of our colleagues working on sidebars. Annie Sweeney wrote a story headlined "Tower Records Pulls Kelly Porn Tapes." They had still been selling the one I bought there on DVD, *R. Kelly: Bump & Grind "You Be the Judge,"* which showed the scenes with Montina Woods and the other partner neither we nor law enforcement ever identified. (The retail chain was not selling the Reshona tape.) Another story led with "The Rev. Jesse Jackson warned Wednesday against rushing to judgment against R. Kelly." The famous activist told reporter Julie Patel, "There are other greater issues in the world."

Mary Houlihan interviewed people in the street, quoting three women and one man who said they weren't surprised by the charges. She also talked to programmers at Chicago radio stations. Dance-pop-oriented B96-FM pulled Kelly's music from its playlist, but the station only played his big pop hits, and he didn't have a new one at the moment. The three top R&B stations kept the singer in heavy rotation. "He's innocent until proven guilty," said Marv Dyson, general manager of both WGCI and V103.

Over the past two days, at my editors' request, I'd written a contextual story on famous cases of pop stars and underage girls. These included Elvis Presley and his fourteen-year-old bride, Priscilla Beaulieu; Jerry Lee Lewis and his thirteen-year-old second cousin and third wife, Myra Gale Brown; Led Zeppelin's Jimmy Page, who first had sexual contact with Lori Maddox when she was fourteen; and Marvin Gaye, who met Janis Hunter when she was seventeen and married her after divorcing his first wife, Anna Gordy. (Hunter later claimed Gaye abused her and forced her to participate in threesomes against her will.)

None of the infamous cases charted in my story can be excused, and there are plenty of others, but Kelly's behavior was of a different magnitude. "The groupies of the golden age who have gone on to write their autobiographies and become famous are pretty different than a fourteen-year-old girl who is being urinated on by a thirty-five-year-old man," then–*New York Times* music critic Ann Powers told me. And the girl on the tape was not the only one Abdon and I had written about.

After the press conference, I started writing the main story about the indictments for page one while Abdon made calls to nail down the details of an AP news alert. Kelly had been arrested in Polk County, Florida, shortly after 4 p.m. EST. In addition to the new mansion he owned in Olympia Fields, Kelly rented two vacation homes in Davenport, Florida, thirty-five miles southwest of Orlando. He used one of the houses as a recording studio and hangout for his crew, while the second was home for his wife, Andrea, their children, and their nanny. Andrea was in the hospital, having just given birth to the couple's third child, a son named Robert Jr.

When Lieutenant Hargesheimer advised Florida officers of the warrant for Kelly's arrest, Polk County sheriff's deputies immediately went to his addresses in Davenport. They arrested him without incident while he sat in a van outside one of the houses. Deputies then led him in plastic zip cuffs to a substation in Winter Haven, where fifteen fans had gathered. "We love you, R. Kelly!" they shouted as reporters and photographers moved in. "I love you," Kelly said. He turned to the media. "Not right now, guys." He arrived wearing white Nike gym shoes, a blue Nike sweatshirt, blue sweatpants, and a denim bucket hat, Abdon noted.

The arrest made headlines worldwide. Most of the stories reported that Kelly had been in Florida with his wife and children, the first time his family garnered widespread mention in the media. The AP talked to some of the neighbors in Davenport, who said Kelly hadn't caused any problems, but full-time residents disliked anyone who rented rather than owned. "Next time, is it going to be a terrorist they let in here?" one homeowner asked.

Abdon emailed me another paragraph of "color," as my features-writing class in journalism school called it. "Kelly was issued the standard orange jail jumpsuit and placed in a private cell. He arrived too late for the 4:30 p.m. dinner." I'd just finished adding that to our story when Hayner told us Ed Genson, the star's new high-powered criminal defense attorney, had just called his second press conference of the day. Genson had not informed anyone from our paper about the first session, held not long after law enforcement's presser at police headquarters. We later read in the *Trib* that the first time he met with reporters to assert Kelly's innocence, Genson angrily vowed, "I'll talk about the *Sun-Times* another day soon."

The copy desk extended our deadline, and Abdon and I hurried to Genson's office in the Monadnock Building, an ornate sixteen-story tower in the Loop designed by celebrated architects Daniel Burnham and John Root. Genson's dark, wood-paneled office had already filled with reporters when we arrived. The sixty-year-old attorney directed camera crews where to stand while he repositioned photos of his family on his desk to ensure they'd be seen on television. A source in the Kelly camp later told me the lawyer charged the singer $750 an hour.

Portly, bearded, and bespectacled, with a famous mop of unruly, sandy-blond hair, Genson was called a mob lawyer by everyone on the Chicago legal scene. He embraced that description, telling AP reporter Mike Robinson, "I have no aversion to organized crime." Genson masked a quick intellect and killer instinct with a bumbling, disheveled persona evoking Dostoevsky's Porfiry Petrovich and Peter Falk's Columbo. Suffering from dystonia, a neurological disorder, he sometimes rode a motorized scooter and sometimes limped with a cane. The cane now sat front and center, propped against his desk. "He told an interviewer years ago he deliberately used his disability to make jurors feel sorry for him," Robinson wrote. "Now he says he didn't really mean it."

Raised in Chicago courtrooms, where his father worked as a bail bondsman, Genson defended crooked politicians in addition to mobsters, but he said he tried to avoid sexual misconduct cases. "I just don't like to be in a case where I have to cross-examine a woman victim," he said. "I feel bad for them." He and his close friend Sam Adam Sr. had nevertheless defended Rep. Mel Reynolds when the congressman was tried for having sexual contact with an underage campaign worker. Reynolds was convicted, and Abdon thought that debacle would have dissuaded Kelly, but the singer had hired Genson and Adam Sr. as soon as he learned indictments were coming.

Genson thought he'd struck a "gentleman's agreement" with the state for how his new, famous client would turn himself in. When the cameras started rolling, he railed about what he called "the grave injustice" of Kelly being arrested in front of his home while his wife and children watched. (Apparently, even Genson didn't know Andrea was in the hospital with a newborn.) "Thirty-five years, and I've never had a state's attorney do this when you offered to bring somebody in. We're talking about a child pornography case where the person they're alleging is the victim of the child pornography says it didn't happen. I've never had an agreement like this breached. I don't know whether it's his race, I don't know whether it's his celebrity, but we were double-crossed!"

I asked Genson if he was saying the girl on the tape told the grand jury it wasn't her. The law requires that grand jury testimony remain secret, and he backtracked. "For the first time, I know who the victim is, and she said it didn't happen." I reminded him that Abdon had been asking him if Kelly had sexual contact with the victim for several weeks. "I've been reticent to talk about it because I didn't think it was appropriate," Genson said, changing the subject. "I'm not the one who put the victim's name in the indictment. They did! It's illegal, as I understand it."

Had the girl signed a nondisclosure agreement with Kelly? I asked. "No. I don't even know what that is." Genson ranted some more about the state not honoring the deal he thought he'd struck for Kelly to turn himself in, and he protested the steep bond of $750,000. "Any ordinary person indicted for child pornography would have been freed on a hundred-dollar bond or a two-hundred-dollar bond!" (I remember thinking, what kind of ordinary person is indicted for child pornography? But I didn't pose that question.)

Before the gentleman's agreement fell apart, Genson said, Kelly's spiritual advisor, the Rev. James Meeks, planned to drive the singer back to Chicago, because he hated to fly. Abdon and I hadn't known about Kelly's aviophobia before this. I asked for clarification, since the *Sun-Times* had reported that Kelly flew to Florida after the wedding with Aaliyah. Genson erupted. "Stop playing these games! Look, I'm a criminal lawyer, I'm not a press-relations person. You write your column about music! I'm talking about a criminal case and people who misrepresented themselves to me. As a matter of fact, and this is really gonna kill you, I'm sixty years old and I have no idea who Aaliyah is! Let's talk about *this* case. She denies she was on the tape and denies she ever had sex with him!"

"Wow, I didn't know you could be such an asshole at press conferences," Abdon said as we cabbed back to the *Sun-Times*. I told him I'd had a lot of experience back in Jersey.

Kelly spent the night of June 5 in jail in Bartow, Florida, and Genson flew there to represent the singer in a Polk County courtroom the next afternoon. The star was led into court in an orange jail uniform, hands cuffed and moist eyes downcast. Judge Karla Foreman Wright agreed to let him return to Chicago on his own recognizance but warned, "You're not to have contact with minor children not related by blood or marriage. Do you understand?" Kelly quietly answered, "Yes, ma'am." Early the next morning, he and Genson flew into Midway Airport on the South Side aboard a rented private jet, then climbed into a silver Lexus.

The luxury SUV pulled up to the Cook County Criminal Court building at West Twenty-Sixth Street and South California Avenue, part of the sprawling legal complex that also includes Cook County Jail, and which most Chicago reporters, prosecutors, criminal defense attorneys and their regular clients simply call "Twenty-Sixth and Cal." When Kelly emerged from the Lexus in front of the waiting crowd of press, Det. Dan Everett of the Special Investigations Unit read the singer his rights, placed him in cuffs for the second time in twenty-four hours, and put him in the back of an unmarked squad car.

Before he could post bail, Kelly had to be fingerprinted and photographed. He was taken to CPD's Marquette District headquarters, "one of the police department's *Hill Street Blues*–era relics from 1926," Abdon wrote, "with marble stairs, mosaic hexagonal tiles, and not enough space for a celebrity, his legal team, his spiritual adviser, his spiritual adviser's driver, and dozens of reporters and cameramen." Kelly then returned to the courthouse to appear before a judge for his release on $750,000 bond. He paid with seven hundred and fifty hundred-dollar bills.

Kelly smiled on his way out of court and told reporters he looked forward to proving his innocence. Standing at his side, Reverend Meeks said he was counseling and praying with the singer. They'd discussed "turning the direction of his music around, looking at other themes other than sex," Meeks said. Then they climbed into the silver Lexus and drove to Salem Baptist Church in the Pullman neighborhood. There Kelly sang for fifty children and their parents at a kindergarten graduation ceremony. Apparently, the *Chicago Tribune* reported, "The no-associating-with-minors stipulation applied to the Florida bond only."

The star continued singing over the next few weeks, hunkering down at Chicago Trax. In early July, Jive Records rush-released a single, "Heaven, I Need a Hug," after Kelly first gave it exclusively to WGCI. Elroy Smith, the station's program director, told me that within ninety minutes of its first airing, it became the station's most-requested song. The lyrics take the form of a letter to Kelly's dead mother, Joann: "Ever since you left, your baby boy's been dealin' with / Problem after problem, tell me, what am I supposed to do?"

Over a mid-tempo groove with lush orchestration and a guitar part credited to Reshona's father, Greg Landfair—after playing on three of Kelly's albums, this would be his last named appearance on the singer's recordings—Kelly takes aim at disloyal former associates and the press: "Get rid of them clowns and get myself a whole 'nother crew / Media, do your job / But please just don't make my job so hard." Finally, he builds to a climactic finale, repeated three times. "Heaven, I need a hug / Is there anybody out there willin' to embrace a thug? / Feelin' like a change of heart / And all I really need is a sign or a word from God / So shower down on me, wet me with your love."

Given the most notorious scene in the videotape, the so-called golden shower that became fodder for jokes and gossip soon after Abdon and I first reported on it, the last line of the song seemed bizarre. "I know Robert, and he knows exactly what he's doing," a former associate told me. "He's smarter than everybody thinks, and what he's doing is, he's fucking with all of us."

CHAPTER 8

VICTORY BY DELAY

"I'm just looking forward to my day in court," R. Kelly had told reporters after he paid his bail at Twenty-Sixth and Cal. In fact, Kelly and his team would do everything possible to delay that day for six years, a wait that broke the record in Cook County for the length of time between an indictment and a trial. Superstar careers have been ruined overnight by accusations far less disturbing and with much less evidence than the video, but the most successful and lucrative period of Kelly's long career came while the charges of making child pornography hung over him. Meanwhile, threats real or imagined and a steady stream of cash settlements kept many who knew about his behavior silent. His lawyers racked up untold billable hours, and the judge assigned to the case seemed happy to accommodate them.

The Cook County courts supposedly assign trials based on a lottery system, though sources in the legal world say the process sometimes seems to be rigged. His fellow jurists appreciated Judge Vincent Gaughan's eagerness to hear the "heaters," the long, stressful cases that got the most public scrutiny. Who needs those headaches? In Kelly's trial, the fix for Gaughan was in from the beginning, five sources told me, because he sought and reveled in the attention. "He said repeatedly in the run-up to the R. Kelly trial that his primary concern was for a 'fair trial' and other concerns were 'secondary,'" the *Chicago Tribune*'s Steve Schmadeke wrote, but my sources said the judge consistently "bent over backwards" for the defense. He was, in a word, starstruck.

Gaughan thought of himself as a star, too, if only on the Chicago legal scene. Like attorney Susan Loggans, he kept a thick file of his press clippings that he proudly showed reporters who visited his chambers. He didn't grant on-the-record interviews, and he refused to speak to me for this book, but he did enjoy attention from journalists he chatted up at his favorite watering holes near Twenty-Sixth and Cal. He also stood out among his peers for employing an assistant who acted not only as an administrator, but essentially as a publicist, regularly reaching out to the press about upcoming happenings in his boss's domain.

In another story, the *Trib* described Gaughan as "an animated jurist known for having a short fuse." Over beers at the Billy Goat Tavern, a different *Trib* reporter preferred "surly fucking nutcase." A much kinder man than many of his peers (or me), Abdon Pallasch called Gaughan "a kook." By the time the judge pulled the Kelly case, my partner had known him for more than a decade. Once, when Abdon had to work but his two youngest sons had the day off from school, he brought them to court. "After the hearing," he recalled, "Gaughan calls out to me, 'Abdon, is that your family?' and makes me bring the boys back into his chamber, where he gave them each veteran pins."

Actually, those were what the judge called "Son of Gaughan" awards. He gave them out twice a year. A member of the team that prosecuted Kelly got one, too. "He didn't ask me, he told me, 'I want you over here.' He has a whole gathering for it. I was awkward about it, but I could never go on record saying that. I managed to cover my contempt for him as we were in there doing the trial. And I manage to cover it to this day."

"The luckiest day in R. Kelly's life was when Gaughan took his case," a legal source told me. Yet another agreed, maintaining, "I couldn't put it any better."

Born in 1942 and raised by Irish immigrants in the Lincoln Park neighborhood on Chicago's North Side, Vincent Gaughan graduated from the University of Illinois in 1964 and enlisted in the army. While Chicago cops cracked the skulls of yippies, antiwar activists, and reporters alike during the 1968 Democratic National Convention on orders from the Boss, Mayor Richard J. Daley, Gaughan concluded a four-year tour of duty with the artillery in Vietnam. He made second lieutenant and earned a Bronze Star. Returning to his old bedroom in his parents' three-story wood-frame house, he resumed the education he'd put on hold to serve his country and enrolled at DePaul University's College of Law.

Around 3 a.m. on April 25, 1970, agitated after a minor traffic accident and a fight with the other driver, Gaughan locked the door of his third-floor bedroom. The twenty-eight-year-old veteran then began firing his M1 Garand service rifle through the window, Bill Mullen reported in a *Tribune* story headlined "A Viet Hero Arrested as a Sniper." Vincent's father said his son suffered from "nervousness," or what might now be called post-traumatic stress disorder. Two bullets shattered the neighbors' bedroom window, lodging in the wall above their bed, and they called the police. As they talked to two patrolmen in their dining room, two more shots came through that window, narrowly missing the officers.

Police swarmed the Gaughan home. Vincent shouted down from his barricaded bedroom that he wanted to talk to a priest who was a friend of his, the vice president of DePaul. Father John Richardson arrived and began to climb the stairs. "I know him well. He wants to talk. He won't hurt me," Father Richardson told police. Suddenly, Gaughan called down again. "Wait, I want a policeman to come, too. An *Irish* sergeant." According to the *Tribune*, "That broke the tension. The policemen smiled, and the guns went down." A classic Chicago case of white privilege, it is impossible to imagine the same outcome—then or now—in the black neighborhoods of the city's South and West Sides for a young man firing a rifle at police.

The outcome of the case is unclear. Gaughan was charged with four counts of aggravated assault and weapons violations, the *Tribune* reported, but a Freedom of Information Act request filed by dogged *Chicago Reader* reporter Steve Bogira came up empty when he tried to determine the resolution of those charges. "They seem to have just 'disappeared,'" Bogira told me, and I had no more luck than he did.

Whatever the resolution to the charges, they did not derail Gaughan's life. After graduating from DePaul and passing the bar in the early seventies, he went to work as a public defender. Over the next two decades, he rose to serve as supervisor of the county office. In 1991, he was appointed to the bench by a panel of circuit court judges during the reign of Mayor Richard M. Daley, who inherited the still-considerable remnants of the political machine built by his father. Gaughan regularly won elections thereafter, because most judges in Cook County do. Few voters investigate the names further down the ballot, and they generally ignore stories like the one Abdon wrote in 1998.

Fresh out of journalism grad school, during his one-year residency at the *Trib*, Abdon reported that Gaughan was one of nine judges deemed "not recommended" by one or more bar groups. That year and every time he ran for reelection thereafter, the Judicial Performance Commission of Cook County praised Gaughan's case-management skills but noted "criticism with regard to his temper, particularly as directed toward attorneys in his courtroom."

With big jowls, a balding pate, and gray temples, Gaughan looked like a bulldog, with a default expression registering some mix of anger, sadness, and chronic indigestion. Many reporters and lawyers compared both his countenance and his demeanor to R. Lee Ermey, who played the drill sergeant in Stanley Kubrick's *Full Metal Jacket*. Some said the judge was much looser, jolly even, when he took off his robes, simply becoming "Vince," and drinking with them in the bars after court adjourned. He was especially friendly with other Irish attorneys, my sources said, a network of "good old boys" rooted in the enduring Daley political machine.

Despite his background as a public defender and his own brush with the law, Judge Gaughan did not prove especially sympathetic to defendants. In 1993, at the end of his first high-profile trial, he sentenced a North Side gang member to thirty-two years in prison for the murder of a nine-year-old boy accidentally hit by gunfire intended for a rival. Three years later, he sentenced the ringleader of a group of five men to death for the murder of a South Side couple during a carjacking. His military background seemed to influence the fifty-eight-year sentence he gave a man who beat to death a Vietnam vet— "He had served our country and fought in one of its worst wars," Gaughan said of the victim, "and all he wanted was to be left alone"—but a few years earlier, in his role as Cook County Commander of the American Legion, he sided against a Korean War veteran who charged racism when he was denied membership at the largely Irish Evergreen Park post two and a half miles from his South Side home and told to apply at an all-black post six miles away.

Gaughan presided over the sensational trials of two men who massacred seven employees at a Brown's Chicken franchise in suburban Palatine in 1993, during a robbery gone horribly wrong. He sentenced one of the killers to death, and the other to life in prison. Those stood as the most prominent trials of his judicial career, until he drew R. Kelly.

Midway through the six-year wait for the Kelly trial to begin, Gaughan traveled to California at Cook County's expense to study how Santa Barbara County Superior Court handled the media attention for another superstar's sensational trial. Michael Jackson had been indicted for molesting a second young boy, thirteen-year-old Gavin Arvizo. Gaughan veered from the handling of that case in a significant way, however. Jackson was charged, tried, and acquitted all within fourteen months, Abdon wrote in a story five years after Kelly's indictment, when his trial still hadn't gotten under way.

"There's no excuse for it, but this is a tried-and-true tactic when it comes to sex-crimes cases," New England School of Law Professor Wendy Murphy told my partner. "Victory by delay." Every day, Abdon said, the fourteen-year-old girl in the video grew a little older. By the time the trial finally started in May 2008, she had become a twenty-three-year-old woman. Jurors would meet a different person than the girl they saw on the video—that is, if she testified.

Some of the delays couldn't be avoided. Gaughan needed time to recover after he fell off a ladder while changing a lightbulb in his home. Lead prosecutor Shauna Boliker took time off for the birth of her third son. Kelly suffered a burst appendix. But most of the long wait remains unexplained. Every few weeks for six years, usually on Fridays, Gaughan held regular status hearings, convening both the prosecution and the defense in his courtroom, then often immediately retiring with both teams to closed chambers. He sealed the records of almost all those proceedings. "He wanted to keep it very tight," said Robert Heilingoetter, a member of the prosecution team.

Representing the *Sun-Times*, the *Trib*, the AP, and WBEZ/Chicago Public Media, First Amendment attorney Damon Dunn petitioned to make all Kelly court records public before the trial. Gaughan rejected the motion, and the Illinois Supreme Court sided with him. To this day, the voluminous record of much of what happened for six years before the opening of the trial, a lengthy docket that includes 168 entries with at least 50 motions by the defense and 56 court orders issued by Gaughan, remains sealed to the public. The only way it can be unsealed is with another legal challenge, and that could fail, too.

"How do I put this diplomatically? This record is a clusterfuck," concluded a legal scholar who reviewed the docket at my request. "I couldn't tell you exactly how many motions there are that he ruled on because I believe a good many of them are not noted. For all I know, some could have been withdrawn or ruled on in chambers. There is no way to know." In 2018, Gaughan oversaw the trial of a white cop who shot a black teenager, Laquan McDonald, sixteen times in the back. He tried to conduct that trial the same way, but this time, Dunn and other media attorneys prevailed when the Illinois Supreme Court scolded Gaughan for "patently unconstitutional conduct."

Much of what happened during the six-year wait for the Kelly trial was procedural. The star had to apply for the court's permission every time he wanted to travel out of state, and Gaughan continually gave his blessing. More problematically, sources told me the judge consistently sided with the defense's contention that prior bad acts should be excluded in any attempt by prosecutors to show propensity, although exceptions do exist to that general rule. In other words, Gaughan ruled as inadmissible any evidence not directly related to the videotape. In the interest of fairness and not prejudicing the jury—noble ideals, to be certain—the judge would allow no testimony about the allegations in the four civil lawsuits filed by Tiffany Hawkins, Tracy Sampson, Patrice Jones, and Montina Woods; Kelly's illegal marriage to Aaliyah; or payments from Kelly to the Landfairs. Jurors would learn very little about the video being part of what the *Sun-Times* had called a pattern of predatory behavior and payoffs. It became an isolated crime.

"Any proof of other crimes in terms of a sexual crime against a minor wasn't coming in, because he wasn't charged with that, even though, you know, that's the extenuation of what our facts did say," a member of the prosecution team later told me. "He reprimanded us on many occasions in terms of any bend in any of the extraneous facts toward that."

In a rare public ruling issued in February 2004, a little more than a year and a half after Kelly's indictment, Gaughan granted a motion by the defense to drop seven of the twenty-one counts against the singer because they cited outdated language prosecutors took from a law the Illinois Supreme Court had declared unconstitutional. Kelly still faced fifteen years in prison if convicted on the remaining fourteen charges of making child pornography, but the ruling gave everyone following the proceedings an early indication that the judge viewed the state's case with skepticism.

The star had another stroke of good fortune in the Florida courts. In June 2002, when Polk County sheriff's deputies arrived to arrest Kelly on the warrant issued in Chicago, they were especially thorough within the bounds of the law as they understood it. While Kelly sat wearing zip cuffs in the back of a squad car, officers searched his two rented vacation homes. One was the house where a nanny stayed with Kelly's two older children when Andrea was in the hospital with her newborn. The other was where Kelly recorded music and partied with his crew. During a search of the "party house," officers found a digital camera wrapped in a towel inside a duffel bag behind a bedroom door marked "Private, Do Not Enter."

Seven months later, Florida police said the camera included twelve images of a naked underage girl, the same fourteen-year-old in the video in the Chicago case. In three of those images, she was having sexual contact with Kelly, and in others, she was engaged in a threesome with him and a legal-age woman, according to Polk County Sheriff Grady Judd. I later learned the woman's identity, but it has never been revealed, and she did not speak to me.

Kelly had traveled to Florida in January 2003 to film the video for "Ignition (Remix)." After he spent a long night on set at the South Beach nightclub Mynt, Miami-Dade police arrested him outside Coconut Grove's Grand Bay Hotel. A warrant had been issued in Polk County charging Kelly with twelve additional counts of possession of child pornography, stemming from the search of his Florida party house. Sheriff Judd told *Orlando Sentinel* reporter Susan Jacobson that it took seven months to arrest Kelly on the new charges only because "we needed to make sure the i's were dotted and the t's were crossed." Each count carried a maximum five-year jail sentence, and Judd didn't rule out additional charges for the legal-age woman in some of the images.

A Florida attorney for Kelly posted $12,000 bail, and the thirty-six-year-old singer walked out of jail three hours later. "At this point, it looks to us like a classic case of piling on," said Kelly spokesman Allan Mayer. "There is nothing new here." Prosecutors disagreed, but in March 2004, a Florida court abruptly shut the case down. Judge Dennis Maloney ruled the digital images were inadmissible because they'd been illegally obtained. Officers had no probable cause to search Kelly's Florida homes for child pornography, Maloney said, even though they were executing a warrant for Illinois indictments on making child pornography. Polk County dropped the charges.

Kelly greeted this incredible stroke of good fortune as if it had never been in doubt. "My faith in our system of justice has never wavered, and with this victory behind me, I look forward to clearing my name in Illinois," he said in a statement released by Mayer. "I am confident that when all the facts come out, people will see that I'm no criminal."

Metaphorical songs about cars, women, and sex had long been a trope in pop music, and Kelly had already gone to the well once. "You remind me of my Jeep, I want to ride it," he sang in 1995. Eight years later, he took things to an absurd and cartoonish new level with "Ignition (Remix)," scoring the biggest hit of his career. "No more hopin' and wishin' / I'm 'bout to take my key and stick it in the ignition," he sang over a hard-driving club groove building to the call-and-response choruses—"Can I get a toot, toot? / Can I get a beep, beep?"—and inspiring everyone at the party to bounce, bounce, bounce.

Jive Records released Kelly's seventh album in February 2003, eight months after his indictment, and *Chocolate Factory* debuted at No. 1 on the Billboard albums chart. The lead single, "Ignition (Remix)," hit No. 2 on the Hot 100 and spent almost a year on the chart. "It's an anthem," Kelly told Chris Heath of *GQ*. "Some even want to call it the national anthem. I don't agree with that, but I've heard it so much."

The album sold more than two million copies and spawned another Top 10 hit and much-loved anthem with "Step in the Name of Love," a tribute to Chicago's stepping scene of primarily middle-aged black couples dressing to the nines for a night of mid-tempo line dancing. Both songs became ubiquitous at backyard barbecues, house parties, family reunions, and weddings throughout the South Side and around the world.

Many fans seemed to have dismissed Kelly's charges, or decided they didn't care and could separate the art from the artist. Critics wrestled with that problem, but only halfheartedly. "R. Kelly's problems start less than thirty seconds into *Chocolate Factory*, when he coos, 'Anything you want / You just come to Daddy,'" Anthony DeCurtis wrote in *Rolling Stone*. "From other R&B lovemen, that would be boilerplate pillow talk, but allegations of participating in child pornography against Kelly provide a distorting filter through which his music will be heard for years to come. That's too bad, because *Chocolate Factory* ranks among the best work of his career."

Pondering the singer's success in the wake of his indictment, *New York Times* Pop Life columnist Neil Strauss asked, "So how has Mr. Kelly pulled this off? He has done it, more or less, by seeming to ignore his legal problems and releasing hit after hit. . . . These are songs that should be on the radio, and Mr. Kelly has found a solution to bad press that even the most expensive publicity agent on earth can't give a client: to excel at the craft that made one a celebrity in the first place." (Strauss would go on to a much more checkered career after the *Times*, writing two books about what he called "the secret society of pickup artists" and "the seduction community," and later seeking treatment for sex addiction.)

While promoting *Chocolate Factory*, Kelly adopted a new nickname: the Pied Piper. A mythical character of the Middle Ages, the Pied Piper worked as a rat-catcher. Hired by the town of Hamelin, Germany, he lured its rats out of their holes with his magic flute, then killed them. When residents refused to pay him for his services, he did the same to their children. Given the accusations against him, Chris Heath of *GQ* told Kelly that some people found the nickname troubling. The singer didn't understand. "I started calling myself the Pied Piper when I started using the flute sound in my music," he said, citing "Snake" and "Step in the Name of Love (Remix)," which includes the line, "Yeah, it's the Pied Piper of R&B, y'all!"

When Heath schooled him on the legend, Kelly maintained that "I never ran into no story like that." ("I do believe that he truly didn't know," Heath wrote.) "It's kind of jokey to me," Kelly added. "It's goofy, because I don't think enough people think that deep into me, they would compare me to some man that leads children out of the community and kills them. There's no way they would buy my albums, there would be no way they would come to my concerts. Anybody that thinks that way is sick. So definitely can't pay them no time."

Separating the myth from the music and discerning fact from fiction consistently challenged Abdon and me as we continued reporting on Kelly through the six-year wait for his trial. In February 2004, a year and a half after his indictment, we talked to one of his closest confidantes, a bright, passionate, thirty-nine-year-old mother of two. Kim Dulaney held a solid corporate job in environmental engineering and pursued a passion for writing children's books during her off hours. She came to the *Sun-Times* wearing a stylish black pantsuit appropriate for any corporate boardroom, and we conducted a long and sometimes frustratingly opaque interview in one of the paper's conference rooms.

Dulaney met Kelly at a Chicago dance club in 1990, and they'd been lovers for a while, she said. What she called their "physical intimacy" didn't last long, because she knew he slept with a lot of women. "You could be fat, skinny; you could be old, young, whatever. He just loves women." A close friendship endured after they stopped sleeping together, she said, lasting for thirteen years, until around the time of his indictment. Dulaney claimed (and other sources confirmed) that she was one of the few people in Kelly's life with whom he shared his most personal secrets.

With his blessing, Dulaney published an illustrated children's book called *I Can Fly: The R. Kelly Story* in 1998, and the star's publicity machine helped promote it. Now, in early 2004, she'd just written and self-published a new book, *Star Struck*, which she called a "thinly fictionalized account" of their friendship. "His story is an amazing story, which is why this is so sad right now. I totally believed in Rob, as everybody around him does. Rob has a personality that's magnetic." But she told us she also believed he needed help for what she called his "sexual addiction."

"There's an element to my character that won't allow me to lie," Dulaney said, "so anything that I say to you, and anything I say in my book, is what I know to be true."

In the pages of *Star Struck*, the narrator, Lela Valentine, is increasingly troubled as her best friend, an R&B superstar, loses control of his sexual impulses. His morals "twisted" by fame and money, "Ben" turns into the manipulative, sexually obsessed monster "Beemo." As we talked, Dulaney referred not to her characters, but to Rob or Robert.

Abdon and I pressed Dulaney on two passages in the book that jumped out at us. The first involved a scandalous videotape. "It passed from the hands of a thief, through the hands of street chiefs, gang leaders," the narrator, Dulaney or "Lela," wrote. "Ben refused to deal. The tape slept with record-industry folks who had grudges against Ben. . . . Through a friend of a friend the tape managed to reach a journalist who'd written several stories on Ben's troubles with women. I dared not call."

Dulaney wouldn't say anything more about the mysterious thief, gang leaders, or record-industry folks, though she did name the journalist. "I knew you were gonna do the story," she told me. "I knew who you were from the beginning, and I was very, um, *instrumental.*" Instrumental in what, exactly, Dulaney wouldn't say, though she did tell us she'd been friends with Sparkle. She'd seen Sparkle's niece Reshona in Kelly's orbit, though she never witnessed anything inappropriate. She'd watched just enough of the tape to be sickened and disgusted, however, and she told us she worried about Sparkle.

The other passage in Dulaney's book that jumped out recounts a conversation between Lela and Ben after the videotape becomes public. Ben complains that the aunt of the girl in the tape is trying to destroy him, "like she's possessed or something." Lela can't believe what she's hearing. "Imagine if someone sexed your niece or daughter. I mean, I understand her." Ben hesitated, "then struck the nail to seal the coffin," telling Lela, "I need her *done.* You know what I mean? I can't say it, in case it ever gets to trial I can say I didn't say it, you know?"

No matter how many times Abdon and I asked, Dulaney wouldn't say whether she'd actually had that conversation with Robert Kelly about Sparkle. "I wrote the book in fiction form so that I wouldn't have to tell specific things that Rob said to me in confidence, and yet I would like to get the message across that we should be thinking critically about these issues." Those in the black community defending Kelly saddened her—"To blindly support Rob does a disservice to Rob"—but she confirmed that some remained silent not out of loyalty but out of fear.

"They're afraid of being murdered or something like that, because it is to protect a great moneymaking machine. I think they have good reason to be afraid, the same reason that I'm afraid sometimes, because you know that a person who is so consumed with saving something, they're not thinking rationally. The people around them have all the money, so they can just pay somebody who has no respect for life and have something done to you."

The author said she'd testify at Kelly's trial if subpoenaed. "I wouldn't lie for him." The last time she'd spoken to Kelly, in late 2003, she told him about the book, and she claimed he hadn't objected. "He knows that the core of the book is true, and he knows that all of my efforts have been to try to save him, so if I wrote it, he knows that I'm not just being malicious. Basically, I'm still his friend. It would surprise me if he was even mad about it."

Abdon and I had a hard time figuring out exactly where Dulaney stood on Kelly, so he finally just asked her, "Should Robert go to jail?" A quizzical look came over her face, and she took her time in answering. "I think he needs to go away, to be by himself away from the glare of stardom. What I'm saying in the book is that this guy is caught up, and his morals are kind of twisted now. I think he can't tell the boundaries of acceptable behavior."

In her book, Dulaney also wrote that Ben had videotaped Lela, shown the tape to friends, and humiliated her. Dulaney wouldn't say if that had happened to her, either, but a few months after we talked to her, Abdon began following the story of yet another Kelly videotape, and I happily ceded that one to him.

On this tape, which we never saw, Kelly had sex with a Chicago woman in her early twenties, gospel singer Deleon Richards, according to the FBI. Richards had been a star since age five, and she held the distinction of being the youngest artist ever nominated for a Grammy. In 1999, she married Gary Sheffield, the Los Angeles Dodgers' (later New York Yankees') star outfielder. In mid-2004, a man from the South Side named Derrick Mosley used the video in an attempt to extort $20,000 from Sheffield, the FBI said.

Sheffield had known his wife had had a relationship with Kelly before they met, and he shut down the attempted shakedown by going to federal authorities. He also released a statement to the New York press: "We will not be blackmailed. I will not have my family be dragged through the mud and filth. I have not seen the alleged videotape, nor do I care to. I love my wife and I vow to stand by her through any trial or tribulation."

Derrick Mosley had become a community activist after attending Kenwood Academy with Kelly. He led protests on behalf of the victims of the stampede at the E2 nightclub, and he frequently spoke to the press to condemn gang violence. His own lawyer called him "a poor man's Jesse Jackson." When Kelly was indicted in 2002, Mosley told Abdon he was hired by Jack Palladino, a high-profile private investigator working for the star. "He spread good PR on Kelly and bad PR on Kelly's critics," Abdon wrote. "Mosley appeared on talk shows on black radio boosting Kelly, until he became convinced that Kelly did what prosecutors claim."

For months, Mosley regularly called Abdon with tips about Kelly. They rarely panned out. After our first big stories in 2000 and 2002, we both got a lot of those kinds of calls, letters, and emails, and they rarely proved legit. We'd report them out, waste a lot of time we didn't have, and wind up with nothing to publish.

In early 2006, a federal court in Chicago convicted Mosley for attempting to extort Sheffield and his wife, and the judge sentenced the poor man's Jesse Jackson to more than two years in prison. Mosley kept calling Abdon from behind bars. The activist turned convict talked about Kelly scandals as yet unreported, promising to tell all if he won his release on appeal, or maybe if Abdon added a little money to his commissary account. My partner finally stopped accepting the collect-call charges whenever his phone rang from prison. There seemed to be no end to the weirdness surrounding Kelly, and we couldn't escape it, even if fans and the music industry largely ignored it.

CHAPTER 9

RECENT UNPLEASANTNESS

While living in his $5 million mansion in Olympia Fields and recording in the new, state-of-the-art studio he'd built in his basement, R. Kelly proved more prolific than ever. Only a year and a half after *Chocolate Factory*, he returned to the charts with *Happy People/U Saved Me*, a double album with one disc of stepping music and another of more gospel-oriented tracks. Released in August 2004, two years and two months after the indictment, the album sold three million copies. Robert Christgau gave it a D+ in the *Village Voice*. "His productivity isn't exuberance, it's greed; his PG rating isn't scruples, it's cowardice. *Happy People* only gets steppin' when it flaunts his wealth, only achieves consciousness on a closing diptych that observes, 'We're so quick to say God bless America / But take away "In God We Trust" / Tell me what the hell is wrong with us?' Nice segue, Mr. Accused, right into the gross God-pop of *U Saved Me*."

The self-appointed dean of American music critics never gave Kelly a free pass, but many others paid mere lip service to the charges against him while rushing to heap lavish, fawning praise on his newest sounds. It infuriated and sickened me. Like the critics I most emulated, Lester Bangs and Roger Ebert, I believe we always should consider the context of the art, and we can't ignore or forgive significant moral wrongs at its core—racism, sexism, misogyny, homophobia, or worse. I once had a long talk with Ebert about *Triumph of the Will*. No critic should praise the work of groundbreaking director Leni Riefenstahl, he said, without giving equal consideration to the evils of the Nazis she depicted so gloriously. Bangs wrestled with the question of separating art and artist constantly, and not always successfully. A lot of my peers either didn't care enough to think that deeply, or didn't see Kelly's actions as fundamentally wrong.

"Kelly makes like the life of several parties," David Browne wrote in *Entertainment Weekly*. "Given the allegations against him, *Happy People* feels either clueless or arrogant, yet there's no denying that Kelly knows record making." In *Rolling Stone,* Jon Pareles wrote, "Kelly is the master of the ultraslow groove, and the songs on *U Saved Me* take their time, then use gospel's strategic buildups to sweep Kelly toward faith. . . . 'After I've been so bad, O Lord / How did you manage to forgive me?' he groans. It's gospel testifying, not courtroom testimony, but where *Happy People* only exercises Kelly's technique, *U Saved Me* adds some heart."

I had a much harder time hearing the heart, or separating the art from the artist's misdeeds. Granted, both the art and the story had become personal. I'd met women who told me how Kelly hurt them, and I'd received the horrifying and disgusting video that got him indicted. Yet Kelly had flouted his obsessions in his music since "(It Seems Like) You're Ready" on *12 Play* and the title track of *Age Ain't Nothing but a Number*, arguably boasting about his behavior in much of his music, on albums as well as in concert.

A month after *Happy People/U Saved Me* arrived in stores, Kelly set out with Jay-Z on the revitalized Best of Both Worlds tour. Overshadowed by Kelly's indictment in 2002, their collaborative album topped out at sales of a million copies, not inconsiderable, but disappointing for the hyped pairing of two superstars. The artists reportedly never worked in the same studio, instead shipping tracks to each other, and critics savaged the result as a merger driven by marketing rather than inspiration and mutual admiration.

Nevertheless, eleven months after his celebrated "retirement party" at Madison Square Garden, Jay-Z announced he'd return to the music world on a joint tour with Kelly. *Unfinished Business*, a second disc comprised mostly of outtakes from the first, would be released by Roc-A-Fella/Def Jam and Rockland/Jive midway through the forty dates, in late October 2004. Trying to determine what motivated the reunion after Jay-Z initially seemed to have turned on Kelly, canceling the first tour after the indictment, journalists got no comment from the stars' labels, but one press rep bragged to any reporter who'd listen that the first two Chicago shows alone would gross $1.6 million.

"We both knew the real money could be made if we toured together," Kelly says in *Soulacoaster*.

My friend Anders Lindall and I sat in the press box at the Allstate Arena in the Chicago suburb of Rosemont on opening night of the tour, September 29, 2004. I had asked the venue's manager if we could review the concert from the perch up in the rafters where sports reporters covered games by the Chicago Wolves American Hockey League team and DePaul University's Blue Demons basketball players. I didn't want to use our reviewers' seats in Section 103 by the stage because I didn't want to be recognized by anyone in the sold-out crowd of more than eighteen thousand people. Ardent fans who still loved and supported Kelly had been sending me hate mail and leaving angry and sometimes threatening voice messages since the first *Sun-Times* story in December 2000. I didn't want to encounter any of them, and I certainly didn't want the artist or his crew to see me.

Neither Anders nor I could believe what we saw. The show started with videos of matching black tour busses speeding to the gig from opposite directions, but a phalanx of Chicago cop cars followed Kelly's. The singer spent very little time together with Jay-Z onstage. Instead, they alternated individual solo sets. During Kelly's first showcase, he flashed a personals ad on the giant video screens. "Looking for a girl. MUST be down for anything. She's got to be at least"—the scroll paused for a beat—"nineteen years old."

The audience laughed uneasily, and later, it delivered only scattered applause when Kelly sought sympathy by complaining about "so-called family and friends" who betrayed and lied about him. "Not only will I continue to give you all what you want," he vowed, "I will continue to give you all what you need."

The strangest moment on opening night came when Kelly selected two supposedly random women (actually planted dancers) from the crowd and seduced them into his prop tour bus. They reemerged clad in orange prison-style jumpsuits, feigning a wild threesome in a barred cell that appeared center stage during an extended instrumental. A native Minnesotan more prone to saying "you betcha" than cussing, my tall, thin, fair-haired friend Anders asked, "Can you fucking *believe* this?" He was not alone in posing that question, or in interpreting the scene as I did. "Kelly re-emerged in a prison cell simulating sex with two writhing women," Greg Kot wrote in the *Chicago Tribune*. Kelefa Sanneh of the *New York Times* flew to Chicago to review the show, and he held that during the threesome scene, Kelly "resembled either a shackled prisoner or a caged zoo ape. Dismayed fans were left to sort out this collision of stereotypes themselves."

Anders had been my intern, transcribing interviews when I wrote my Bangs biography, and he'd gone on to freelance music reviews for the *Sun-Times* afterhours from a more reliable day job. He handled the straightforward critique. "It should have been bigger than the War of the Worlds, the Clash of the Titans, and Godzilla vs. King Kong all rolled into one," he wrote, "but the pair couldn't escape the shadow of the elephant in Kelly's boudoir." My editors assigned me to provide context and commentary. Under the headline "R. Kelly Flouting His Foes," I observed that the line between Kelly's public art and personal obsessions had always been blurry. During the show, he referenced the charges hanging over him by alternately playing his alleged crimes for laughs, using them to evoke sympathy as a victim unjustly persecuted, or bragging that nothing would stop the Superfreak.

Ed Genson, Kelly's lead attorney, took umbrage with my column and promptly faxed a letter to the paper. "Jim DeRogatis, *Sun-Times* rock critic, ran his interpretation of the message R. Kelly intended to deliver at his show. The article was incorrect." He took special exception to my description of the cell skit. "Apparently, DeRogatis is so focused on Kelly's criminal case that he sees it everywhere, even in places it is not." Kelly and the two female performers "danced not in a jail cell but in a cage." The defense attorney didn't bother to correct the *Trib*'s Greg Kot or Kelefa Sanneh at the *New York Times*. He targeted me.

Abdon Pallasch and I had always given Kelly every opportunity to comment, and if we tried three times and failed for any story, city editor Don Hayner didn't publish until we tried a fourth time. The *Sun-Times* intended to publish the letter, but I objected to a sentence that took a shot at my punk band. Arguing that Kelly's First Amendment right to express himself was the same as mine, Genson referenced lyrics in my band's songs and photos on my website. I found that chilling. I had learned the Kelly camp hired private detective Jack Palladino to look into many of my sources, and I assumed they looked into me and Abdon, too.

Then there were the gangster affectations of some of Kelly's crew. "I know you have a six-year-old daughter," Kelly's manager Derrel McDavid said apropos of nothing when he called me at home on a Saturday afternoon. He also told Abdon that he'd seen me with my daughter at the Old Orchard shopping mall in Skokie, and he'd wanted to beat me up. Abdon and I made a point of documenting these comments in memos to our editors.

"Jim: Don't worry, you are right to be concerned about the personal stuff they're trying to get at," Cooke responded via email after I complained about Genson's reference to my band. He cut that sentence but ran the rest of the letter verbatim as a thousand-word op-ed. Kelly's crisis manager Allan Mayer moved it on the PR Newswire with the heading, "*Sun-Times* Publishes Column Refuting R. Kelly Critic."

I had no love for Kelly and his crew, and as the Best of Both Worlds tour rolled on, it became apparent that Jay-Z and his camp didn't, either. During one of his sets, the rapper included what some saw as a dig at his co-headliner. When Jay-Z paid tribute to fallen stars, he solemnly stood as images flashed on the video screens of the late Tupac Shakur, Biggie Smalls, and, to the biggest reaction from the crowd, Aaliyah. The Allstate Arena, where the tour started, stood less than a mile from the Sheraton Gateway Suites, where Kelly had married his underage protégé a decade earlier. At the time of her death, Aaliyah had been dating Damon Dash, who co-founded Roc-A-Fella Records with Jay-Z.

After opening night, the threesome in a cell disappeared from Kelly's sets through the rest of the tour. The singer arrived two and a half hours late for night two, and he left early, before the closing bow with Jay-Z. Kelly complained that Jay-Z's sound and lighting crews sabotaged his parts of the show. The tour's producers canceled the next date in Cincinnati. A week later, Kelly stopped a show in St. Louis and got into a screaming match with the tech crew, *Post-Dispatch* music critic Kevin C. Johnson told me. Jay-Z finished the performance with his tribute to dead legends, while Kelly went to a nearby McDonald's that had just closed for the night.

The singer persuaded the Mickey D's manager not only to reopen for his crew, but to allow him to hand orders to customers at the drive-through window. "It was on the radio," Genson bragged to Abdon. "People were running out of their houses to have R. Kelly serve them."

Kelly seemed to be coming undone. The production company canceled the next two shows in Milwaukee and Hartford, then the tour lurched forward again, arriving in Jay-Z's hometown for his triumphant return to Madison Square Garden on October 29, 2004. During his second solo set, Kelly fled the stage, saying two people in the crowd were waving guns at him. When he tried to return, Jay-Z's friend Tyran Smith pepper-sprayed him. The singer went to St. Vincent's Hospital while Jay-Z ended the show with several superstar guests from the audience.

The next morning, the best of both worlds gave separate, dueling interviews to New York's Hot 97 radio station. Jay-Z said audiences preferred him to Kelly, which made his partner jealous. Kelly complained again about production issues. The rapper kicked him off the tour, rebranded it as Jay-Z and Friends, and tapped Pharrell Williams, Snoop Dogg, and Kanye West to complete the remaining dates. Kelly sued Jay-Z, and Jay-Z sued Kelly. A judge dismissed the rapper's lawsuit, and Jay-Z settled Kelly's claim out of court. Lawyers did not disclose the terms, and Jay-Z never has spoken publicly about Kelly since.

Through all the reporting Abdon and I did on R. Kelly for the *Chicago Sun-Times*, our colleague Mary Mitchell was one of our staunchest allies, and an inspiration whenever we felt as if we were banging our heads against the wall. Mary grew up in public housing on the South Side, raised four children, and spent two decades working as a legal secretary before enrolling at Columbia College Chicago in 1989 at age forty-one. She found her passion in journalism, and she was badass. "There are voiceless people in the world," she said, "and I was a natural at hearing those stories." Since starting at the paper in 1991 as an education reporter, she'd risen to become a member of the editorial board and a columnist. Dedicated and fearless, she'd also battled and beaten cancer. I knew I'd earned my bona fides after the first story about

Kelly when Mary stopped me in the hall and said "Great work." Previously, we'd never even talked.

In her columns, Mary questioned Kelly flouting his spirituality as if it forgave his continued sinning. She hammered the Congressional Black Caucus Foundation for booking Kelly for a benefit concert; criticized mothers "who were either so impressed with Kelly's stardom or so negligent of their daughter's activities that they failed to protect them from a sexual predator"; and blasted absent fathers "not there to protect their daughters from lecherous older men." She compared the situation with Kelly to that of predatory Catholic priests, holding readers partly responsible. "Both the church and the community failed to hold the offenders accountable until the complaints erupted like a volcano." She also repeatedly noted that the singer was emblematic of a much larger problem. "Kelly may be the mama's boy who can do no wrong in the black community, but he is also the poster child for the dysfunctional relationship that has developed between adult men and girls in our society. Despite statutory rape laws, a growing number of girls are getting pregnant by grown men." And that was all within the first two years after our first story.

"I got a lot of hate mail. The community was after my head," Mary told me years later. "There's this desperate need for the black community to have a hero. That's why Bill Cosby was out there for so long. Same thing with Kelly. The black community didn't want to deal with this being a form of sex-trafficking girls. I was trying to get them to understand the seriousness of it, that it wasn't just two white guys, you and Abdon, trying to bring down a black guy. I always saw that as a problem."

"We failed as a community," Common told TMZ in early 2019. The Chicago rapper is known as one of the most conscious men in hip-hop, and he's always been one of my favorites. Even he didn't see the problem with Kelly until too late. "We knew these things were happening. Instead of trying to free these young ladies and stop this thing going on, we were just, like, man, rocking to the music. I'm guilty of that, too, myself. I didn't speak out against it."

Mary Mitchell did, and she was never alone among black women in Chicago and elsewhere. "I just had a loud megaphone," she told me. "So did you, and you used it. You made victims visible and amplified their voices. That's what journalism is supposed to do."

In April 2003, ten months after Kelly's indictment, Mary scooped Abdon and me when she interviewed three of the singer's in-laws for a disturbing story about how he treated his wife, Andrea. Kelly married twenty-two-year-old Andrea Lee, a dancer in his touring troupe, in 1996. By age twenty-nine, she'd given birth to his three children, Jaya, born in 1996; Joann, born in 1998; and Robert Jr., born in 2002, but sources in his crew told me she was almost a nonentity in his life. They called her "Puppydog," rather than her preferred nickname, "Drea." They said (and she later confirmed in many print and television interviews) that she had to knock before entering any room in the house on George Street or the mansion in Olympia Fields. Photographers almost never captured the couple together in public, and many of Kelly's fans didn't know he was married until the widespread publicity after his indictment.

"His wife was still excusing Rob, Rob and his friends," the singer's confidante Kim Dulaney said in 2004. "His wife was a Stepford." (Ira Levin's 1974 novel and the subsequent film *The Stepford Wives* portrayed the robotic women of a Connecticut suburb who submitted totally to their controlling husbands.) "I think she knows Rob, I can say that. I think she knows," Dulaney said of Kelly's sexual contact with underage women.

When Mary Mitchell talked to Andrea's mother, grandfather, and aunt, they said Kelly didn't allow them to visit her at home, and he didn't permit Andrea to speak to them on the phone. In 2003, they still hadn't met their sixteen-month-old grandson, Robert Jr. "The last time I talked to her was over two years ago on the phone," said Gerri Cruz, Andrea's mother. "She was crying hysterically and violently. Of course, you are worried when you go from talking to a person every day to not talking to them, period."

Cruz had recently asked the Olympia Fields Police Department to perform a well-being check on her daughter, and they reported Andrea was fine. "I don't know if my child is under the influence. I don't know if she is being controlled. I don't know if people are watching her. I don't know if she is being brainwashed," Cruz told Mary. "If everything is all right, then she should call her mother and her father. I find this behavior bizarre."

In September 2005, thirty-nine months after Kelly's indictment, Andrea petitioned Cook County Circuit Court for an order of protection from her husband of nine years. She charged that he repeatedly slapped and hit her when she asked for a divorce. "I'm now fearful of him and I want to get away safe and be happy," she wrote in large, looping handwriting. "No, I never called the police, I thought it would get better." In even larger scrawl, Andrea requested "No contact by any means!" for herself and "Supervised visits only!" for her children. Several weeks later, after the couple reportedly reconciled, she rescinded the request for a protection order.

"Robert needed her to play a role during the trial, or at least make it be like he had this happy family at home," one of Kelly's former associates told me. (Andrea did not attend the trial.) "One way or the other, he convinced her to stay a little bit longer."

Almost five years after Robert's indictment, in May 2007, journalist Natalie Moore asked Andrea about her husband's case during a lengthy interview that ran as a cover story in *Essence*. "C'mon. Who would believe all that?" Andrea said of the charges. "That's why they call them allegations." She grew indignant when Moore asked if she'd seen the videotape. "Why would you ask that question of a woman married with children? It's ludicrous to ask me a question like that."

The couple finalized their divorce a little more than a year later, weeks after the end of the trial. In 2018, Andrea began to speak to the media about the physical and mental abuse she says she suffered from Kelly during their marriage. She once contemplated suicide because things got so bad. Her friend Gem Pratts and manager Eric France—both accompanied her to speaking engagements for a time, along with another friend who serves as her stylist—told me Andrea could not talk to me because "some things are still just too painful for her." In dream hampton's 2019 docuseries, *Surviving R. Kelly*, Andrea says there are "certain things here I'm not willing to talk about." Asked if she ever saw underage girls with her husband or in their homes, she says, "He never brought any of them around me. He kept it away from me for a reason."

After that series aired, a key member of the prosecution team for the 2008 trial told me one of their biggest regrets was that they could not convince

Andrea to testify. "Even at the end when you could tell their marriage was breaking down, we made some last-ditch efforts to get her on board, and we were told in no uncertain terms, 'Get the fuck out of here.' To see her now, talking about what a monster he was . . . Maybe even just having her on our side could have changed that."

As he continued waiting for his day in court, Robert Kelly had plenty of other problems with both blood relatives and people he considered family. In early 2006, three and a half years after his indictment, his younger half brother, Carey, released an interview with *Drahma*, a DVD-based music magazine, claiming Robert emotionally and physically abused Andrea, had "a problem" with underage girls, and often showed the videotape at the heart of the indictment to his friends. He also tried to convince Carey to take the blame as the man who appeared on the tape, Carey said, even though the half brothers don't resemble each other very much. "I got a call a year, year and a half ago from my older brother who wanted me to do some shit pertaining to this case that was going to leave me behind bars," Carey says in the *Drahma* interview. "I turned it down. The nigga offered me $50,000, a bullshit record deal, and a house to lie, to perjure myself in a court of law, and I felt this shit wasn't worth it."

According to Carey, Robert had long documented his obsession with underage sex, in "Age Ain't Nothing but a Number" and other songs. "He's been telling, 'I've got a problem, because if I love this girl and she's twelve, that's all that matters.' He's been saying it in his songs, and that's what makes him the genius that he is," Carey says. "He speaks shit that other motherfuckers who are on his level can relate to. And I say to America, the criminal justice system, if you let that nigga off, he's going to do it again, trust me. I bet my life on it."

By his own admission, Carey had struggled—he was homeless for a time—and he resented Robert for not helping him launch a rap career. "This is not the first time Carey has made ridiculous accusations against his brother," R. Kelly's spokesman Allan Mayer said in response to the *Dhrama* interview. "We're not going to dignify them with a comment."

Robert's other half-siblings, Bruce and Theresa, worked on and off for their superstar kin, Bruce as a bodyguard and runner, and Theresa—who has never spoken about Robert publicly—cleaning Robert's house. In 2015, Bruce sued Robert, claiming he was owed $11,000 in back wages for working as a driver and an assistant, but he continued to defend Robert after they settled that case. Interviewed for *Surviving R. Kelly* while being held in Cook County Jail on $100,000 bond for theft, burglary, and possession of a controlled substance, Bruce said, "Robert likes younger women. You have people who have fantasies about different things. . . . But that's just a preference. Everyone has preferences. What is the big deal about my brother?"

In the fall of 2006, more than four years after the indictment, I got a call from Henry Vaughn, a Chicago man who wanted to give me a scoop about the lawsuit he'd just filed. The son of a South Side Democratic ward boss, Vaughn worked as a security guard, and he claimed to have been a mentor and "uncle" to Robert since Kelly's teens. They were not actually related, but the singer and his crew called Vaughn "Uncle Henry Love." He arrived at the new *Sun-Times* offices in rented space at 350 North Orleans Street wearing a crisp white shirt beneath an impeccably tailored red suit, tie, and top hat, the living embodiment of the city's stepping scene. Abdon, Mary Mitchell, and I sat with him in a small, gray conference room as he told us he'd gone to a party at Kelly's Olympia Fields mansion months earlier on February 19 to watch the NBA All-Star Game, and he'd been beaten by Kelly and his bodyguards.

Uncle Henry showed us an Olympia Fields police report, photos of a bloody lip and other injuries, and paperwork from Advocate Christ Medical Center in south suburban Oak Lawn to back up the account in his legal claim, which demanded compensation for "permanent injuries" from the beating, as well as money he said Kelly promised to pay him for sharing his stepping moves and inspiring the hit "Step in the Name of Love." Myriad are the accusations against pop stars for stealing other people's ideas, and every journalist on the beat soon learns to ignore them, but the original version of Kelly's song does end with the line, "Dedicated to Uncle Henry Love, thank you," and the remix includes the shout-out, "Henry Love, I see you, yeah!"

Asked what prompted Kelly to allegedly beat his friend, mentor, and dance instructor, Uncle Henry said he couldn't be certain, but the argument started when Kelly's young daughter Jaya danced to amuse his friends at the party, and Uncle Henry criticized Kelly for encouraging her to do it. (Jaya came out as transgender in 2014, and now prefers to be called Kelly's son, Jay.) "She was all dressed up with tight jeans and makeup on, a seven-year-old girl, dancing on top of the pool table," Uncle Henry said. "It was ridiculous. She told my lady, 'I'm having a show next week. When you come, bring a hundred dollars.' Nobody would tell this, but I ain't scared to tell the truth. Shame the devil!"

Olympia Fields police told Abdon they responded to a call from the mansion the night of the party but declined to file charges when Kelly's bodyguards and others at the gathering said Uncle Henry had gotten drunk and had to be subdued. They found the singer's children upstairs, sleeping. Kelly's spokesman Allan Mayer described Uncle Henry as "a disgruntled former employee and hanger-on" and called the lawsuit "a pathetic collection of half-truths, distortions, and outright lies." He dismissed the story about Kelly's daughter dancing at the party as "outrageous nonsense," but Kelly nevertheless settled Uncle Henry's claim out of court for an undisclosed sum. Vaughn never spoke about Kelly in public again.

Kelly's new spokesman, Mayer, had replaced Regina Daniels, who for years had stood among Kelly's most ardent defenders. Regina and her husband, George, split from the star not long before his indictment in 2002, issuing a press release saying they'd severed all ties with Kelly, and cryptically adding, "a line has been crossed." In 2008, George Daniels talked to a Los Angeles radio station and explained what that meant. "He crossed the line with my daughter. It didn't get to the extreme of that video or else I wouldn't be here, if you know what I'm talking about." Slamming his fist on the table, he made it clear he would have beaten Kelly to a pulp. "The reason that I'm talking about this, it's not just for me, it's not for my wife, it's not for my daughter, but it's for other fathers and mothers, because it doesn't have to be a superstar, it could be the dude on the corner. There are guys who sit around and give your child a couple of bucks to go to school and then wait until they get a little older, then they set that trap."

Maxine Daniels, George's daughter and Regina's stepdaughter, talked to World Entertainment News Network several weeks later, detailing the affair she said she had with Kelly when she was twenty years old. "My stepmother and father didn't know about my relationship with the singer because I knew and he knew that they wouldn't approve . . . so I tried to keep it a secret, but when my stepmother found out about our relationship, she resigned because she felt that Rob had 'crossed the line' by dating a girl that he has known since she was seven years old. . . . She was Rob's publicist for fourteen years and always considered Rob not just a client, but family. And Rob thought of my dad like a father."

Maxine Daniels said the affair with Kelly had been a "serious misjudgment," but she'd been "swept up by his charming and generous ways."

"It's hard to take seriously the moral outrage expressed by George and Regina Daniels over R. Kelly's relationship with Mr. Daniels's adult daughter, Maxine," spokesman Allan Mayer said. "The fact is that they had no problem with the relationship—indeed, they encouraged it—while Ms. Daniels was on Mr. Kelly's payroll."

When the Best of Both Worlds tour fell apart in the fall of 2004, Kelly came off the road and did what he always did, returning to the recording studio in the basement of his Olympia Fields mansion. Nine months after his last show with Jay-Z, and thirty-seven months after his indictment, Kelly released *TP.3 Reloaded*. The title harkened back to his earlier, most lascivious Jive Records releases, *12 Play* and *TP-2.com*. With songs such as "Sex in the Kitchen," "Sex Weed," and "(Sex) Love Is What We Makin'," Kelly didn't hide his obsession, but the first five chapters of "Trapped in the Closet," his soon-to-be-notorious, never-ending "hip-hopera," garnered the most attention. Many music critics loved it.

Writing for *Pitchfork*, Rob Mitchum asked, "Is R. Kelly a joke or a genius? Does he really expect us to forget his recent unpleasantness"—an exceedingly poor choice of words for allegations of statutory rape and making child pornography—"or does he just not care what we think? Given the charges against him, how is he still recruiting A-list guest stars? How many metaphors for sex can one man think up?" The review's rating of 7.8 on *Pitchfork*'s 10-point scale answered the critic's rhetorical questions. "For all the absurdity of his 'Trapped in the Closet' cycle and his endless stock of creative horniness, the man is an absolute master of his medium."

Kelly had a deep connection to closets, both physical and metaphorical. He'd spent countless hours honing his music in the closet-size "guitar room" at Kenwood Academy, and he said he often slept in his closet, as he did for a month after Aaliyah's death. "Everyone has a secret," he says of the closet as metaphor in *Soulacoaster*. "Everyone has a closet that he or she is trapped inside of, and everyone—believe it or not—wants out of that closet."

"Trapped in the Closet," which Kelly also called "a ghetto soap opera," kept expanding. Eventually, it followed the peccadillos of a horny and adulterous cast of dozens, including a pastor, a cop, a midget, and a central protagonist named Sylvester. Kelly sang almost all of the roles himself.

In addition to his own prolific output, Kelly continued writing for and producing other artists, including rappers Ludacris, LL Cool J, and Lil Wayne; singers Ciara and Syleena Johnson; and, in perhaps the most unlikely collaboration, Missy Elliott, who'd coproduced the album Aaliyah made after she split from Kelly. Talks were even under way for Kelly to work with Whitney Houston (which finally happened after the trial). *Double Up*, Kelly's ninth album for Jive Records, included guest appearances by Snoop Dogg, Nelly, Usher, T.I., T-Pain, Chamillionaire, Kid Rock, Swizz Beatz, Keyshia Cole, and Polow da Don.

Few of Kelly's peers seemed to have a problem working with a man accused of making child pornography. For some, the accusations even became a joke. As Aisha Harris wrote years later in the *New York Times*, "[T]hose who laughed at Kelly were able to ignore the charges against him."

Near the top of his opening monologue at the MTV Video Music Awards in 2003, host Chris Rock pointed out three of the many celebrities in the audience. "Sit the Olsen Twins down here, you gotta sit R. Kelly way up there!" For years, Cedric the Entertainer's stand-up routine included a bit in which he imagined Kelly as a horny preacher, and in the 2004 film *Barbershop 2: Back in Business*, he cracked, "Yeah, R. Kelly was set up. He set up the camera!" Comedian Dave Chappelle mocked Kelly in 2003 on his Comedy Central sketch show with a video entitled "(I Wanna) Pee on You," and the same year, cartoonist Aaron McGruder took aim at Kelly in the second episode of *The Boondocks*, the animated series based on his comic strip.

In an episode called "The Trial of Robert Kelly," airing on Cartoon Network's Adult Swim, McGruder's version of the singer wears the bandit mask he first sported in the video he made with yet another collaborator, rapper Cassidy. He's defended by an animated lawyer resembling civil rights activist William Kunstler (voiced by Adam West), while a trio of black activists protesting Kelly resemble Cornel West, Tony Brown, and Dick Gregory. Defending the singer are a group of people grilling on barbecues, listening to R&B, and holding misspelt signs such as "Not Gilltee." One overweight black woman swoons over her musical heartthrob. When asked why she supports Kelly, she says, "'Cause he good!" Kelly is acquitted, and in the end, Chicago-born Huey, the perpetually vexed ten-year-old hero and political conscience of *The Boondocks* voiced by Regina King, declares, "Every famous nigga that gets arrested is not Nelson Mandela. Yes, the government conspires to put a lot of innocent black men in jail on fallacious charges. But R. Kelly is not one of those men."

Even though some of the many jokes about Kelly had an edge, most reduced his crimes to his fetishes—urination and videotaping sex acts—ignoring the far more troubling charges of a pattern of pursuing underage girls for sex. The insidious fact, Aisha Harris wrote in the *New York Times*, is "it's easier (and safer) to poke fun at a grown man's fetish than to wrestle with claims that he performed his fetish on a minor."

Kelly continued to sell new music and, some said, join in laughing at himself. *Double Up* was released in May 2007, almost sixty months after his indictment; he intended the title as a pun on the joys of both double albums and threesomes. Tracks such as "Get Dirty," "Freaky in the Club," "Sweet Tooth," and "I'm a Flirt (Remix)" once again mined familiar hot-and-horny themes, and Pitchfork rated the disc a 6.7. "In a sense, it seems more apropos to judge *Double Up* as a comedy record than as a pop record," critic Ryan Dombal wrote.

In *Soulacoaster*, Kelly brags, "The two songs that got lots of attention were the lines where I once again messed with the metaphors. 'The Zoo' was my very own version of the film *Jurassic Park*: 'Girl, I got you so wet, it's like a rain forest / Like *Jurassic Park* except I'm your sex-a-saurus. . . .' The other song was 'Sex Planet': 'Jupiter, Pluto, Venus, and Saturn / I'm leaving Earth to explore your galaxy / Ten to zero, blast off, here we go / We'll be climaxing until we reach Mercury.' For reasons I can't explain, the song became a big hit with indie-rockers and made a number of their Top 10 lists in 2007."

Only three months later, in August 2007, Kelly released a new "video album" with ten more chapters of "Trapped in the Closet," and cable television's Independent Film Channel ran a compilation film of all twenty-two chapters in heavy rotation. The list of all the music Kelly recorded between his indictment and his trial still doesn't end there. His "official" releases sold a combined eight million copies in the United States, according to the Recording Industry Association of America, impressive business in the dying days of the old-school music industry, when physical product yielded to digital downloads (and, eventually, to streaming). But Kelly also recorded two other albums that he floated to fans for free on the Net: *Loveland* in 2002, and *12 Play: 4th Quarter* in 2008.

"Sources close to the Kelly camp said that some of the *Loveland* themes and lyrics would present awkward connotations in the context of the singer's legal situation," Geoff Boucher reported in the *Los Angeles Times*, and that's why Kelly decided not to release it as a CD. Age seventy-seven and dying of cancer in March 2019, Ed Genson told *Sun-Times* columnist Neil Steinberg that he "vetted" Kelly's recordings while serving as the star's attorney. "I listened to them, which ones would make a judge mad," Genson said. Some critics thought the problem was hypersexualized jams such as "Come to Daddy" and "Make You My Baby," but the most remarkable and problematic song may have been "I Believe I Can Fly (Remix)," a nearly ten-minute operetta in a similar mode to "Trapped in the Closet," with Kelly portraying all of the characters.

The remix sounds very little like the original "I Believe I Can Fly," and it amounts to a lengthy confession to unnamed sins as a character named Robert appears before St. Peter at the pearly gates on the day of reckoning. The music is ornate and mock-classical, as perhaps befits the soundtrack in heaven. "I'm sorry for all of the wrong I've done / So can you please forgive me / And deliver me from my ways?" Robert sings in his familiar range. Then, he responds as St. Peter in a basso profundo. "We don't welcome sinners in this place. . . . You are a heartless thug and we don't want you here!"

Turning to his dead mother, Robert pleads for her to intervene, but she asks, "Now, son, tell me, do you believe the Truth?" He assures her he does, and Jesus finally comes to his rescue, offering absolution, and encouraging him to "stand up and claim victory."

CHAPTER 10

THE STATE OF ILLINOIS V. ROBERT SYLVESTER KELLY

With R. Kelly's defense team having exhausted their delaying tactics after six years, and with Judge Vincent Gaughan often siding with them in sealed rulings limiting the evidence and testimony he would allow in the trial so as not to prejudice the jury, *The State of Illinois v. Robert Sylvester Kelly* finally was set to begin in the spring of 2008. It would take place at Twenty-Sixth and Cal on the fifth floor of the Cook County Criminal Court Building, one of the grandest, most storied structures in Chicago, a city lousy with such places. Constructed of limestone trucked in from Indiana, the seven-story tower opened a few miles south of the Loop in 1929, weeks after the Saint Valentine's Day Massacre. Built at the then-staggering cost of $7.5 million, it sat on a strip of land that, not coincidentally, happened to be owned by the family of Anton Cermak, leader of the Cook County Democratic Party, and a future mayor of Chicago.

The county courts had outgrown their previous home in the Loop, and the new courts building bordering the West Side neighborhood of Little Village, rapidly becoming one of the city's most vibrant Latinx communities, quickly became one of the busiest judicial centers in the United States. Judges in the tower's thirty-one courtrooms decide twenty-two thousand cases a year, from street-corner busts for possession of weed, to multiple murders like the Brown's Chicken massacre. Al Capone made numerous appearances there, and his sneering picture hangs in one of the marble hallways between two solid-brass light fixtures. John Wayne Gacy also strolled the corridors in chains, but court clerks preferred not to think about his trial for the brutal sexual assault, torture, and murder of at least thirty-three teenage boys and young men in the seventies. They were more likely to mention rubbing elbows with Harrison Ford during the filming of *The Fugitive* in 1993.

Designed to impress upon visitors the awesome power of the law, Greek and Roman flourishes abound. The building boasts eight huge columns on its front façade, and its top-floor windows are framed by statues of classical figures symbolizing law, justice, liberty, truth, might, love, wisdom, and peace. Judges preside from thronelike benches that look down on courtrooms filled with dark rosewood paneling, but the building isn't always as regal as it appears at first glance. Stifling in the summer, it's freezing during the winter. Scurrying mice sometimes distract lawyers as they address the court, and jurors have been known to shriek when a huge cockroach drops from the ceiling.

In the weeks before jury selection began in the Kelly trial, Judge Gaughan demanded that the county paint Courtroom 500 and spiff up the hallway leading from the elevator. He said he wanted the facility to look its best for the world's press. At his urging, a maintenance crew also reopened and repaired an unused handicap ramp on the ground floor, and he devoted that entrance exclusively to Kelly and his entourage. The judge anticipated throngs of fans and protestors filling the street, and he didn't want them to harass Kelly. "Not even Oprah Winfrey—who sat on a jury in a murder trial here two years ago—got her own entrance," Stefano Esposito wrote in the *Sun-Times*.

A crowd of about a hundred people came on the trial's opening and closing days, but most times, only about a dozen diehard Kelly fans and two black activists stood on the sidewalk at Twenty-Sixth and Cal. Najee Ali, executive director of Los Angeles–based Project Islamic HOPE, carried a sign proclaiming "R. Kelly, World's Greatest Pedophile," but he failed to attract other protestors. "This has been the loneliest fight I have ever been in," he told Kayce T. Ataiyero of the *Trib*. For the first few years of pretrial hearings, Kelly's spiritual advisor, the Rev. James Meeks, had brought a yellow school bus full of kids from the Rainbow/PUSH Coalition wearing "Free R. Kelly" T-shirts. By the start of testimony, they'd stopped coming.

Some fans paid a price for supporting the singer. On the first day of the trial, Gaughan threw Kelly's spokesman Allan Mayer out of the courtroom and threatened to jail him for contempt if he returned. Mayer had angered the judge by giving yet another quote about the star's innocence to one of the daily papers, violating the gag order Gaughan imposed on both legal teams when proceedings started. One day after the lunch break, as the jury exited the elevator on the fifth floor, a woman who appeared to be homeless and mentally disturbed shouted, "Free R. Kelly!" Jurors said they hadn't heard her, but the judge ordered sheriff's deputies to put the woman in cuffs. He sent her to Cook County Jail, right next door to the courthouse, and set bail at $50,000.

"Only God can judge him," two older Kelly fans told reporters who asked why they prayed in front of the courthouse on some mornings. The media preferred interviewing two young female regulars who called themselves "R. Kelly's biggest fans." Streamwood resident Jerhonda Johnson, who claimed to be eighteen, told anyone who'd listen that prosecutors "don't have a case, it ain't him on that tape." She and her friend, a twenty-three-year-old criminal-justice student at Harold Washington College, shouted, "I love you!" when Kelly walked in or out of his special entrance. The star always smiled and waved. One day, a reporter asked Johnson if she'd date the singer if he asked her out. "Yes! He ain't even gotta finish the sentence." And if he wanted to tape her? She paused, then smiled wide. "Just don't let it go public."

Because *Sun-Times* city editor Don Hayner and media attorney Damon Dunn urged me to stay away, I attended the trial only once. They told Abdon Pallasch to steer clear, too, but he kept "popping in for just a minute," despite ceding daily coverage to our colleagues Eric Herman and Stefano Esposito. My account of the trial is based on their reporting, as well as Abdon's observations and interviews I conducted with the attorneys, jurors, reporters, and court personnel. Cameras, video, and audio recorders were not allowed in Cook County Criminal Court, but transcripts of the proceedings are available (at the exorbitant price of four dollars per page). I also relied on some of those, in addition to frequent reports during and after the trial by Jennifer Vineyard for MTV News; Kathy Chaney for the *Chicago Defender*; Kyra Kyles for *RedEye*; Josh Levin for *Slate*; Edward McClelland for *Blender*; Azam Ahmed, Kayce T. Ataiyero, and Stacy St. Clair for the *Tribune*; and Kim Janssen for the *Daily Southtown*.

"As you know, this is a high-profile case, and if you don't know, God love you, you're probably the only person on earth that doesn't," Judge Gaughan said with considerable hyperbole at the start of jury selection on May 9, 2008. Picking a jury of twelve of Kelly's peers and four alternates from a pool of one hundred fifty people took four days and proved contentious. The lawyers and the judge started by quizzing potential jurors if they knew or knew of anyone on the witness list.

One woman said she knew of Kelly's former manager and Aaliyah's uncle, Barry Hankerson. "He was married to Gladys Knight, right?" She remained through several more rounds of questioning before she was excused. A man said he liked my music columns in the *Sun-Times* and *Sound Opinions*, the radio show I co-host with Greg Kot of the *Trib*, thereby disqualifying himself in court (though not in my heart). Asked if she knew anything negative about Kelly, a black female postal worker said, "He and Jay-Z don't get along." Lead prosecutor Shauna Boliker disqualified her because she also called Kelly "a musical genius, a pied piper."

While attorneys wrangled over the jury, the Pied Piper of R&B sat in court looking disinterested, occasionally doodling on yellow Post-it notes that he shoved into the pockets of his expensive-looking, perfectly tailored suits. Reporters were awed by what seemed to be his endless closet full of these, though given the way most reporters dress, it doesn't take much to impress them, fashion-wise. The only time Kelly reacted during jury selection came when a middle-aged white woman responded to whether she had an opinion about the singer by saying, "Yes, he's not very smart." Kelly turned to her and looked hurt.

Four well-paid lawyers sat with Kelly at the defense table throughout the trial: Genson, the self-professed dean of local defense attorneys; his office-mate, forty-six-year-old Marc Martin; the rotund, seventy-two-year-old Sam Adam Sr.; and his equally beefy thirty-five-year-old son, Sam Adam Jr. At one point, the defense angrily charged the prosecution with excluding black jurors, although they well knew federal law prohibits discrimination on race or gender. Adam Sr., a white man married to a black woman, angrily made the argument to Gaughan. "They've used fifty percent of their challenges on African Americans!"

Writing in *Slate*, Josh Levin compared the bellicose elder member of the Adam family to Uncle Fester. "I like to dress like the jurors," Adam Sr. said when asked about the old burgundy sport coat he often wore to court. In *Blender*, Edward McClelland compared him to "a wine stain with arms." During his long career, Adam Sr. had represented almost as many mobsters as his good friend Ed Genson, and the two had partnered to represent Rep. Mel Reynolds in 1995 and lost. Genson had also lost another, more recent high-profile case that resonated with Abdon and me, when he defended Lord Conrad Black, the Canadian press baron who owned the *Sun-Times*. Black was convicted of securities fraud in 2007 and eventually sentenced to forty-two months in prison and a fine of $125,000.

In response to the defense's charge of racism during jury selection, lead prosecutor Shauna Boliker pointed out that all six of the peremptory challenges by Kelly's team had removed white jurors. Judge Gaughan deemed both sides "race-neutral" and kept jury selection moving. Now that the trial had finally started, he was not going to let anything slow it down, and he tolerated no distractions or infractions of his rules. On day one, Gaughan ordered Genson to leave the motorized scooter he rode because of his physical disability outside the courtroom. At one point, when Adam Sr. moved a chair in front of the bench so his friend could sit while addressing the judge, Gaughan snapped, "Oh, no, this ain't the ADA here!" The judge demanded that Genson stand at the lectern like all the other attorneys, and to hell with the Americans with Disabilities Act.

In the end, Kelly wound up with a jury of eight whites and four blacks, nine men and three women, half middle-aged and half young adults. Hailing from throughout Cook County and working a wide variety of jobs, the jury presented a panoply of Chicago.

Juror No. 69 worked as a vice president of national accounts, listened to NPR, read the *Wall Street Journal*, and thought "child porn is as low as it gets." The wife of a Baptist preacher, No. 6 lived near Kelly's mansion in Olympia Fields, but said she didn't know about the case and had "not heard the local scuttlebutt." No. 9, a devout Christian, worked in telecommunications and knew Kelly only from "I Believe I Can Fly." Asked about pornography, he said, "I don't like going to 7-Eleven and seeing it, but if a person wants it, it's their right." No. 21 studied criminal justice and wanted to become a cop. Gaughan delayed the start of the trial by a day so she could take her final exam.

Juror No. 22 said he read the newspaper every morning, but he hated the *Sun-Times*. No. 23 worked as a compliance officer at a downtown investment firm, sported an "Impeach Bush" button on his book bag, and knew a victim of sexual abuse. He assured the court he could be fair. No. 32 was a teaching assistant at Saint Agatha Catholic Academy in the Lawndale neighborhood, where Rev. Daniel McCormack had served before pleading guilty in 2007 to sexually abusing five boys ages eight to twelve. That case had been overseen by Kelly's chief prosecutor, Shauna Boliker.

A culinary student, Juror No. 40 heard about the Kelly case on TV and radio, but assured the judge he'd paid little attention. No. 44 had seen a blurred clip from the video on TV, but the man, who owned a financial company, said he had no opinion. No. 48, a recent graduate from the University of Kansas, had been arrested for underage drinking (paying a $450 fine) and possession of marijuana (paying $350 on top of serving five days in jail). He thought people with money can "afford better lawyers." A Romanian immigrant who retained a thick accent, No. 61 believed in this country's justice system, but expressed confusion about how much the prosecution had to prove. "I'm probably not the smartest guy," he said, "but I will do what is best and fair."

The final juror, No. 68, was a rape survivor who assured the court she could set aside her personal trauma and remain impartial. With typical chutzpah, Genson asked Gaughan for an extra peremptory strike. When the judge asked why, Genson said, "Because we've run out of them!" Gaughan scowled and denied the request.

The morning the trial began, both Chicago dailies quoted legal experts about the makeup of the jury. "It was amazing how few people knew about it," prominent defense attorney Terry Ekl said, skeptical of the number of jurors who claimed ignorance of a case that had been big news in Chicago for six years. Noting that the jury represented "a broad spectrum," Kent College of Law Professor Richard Kling said it gave both sides reasons to be hopeful, but he noted the defense might have reason to worry about the rape victim.

Just before opening statements, Judge Gaughan dismissed the woman who'd been raped, not because of her history, he said, but because her boss wouldn't pay her during the trial. One of the alternates, No. 66, took her place. The twentysomething man had interned at a radio station, then applied for a job with the Chicago Police Department. His uncle had been convicted on child porn charges, but he swore he could be fair.

Solicitous of the jurors throughout the proceedings, the otherwise stern judge generally spared them his flashes of wrath, frequently asking if they'd slept well in the sequester hotel, or if they enjoyed their state-provided breakfast, lunch, and dinner.

In opening statements on May 20, 2008, both sides presented their versions of what jurors would see when the video was screened in court. "It is Reshona Landfair and Robert Kelly that you will see on this videotape," Assistant State's Attorney Shauna Boliker said, her usually chipper trill wavering at times. "You will see the sex acts that he commanded Reshona Landfair to perform, vile and disturbing and disgusting acts. You will see that underage child performing acts that you have never seen before. A child doesn't choose to be violated and placed on a videotape, a videotape that will live on forever, long after this child becomes an adult. The case is laid out for you, frame by ugly frame. Frame by disgusting frame. You don't have to put the pieces together, because he already has done that for you."

A mother of three boys in her late forties, Boliker served as the face of the prosecution. A then–junior attorney, Mary Boland, sat taking notes or handing files to her colleagues; another, Kim Foxx, was overseeing other sex-crime prosecutions, but she occasionally visited the courtroom to observe. Robert Heilingoetter acted as Boliker's deputy, since he'd gotten that first call to the state's attorney's office from Sparkle by chance. "Poor Bob never wanted to be part of that case, but he got pressed into service," a source told me. Heilingoetter laughed and confirmed that when I asked him. The Kelly trial would be his last before retiring.

Chief of the state's attorney's Sex Crimes Division for a decade, Boliker had made headlines a year earlier for prosecuting the Rev. Daniel McCormack. A Catholic herself, the plea bargain she struck landed the priest in jail for five years. (Later, a judge designated McCormack a "sexually violent person," and he will be held in a state prison for sex offenders indefinitely.) In *RedEye*, the free tabloid started by the *Trib* for young commuters, Kyra Kyles described Boliker's "radiant smile" and "blunt bangs," suggesting she could be played in a movie by Meg Ryan. "She has one of the grimmer assignments among county prosecutors," the *Trib's* Kayce T. Ataiyero wrote, "yet she is widely regarded as one of the friendliest lawyers in the courthouse."

Boliker's voice could sound incongruously cheerful, almost musical, even when discussing the most horrible sex crimes. In *Blender*, Edward McClelland called her "a high-school homecoming queen who grew up to prosecute pervs and creeps." The only part of that description with which she disagrees is that "homecoming queen" evokes a party girl, while she had been a nerdy straight-A student from grammar school in her native Gary, Indiana, through DePaul University's College of Law.

"Robert Kelly is not on that tape!" Sam Adam Jr. bellowed at the start of opening statements for the defense. Although he was the least experienced lawyer on Kelly's team, his father and Genson wanted to "give the kid his chance," a source told me, adding that it didn't hurt that the biracial Adam Jr. was often the only lawyer of color in the courtroom. Displaying a shirtless photo of Kelly taken by Chicago police after they fingerprinted the singer at the Marquette District headquarters in June 2002, Adam Jr. pointed to a caterpillar-shaped mole on Kelly's back, a stratagem straight out of the O. J. Simpson trial. He tried to channel one of Simpson's lawyers, Johnnie Cochran, comparing the mole in the photo to what jurors would see in the video. "Either Robert isn't the man on that tape, or he's a magician, because there's no mole!"

That line didn't quite have the ring of "If it doesn't fit, you must acquit," but reporters agreed Adam Jr. made a game attempt. After graduating from Lake Forest Academy in the exclusive North Shore suburbs, he went to the University of Wisconsin's law school in Madison, but he bragged about working from a basement office behind a battered door and a weather-beaten mailbox on the South Side, "keeping it real." His voice could be musical, too, but where Boliker sounded like Karen Carpenter, Adam Jr. evoked KRS-One.

Adam Jr.'s opening began a three-pronged defense in which the arguments sometimes conflicted. One, the man on the tape wasn't Kelly. Two, it *was* Kelly, but the video was fake, allegedly produced by a shadowy conspiracy of people out to destroy the star, led by Barry Hankerson and including Sparkle and the journalist who received the tape (that is, me). Three, the girl wasn't who prosecutors said she was. "Reshona Landfair is sweet and nice, a wonderful person. The woman in this tape is a prostitute, paid with money," Adam Jr. said. He questioned why the twenty-three-year-old woman wouldn't testify for the state. "She's right here in the city. Right here on the South Side of Chicago. Now why wouldn't they bring her in? If she's not here for you to see her, for you to hear her, there's one reason for that. It's not her on that tape!"

Actually, there was another reason. If the prosecution won, and it turned out Reshona had perjured herself before the grand jury or in Judge Gaughan's courtroom, she could wind up behind bars, too, like the girl in Rep. Mel Reynolds's case. The prosecutors certainly did not want to do that to a young woman they'd seen violated on video, and State's Attorney Dick Devine wouldn't want that, either. The bad publicity from the Reynolds case had been a political nightmare for Devine's predecessor, Jack O'Malley.

Adam Jr. didn't say why the defense wouldn't call Reshona to repeat her denial to the grand jury, which five sources told me about, but his bombast often covered his lapses in logic. During a public hearing five months earlier, Judge Gaughan had ruled prosecutors could not call a renowned expert, Dr. Sharon Cooper, to testify that such denials aren't uncommon for victims of child sexual abuse. Gaughan agreed with the defense: Reshona spoke to the grand jury under oath; she presumably told the truth; the trial would not question her credibility or motives. "It was a significant blow to our case," a member of the prosecution team told me.

Dr. Cooper, the CEO of North Carolina–based Developmental and Forensic Pediatrics, saw the videotape and spent weeks preparing the testimony she never delivered in 2008. More than a decade later, she told me what she'd been prepared to say on the stand: "Many times, children will deny, because the presence of these images is so shaming. The reason that victims don't acknowledge that those images are them is because of the guilt, self-blame, and shame. . . . A second part of this is that you don't know what degree of brainwashing may have occurred for this young person by the offender. Very often, just like in sex-trafficking victims, they are sworn to secrecy. The individual uses love and affection as the piece that makes this child or adolescent become devoted to that individual."

If Reshona Landfair's parents were discouraging her from speaking out, that was another big problem, Dr. Cooper said. The media attention would also have been daunting. Finally, "as we see in sex-trafficking cases where images also exist," Dr. Cooper said, "there's often a degree of witness-tampering that occurs. I suspected or was concerned that there was some degree of witness tampering that may have happened in this particular case, because the witness was nowhere to be found." Although she continued to follow the Kelly story, she wasn't disappointed she never testified, "primarily because Chicago has such a reputation for corruption. And you always worry when you go into a high-profile case like that. You worry about your personal safety."

In other sealed rulings in closed chambers, my sources said, Gaughan ruled as inadmissible any evidence or testimony that Reshona; her mother, Valerie; and her father, Greg, worked for Kelly and were on his payroll. None of the lawyers Abdon or I spoke to could understand why the prosecution wouldn't be able to follow the money from Kelly to the Landfairs, or offer testimony on the connections, and why the jury wouldn't be able to hear about the singer's history of buying silence from his victims. Greg Landfair played on Kelly's albums, Valerie worked as an office assistant, and Reshona, who dreamed of stardom as a singer, sometimes babysat for the star, our sources said. Again, the Landfairs have never spoken.

After opening arguments and a break for lunch, the trial reconvened at about 1 p.m. on May 20. Sheriff's deputies dimmed the lights and drew the blinds as a technical assistant wheeled a six-foot projection screen worthy of a sports bar in front of the jury box. A smaller TV faced the spectators. Judge Gaughan's assistant and de facto publicist, Terry Sullivan, warned courtroom artists not to sketch what they saw. "Anyone who draws a depiction or a simulation can be committing the act of child pornography," he said, "and you don't want to do that." Tense with anticipation, everyone watched as the tech hit PLAY. And nothing happened.

Only after tinkering with the wires for a few minutes did the twenty-six-minute, thirty-nine-second video begin to screen, and not for the last time. *Sun-Times* reporter Eric Herman told me the video eventually would be shown in its entirety or in part more times than he could count.

During the first viewing, the jurors stared intently, some taking notes, and others resting their heads on their hands. One of the male jurors broke into a nervous smile, and another busily chewed gum. An older female juror pinched the bridge of her nose, while the Baptist minister's wife kept her hand over her mouth. In the gallery, Kelly's entourage filled most of two rows, all men, and all attired in seemingly expensive suits. They kept their eyes downcast. Two dozen reporters covering the opening day took notes, documenting the action onscreen, minute by minute. An older male spectator clenched his arms tight, his bald dome turning red, while a young woman crossed her legs, her face registering disgust. Abdon, who'd "popped in," said he'd forgotten the impact of seeing the video for the first time, but it registered on everyone in court.

The reporters all agreed about what Kelly wore that day—a dark pinstripe suit and a blue tie with diagonal orange stripes—but they differed wildly when describing his reaction. He was (choose one) bored; sad; appalled; concerned. Chin in hand, he tilted his braided head, looking from different angles. Occasionally, he whispered to his lawyers.

The prosecution followed the video with its first witness, Detective Dan Everett of the Youth Division of the Special Investigations Unit. He had since retired, but he testified that he obtained the tape in February 2002 from a *Chicago Sun-Times* reporter. He did not know where the reporter got it. Prosecutor Robert Heilingoetter asked Everett if he recognized the girl on the tape, and the detective said he did, from a previous investigation.

Chiseled, square-jawed and the epitome of a veteran law-and-order man—very much like Everett himself—Heilingoetter had neglected to tell the detective that the judge ruled witnesses for the state could not mention the years-long police investigation into Kelly's allegedly predatory behavior. Judge Gaughan sent the jury out of the room, then erupted. "If you do it again,

I certainly am going to grant a mistrial!" he roared at Everett, rocking so hard in his chair, it seemed as if he might fall out of it. "It's an egregious mistake!"

When the jury returned, a crimson-faced Everett said he'd been "mistaken" in characterizing "an interview" as "an investigation." The significance of what happened with Everett struck every journalist in the courtroom. In Slate, Josh Levin wrote that "the facts of this particular case don't come close to speaking to the nature and magnitude of Kelly's alleged crimes. On the basis of today's proceedings, Judge Vincent Gaughan seems to have ruled that none of them is fair game."

The rest of the case Gaughan allowed prosecutors to present unfolded over six more days, though the proceedings stalled several times for squabbles out of the presence of the jury. Whether other witnesses had been ruled out by Gaughan, or Boliker's team didn't want to bore the jury with repetitious testimony, the fifteen called by the state represented a fraction of the fifty we heard testified before the grand jury. The state called fourteen people after Detective Everett, including a woman who said she'd engaged in videotaped threesomes with Kelly and Reshona, four of Reshona's relatives, six of her friends and their parents, her high-school basketball coach (a former cop who had since become Oak Park's school board president), and three photo and video experts.

Twenty-four-year-old hair-stylist Simha "Punky" Jamison gave the most convincing testimony of Reshona's friends, corroborated by Peter Thomas, who'd been her legal guardian. Jamison and Reshona started hanging out in fourth grade. When Boliker asked if they saw each other every day, Jamison laughed as if to say, "*Duh.*" Reshona ended the friendship abruptly not long after the singer she called her godfather was indicted.

Jamison said she'd been introduced to Kelly by the Landfair family when she was twelve years old. She and Reshona began spending time with the star at a West Side gym, Hoops, watching him play basketball. They also went to Chicago Trax recording studio, and they visited his house on George Street. Sometimes, Jamison went home alone, while Reshona stayed for the night. Jamison said she never saw Kelly touch Reshona inappropriately, but she did see the star give her friend cash, "never less than a hundred, never more than five hundred." The prosecution also implied that Kelly bought Reshona a PT Cruiser, years before she'd even obtained a driver's license. These two statements made it into the record despite Judge Gaughan's rulings that any possible payments to the Landfairs for their silence were inadmissible.

Reshona never discussed having a sexual relationship with Kelly, her friend Jamison said. "There were things I wouldn't tell her, as I'm sure there were things that she wouldn't tell me." She testified that she saw the tape twice, once when friends showed it at Oak Park and River Forest High School—she didn't specify exactly how or where that happened—and again in court. She had immediately recognized Kelly and her best friend during the first viewing. "I know her like the back of my hand," she said, adding that she cried herself to sleep that night. Based on her hair style, a mullet cut they once shared, Jamison believed Reshona appeared in the video at age fourteen.

During cross-examination, Adam Jr. tried to make a point about Jamison relying only on her friend's hair style to identify her. "You can't tell by looking at a person's vagina how old they are, can you?" Sensing how poorly that bizarre question played, he moved on to part two of the three-pronged defense, the fake tape. He asked Jamison if she'd seen a "Waymon [sic] Brothers" movie called Little Man. "They took the head of Marlon Waymons [sic] and put it on a midget, and it looked real, didn't it?" Jamison looked at him like he was nuts. "Not really," she said, drawing out the last word, and jurors and spectators laughed.

The 2006 comedy Little Man digitally morphed the head of an adult comedian, Marlon Wayans, onto the body of a dwarf actor playing a baby. Made at least six years after Kelly's home recording at the heart of the trial, Little Man had a $64 million Hollywood budget, and it still looked absurd. (It also wasn't remotely funny.)

Striking out again with the Little Man question, Adam Jr. tried the missing mole. Looking at the photo of Kelly's back, Jamison suggested it could have been a mark on the print, or "a cancerous mole, maybe." Kelly laughed, his usually stoic court façade cracking. Cross-examination ended after Jamison admitted that, yes, she also received gifts from the star, including a hundred dollars on her thirteenth birthday.

The parade of people identifying Reshona continued with Aubrey Hampton, a member of the girls' high school basketball team. "There's no question,"

Hampton said, pointing out the unique way her friend and teammate licked her bottom lip. Hampton's mother, Mary Kay Jerit, worked for the Illinois Department of Children and Family Services, the state's child protection agency. Jerit testified that she recognized Reshona when she watched an unmarked copy of the tape she found in her daughter Aubrey's room, and immediately "threw it in the trash." She did not say if she did anything else, like bringing the case to the attention of her bosses, but Abdon and I wondered if she'd been the anonymous source at DCFS who'd emailed us about Reshona years earlier.

Tjada Burnett, best friends with one of Reshona's aunts, Charlotte Edwards, also identified the girl in the tape, but Adam Jr. tried to confuse her chronology on cross-examination. She said Reshona got braces after she appeared in the tape, but the defense attorney showed jurors a photo of Reshona looking younger and already wearing braces.

Raven Gengler had been another of Reshona's best friends since junior high, and they went on to become star players on the Huskies, their high school basketball team. Sitting in the witness box, Gengler was nearly as tall as Judge Gaughan, though his chair stood a foot higher than hers. She was "one-hundred-percent sure" Reshona appeared in the tape, she said on direct examination, but she broke down in tears when Genson questioned her on cross, doubting her ability to identify the victim because she hadn't seen or spoken to Reshona in six years. That didn't make a lot of sense, since the tape was now at least nine years old.

Gengler acknowledged that she hadn't wanted to testify. "It's very upsetting. It's very upsetting to my family. I just wanted it go away." Finally excused, the twenty-three-year-old woman let out a very teenaged "*Oh, my God,*" expressing exasperation, disgust, amazement at the spectacle, or all three.

Jacques Conway identified the girl in the video as the starting point guard on the basketball team he coached in 2000. The United Methodist pastor, school board president, and retired police sergeant said Reshona had been fourteen or fifteen in the video, and that Kelly came to the team's final home game to see her play. "She was as sweet and nice a person as could be?" Adam Jr. asked. Clearly a man who actually knew teenagers and their mercurial moods, Conway elicited a laugh. "At *times,*" he said. He added that he never saw anything inappropriate between Kelly and Reshona, but he did notice that her parents seemed very concerned about her.

The defense had mixed success during cross-examination while trying to refute the testimony by Reshona's relatives. Her uncle, Sparkle's forty-four-year-old brother, Bennie Edwards Sr., admitted he'd recently been arrested for possessing crack. He had trouble recalling significant events. He took ten seconds to remember when he was born, and he got his son's birthday wrong. "I don't recall," he replied to most of Genson's questions, including some he had just answered for the prosecution.

Genson asked Edwards Sr. how he could say his niece appeared on the tape if he had such a hard time retaining information. "She's my blood. Why wouldn't I remember? Am I on trial here? I told the truth. It looks like Reshona is on the tape. It looks like R. Kelly is on the tape."

While we were admittedly armchair quarterbacks, Abdon and I always wondered why the prosecutors didn't ask every one of their witnesses if they'd heard Kelly call the girl on the tape "Shona." That struck us as pretty strong evidence.

Chicago Police Officer Delores Gibson held up better on the stand than her former husband, Bennie Edwards Sr. She said she and Bennie learned about the tape in December 2001, the same time Sparkle called to tell me about it. Sparkle had told me she'd called her brother Bennie and asked him to call their sister, Reshona's mother. Gibson admitted she didn't immediately report the tape to her superiors at CPD. "It was very sensitive. The mother didn't want to cooperate, and neither did the father."

Adam Jr. tore into Gibson on cross, attacking her credibility, suggesting the family intended to use a phony tape to extort money from the singer, and hammering away at why she didn't file a police report. "You are a police officer and your niece is severely violated and you're telling us you didn't want anything to do with it? Come on, officer! You can do better than that!" Gibson calmly replied that she did speak to investigators only a few weeks later. "You knew Sparkle had an ax to grind and was running around with the tape so she could try to make money, didn't you?" Adam Jr. asked. Officer Gibson stayed cool. "What I do know: That there was an act committed that involved a family member. Something needed to be done about that. I took the action that was needed at the time."

Like almost all of Kelly's alleged victims, Reshona had been an aspiring musician, a member of a quartet called 4 the Cause with three of her cousins, including Bennie Edwards Jr., who played bass with Lionel Richie at the time of the trial. Prosecutors showed a 1998 music video for the group's cover of Ben E. King's "Stand by Me," which became a minor hit in Germany. Contradicting the photo the defense showed, Reshona didn't wear braces in the clip. Edwards Jr. testified that the girl in the tape "favored" his relative, and the man "favored" Kelly. Genson criticized him for not definitively identifying them. "It wasn't her, was it?" Reshona's cousin and bandmate shifted uncomfortably. "It *looks like* her," he said.

Reshona's aunt, thirty-three-year-old Stephanie "Sparkle" Edwards, took the stand in full, glamorous pop-star regalia, the same way she'd come to the *Sun-Times* the day we watched the tape in the paper's video closet. As she had that day, she cried often while prosecutors led her through her story. A sheriff's deputy handed her a box of tissues.

Many members of the Landfair and Edwards families had big musical ambitions, Sparkle said. She split from Kelly after the release of the self-titled, half-million-selling debut he produced for her in 1998. Before that falling-out, she introduced the star to her niece Reshona one night at the house on George Street, when they gathered to watch the Chicago Bulls in the NBA Finals. Sparkle wasn't sure if it was the team's fifth or sixth championship run, in 1997 or 1998, so her niece was either twelve or thirteen. "He liked her spirit," Sparkle said. "She was a very jolly person at the time. She was my heart."

After Sparkle broke from Kelly, she said his manager Barry Hankerson facilitated her move to Motown Records for her next album, *Told You So.* It was a better record, but a commercial disappointment. For the last few years, she'd been singing backing vocals in concert for another Hankerson client, Toni Braxton. The Landfair and Edwards families had been "thick as thieves, you couldn't break the chain," but Sparkle testified that a rift opened after she got a call from a lawyer, "Buddy something," who sent someone to her apartment to show her the videotape, then left with it.

That testimony differed slightly from what Sparkle told me in 2001, and I went back to my notes and recording of that interview. She had not mentioned a call from Buddy Meyers, just that the man who visited her left Meyers's card. Maybe she said "call" on the stand and meant "visit from a man who claimed to have been sent by Buddy." Then again, Sparkle has now given several different versions of her first encounter with the tape. After the trial in 2008, she did not talk publicly about it again until *Surviving R. Kelly* in 2019. After it aired, she began doing a lot of interviews to talk about the docuseries and her single "We Are Ready," a powerful anthem dedicated to women who have fought and survived abuse. In some of those interviews, she said she learned about the tape when a reporter called her. It was the other way around. Unfortunately, she declined to talk to me again for this book.

Sparkle told the court she recognized Reshona in the video, but her sister and brother-in-law didn't seem to care, and she hadn't spoken to them since. She later told McClelland in *Blender* that the last time she'd seen Reshona, at her grandparents' home in 2006, her niece had looked away, put her head down, and walked out of the room. In *Surviving R. Kelly,* she says the singer offered her "in the high six figures" to praise him in the media instead of testifying. "I didn't take the money because I can't be bought. I'ma stand up for my family." She wasn't asked about this attempted payoff on the stand, sources told me, because Judge Gaughan had ruled it inadmissible.

Defense attorney Ed Genson once bragged to Abdon that Kelly's legal fees would pay to put his grandkids through college, and he earned his money cross-examining Sparkle. He attempted to paint a portrait of a disgruntled artist blackmailing the star for revenge. Sparkle kept her composure, insisting that despite her split from Kelly, "He was my homeboy. We were still cool." Genson scoffed. "You weren't angry you'd been terminated?" Sparkle said no, repeating that Hankerson helped her land a new contract at Motown, the label that had made his ex-wife, Gladys Knight, a star. "Was part of the deal you were talking about doing something bad to Robert?" Genson asked. Absolutely not, Sparkle insisted.

The tension mounted as Genson turned to the tape, reprising the *Little Man* defense. "You have no idea if that tape was put together from tapes of old footage, tapes of other people, in order to make money off Robert, do you?" Sparkle held firm. "Sir, that's Robert and Reshona on that tape. I know my family." Genson persisted. "You know and believe that your niece had Robert give her money to have sex?" he asked. "Just like he made her do! She's a robot on this tape." Genson wouldn't back down. "You know that your niece is taking money for sex?"

"I know who made the tape. Robert made the tape!" Sparkle said. "He passed her money—" Genson began, but Sparkle cut him off. "Like a prostitute!" That thought triggered her the same way it did when she and I watched the tape in the video closet. "You don't like Robert!" Genson shouted. He suggested again that Sparkle hoped to profit from the video. "Sweetie, I am not trying to get any money with this," she sneered. "I am not your sweetie!" Genson shot back. Judge Gaughan interrupted as the exchange escalated, but Genson kept talking. "Mr. Genson, you're not listening!" the judge snapped. Kelly, who rarely looked at Sparkle, stared straight ahead, expressionless.

The week ended on a quieter note, with the prosecution's three technical witnesses. State investigator Alexandra Guerrero testified about photos she took of the Looney Tunes mural in Kelly's basketball court on George Street—reporters didn't know why, but it would become apparent—and two video experts authenticated the tape in an attempt to deflate the missing mole and *Little Man* arguments. Grant Fredericks of Spokane, Washington–based Forensic Video Solutions played the video in slow-motion, concentrating on seventeen frames where the man turned his back, clearly displaying a dark spot. He compared the video with the CPD booking photos of a shirtless Kelly. "There's something dark there on his back in that position," he said, matching the video to photos of the mole to the left of Kelly's spine, a few inches above the waist.

Digitally altering the tape "would have been impossible," Fredericks said, taking a professional forty-four years to change every frame. He also testified that the log-cabin playroom on George Street matched the one in the video, based on a comparison of knots in the wood. "It's kind of like looking at the stars. You can then map them all out."

Questioning Fredericks on cross, Genson asked if the spot could be a glitch. "It comes and goes." The lawyer showed the tape again at half-speed. "There; not there. There; not there." Fredericks seemed amused, refuted that theory, and said the spot "tracks with him and moves with his body." George Skaluba, a video expert with the FBI, confirmed that he also found no evidence that the tape had been altered or generated by a computer.

The prosecution resumed on Tuesday, May 27, after Memorial Day. The state called Lindsey Perryman, a twenty-seven-year-old Chicago woman who worked as a personal assistant to Kelly for seven years, until 2006. She started by praising the star as a "great boss . . . I think so highly of Mr. Kelly and his family." She paid little attention when she first heard the rumors of a tape with Kelly and Reshona, whom she met in 1999, introduced as the goddaughter of her boss and his wife, Andrea. Perryman said the singer often dispatched her to pick Reshona up after high school in Oak Park and drive her to one of his homes, on George Street or in Olympia Fields, or to Chicago Trax studio.

Perryman said she never suspected anything untoward in the relationship. Reshona sometimes babysat Kelly's children in Olympia Fields. Her father, Greg, played guitar and bass for the singer on tour and on his recordings, and he often came by the studio, where Reshona's mother, Valerie, had an office and did paperwork for Kelly. Perryman didn't even question when she saw Reshona bring a pillow and an overnight bag to the studio one night, because her parents and her younger brother accompanied her. "I had never seen him be inappropriate with anyone, and he had never been inappropriate with me. There's never been any reason to walk away."

That changed when investigators showed Perryman the video. "I didn't want to think it was them," but she was "one hundred and ten-percent sure" she recognized Kelly and Reshona. "She has distinct cheekbones, and the way she moves her mouth, the way she smiles, it's all very distinctive. The image I saw looked exactly like her, it sounded exactly like her. I was shocked. I was disturbed. I didn't want to see any of this." The former assistant added that she had seen another woman, Lisa Van Allen, visit Kelly in the studio, setting the stage for what many in the media called the prosecution's "bombshell witness."

Judge Gaughan postponed Van Allen's appearance several times during week two as the defense made a last-ditch attempt to exclude her testimony. The judge heard the back-and-forth between both sides out of the presence of the jury. Reporters and spectators were eager for the action to resume, and jurors sat waiting and watching TV, but not the news, they promised the judge. Finally, in a rare win for the prosecution, Gaughan ruled that the jury would hear from Van Allen on Monday, June 2, at the start of week three.

The single mother of a five-year-old daughter, four months pregnant with her second child, twenty-seven-year-old Van Allen took the stand in a low-cut black dress. "I want to do what is right," she said, starting by identifying the couple in the tape. Reshona looked "just exactly how I remember her—her body, her face, her breasts. Back then, I felt they were so much bigger than mine." She identified Kelly by "everything from his face, to his bald head. His genitals, back, everything." Then she began telling her own story, which started at age seventeen when she met Kelly while working as an extra in the video for "Home Alone," a duet with rapper Keith Murray shot in 1997 near her home in Alpharetta, Georgia.

Summoned to Kelly's trailer by "his cousin, Blacky," Van Allen said she and the star started talking, then they had sex. She was a year older than the age of consent in Georgia, sixteen. Kelly was "a nice guy," and she was smitten by his charms and awed by his talent. Kelly asked Van Allen if her mother would mind if she came to Chicago, and Van Allen told him traveling wouldn't be a problem. Several visits followed. The singer put her up at hotels in the Loop or at Trax studio because his wife, Andrea, was at home with their children. Kelly asked her to call him "Daddy." Eventually, Van Allen quit her job in Atlanta, came to Chicago, and "just never left. I traveled with him. We went to the mall, movies. I went on tour with him. He would pick me out of the audience at the shows, and I would do the bed scene at the end of every show."

Kelly introduced Van Allen to Reshona in late 1998. She said he told her Reshona was sixteen, though prosecutors contended she was thirteen or fourteen at the time. The three of them went to the log-cabin playroom on George Street, and the singer set up a video camera to record them having sex. Prosecutors granted Van Allen immunity for that testimony, since she committed a crime by having sexual contact with a minor. A year later, Van Allen, Kelly, and Reshona had another threesome on a futon in front of the Looney Tunes mural in the basketball court on George Street, Van Allen said. When she started crying, Kelly railed at her for ruining his video, and she cried again on the stand as she recalled that moment. "I didn't want to do it. He got upset. He said he couldn't watch that. He couldn't do anything with me crying. He stopped the camera."

Van Allen appeared in the 2000 video for "I Wish," braiding Kelly's hair as he sat on the stoop of a house that looked like one of his childhood homes, in the area near West 107th Street and South Parnell Avenue. (The star's half brother Carey told me the new owners wouldn't allow filming at the actual house.) Van Allen had a third threesome with Kelly and Reshona in the trailer parked on set. Someone knocked on the door and interrupted, Van Allen said, and Kelly ordered Reshona to run "into the bathroom naked" to hide. The star did not record that encounter.

In 2001, Van Allen moved back to Georgia, but she stayed in touch with Kelly. They spent a weekend shopping and having sex at the Swissôtel in Atlanta later that year, and "before I ended up leaving, I took a Rolex watch from him," she said, confessing a $20,000 theft. She heard about the indictment in 2002, but didn't call authorities. "I had just had my daughter. My mind was not on getting involved."

During her testimony, a stone-faced Kelly sometimes locked eyes with her, shaking his head at some points, and conferring with his lawyers at others.

Cross-examination found Adam Sr. at his most brutal. He portrayed Van Allen as yet another liar out to blackmail his client. "If it was the right thing to do," he asked, why didn't she go to authorities in 2002? "I was young then," Van Allen said. Six years had passed since the indictment, Adam Sr. said, but "the spirit didn't move you to do the right thing, this, until today?" She repeated she'd been focused on her infant daughter. Then the two got into the tale of one of the videotapes she'd made with Kelly.

Van Allen said she grabbed the video of her first threesome with Reshona from Kelly's duffel bag when he left it on the sidelines of the basketball court at Hoops. "He carried it everywhere with him. Wherever he was at, the bag would follow," she said on the stand. ("I just didn't want that tape out there," she further explained to me years later.) In March 2007, she told Kelly she'd taken the tape. He flew her and her hulking fiancé, Yul Brown, to Chicago, putting them up in a hotel near the Olympia Fields mansion. The singer offered her $250,000 for the tape, but she said she'd given it to Keith Murrell, a friend from Kansas City. Murrell, also known as "Casino," sang with a trio called Talent that Kelly produced. It released one album, *Bull's Eye*, on Kelly's Rockland imprint with Interscope Records in 2001. It flopped.

Kelly's "people" arranged a meeting with Van Allen and Murrell in the presidential suite of a downtown Chicago hotel, Van Allen said, and Derrel McDavid, the accountant who took over as Kelly's manager when Barry Hankerson quit, gave her and Murrell $20,000 each after they showed him a copy of the tape. McDavid promised $210,000 more when they returned with the original tape, Van Allen said. She also mentioned another man in connection to that tape. A private investigator from Kansas City named Charles Freeman had apparently been hired in May 2002 as a subcontractor by Kelly's chief private eye, Jack Palladino, to track down that videotape and others "on the streets." The Kelly camp stiffed Freeman, paying him only $75,000 of a promised $140,000, and he sued the star in July 2002.

The day after Van Allen's testimony, Freeman and Murrell—reporters covering the trial called them "Chuck and Keith from Kansas City"—promised to hold a press conference that would be "big news" and "reveal all." The press conference never happened. Neither man was called to the stand, and what became of any other videotapes they had remained a mystery. (Nine months after the trial ended, in the spring of 2009, Freeman sued Kelly and his accountant Derrel McDavid a second time for failing to pay him everything they owed for his tape-tracking services.)

"In July 2007," Adam Sr. said, "you tried to extort some money, claiming you had a sex tape of Mr. Kelly." The witness stayed cool. "He tried to offer me money. I did not extort him," though the scenario she herself described seemed to suggest otherwise.

When Van Allen left the stand, McDavid released a statement through Kelly's spokesman, Allan Mayer. "Lisa Van Allen is an admitted thief and a liar, who wouldn't know the truth if she tripped over it. If there was any crime committed here, it was her attempt to extort money from R. Kelly." The Kelly camp did not deny it had paid Van Allen and Murrell, however, and it didn't say anything about any of the other tapes the jurors had just heard about.

The prosecution rested its case with Van Allen, and Abdon and I compared notes as we huddled at the *Sun-Times* on the evening of June 3. Some of the state's witnesses had contradicted themselves or behaved problematically, taking money from Kelly, or failing to promptly contact authorities. People are complicated; motives are complicated; sexual relationships are *really* complicated, and no victim is "perfect." So many people Kelly considered friends seem to turn on him and shake him down for cash that we almost felt sorry for him, until we remembered it was his own behavior that left him vulnerable and put him in that position. The testimony echoed what we'd learned during years of reporting, that the star allegedly preyed on and manipulated young girls for his pleasure, in the process ruining lives and destroying families. Of course, thanks to Judge Gaughan, the jurors weren't hearing evidence of that pattern of behavior, nor would they hear from several key witnesses who *had* been mentioned in court.

Prosecutors never called to the stand four men who'd been cited in sworn testimony in relation to tapes, shakedowns, and pay-offs: attorney William "Buddy" Meyers, who allegedly sent someone to Sparkle with the tape of Kelly and her niece; Keith "Casino" Murrell and private eye Chuck Freeman, who allegedly had *something* to say about at least one other videotape; and Kelly's manager Derrel McDavid, who allegedly paid Van Allen and Murrell for that tape. Van Allen told me years later that prosecutors never seemed all that interested in the second tape showing the girl at the heart of their case, and they did not even try to track down that tape or any others (perhaps because Judge Gaughan would not have allowed them to be submitted as evidence).

Most curiously, the state never called Barry Hankerson, the former community activist and husband of Gladys Knight; Kelly's ex-manager; Aaliyah's uncle; Sparkle's champion at Motown and with Toni Braxton, and, most important, the alleged head of the shadowy conspiracy to bring Kelly down. Hankerson told prosecutors he would refute that and answer any question if called to the stand, sources told me, but he never received a subpoena. In chambers, Judge Gaughan had sided with the defense. "The trial was never gonna get into the Aaliyah stuff," a member of the prosecution team told me years later, while I struggled to connect the dots for this book. The state decided that if Hankerson could not testify about Aaliyah, there was no reason to bring him to Chicago. At the same time, a member of Kelly's crew told me in a menacing tone, "He probably wouldn't have made it to Chicago."

Really? "Barry's alive still. The Minister protected him at one point. But the Minister won't protect him anymore."

By "the Minister," that source meant Minister Louis Farrakhan, leader of the Chicago-based Nation of Islam. I'd heard from several sources over the years that Hankerson had a friendship with Farrakhan. I'd also heard from two sources, neither of them particularly reliable, that the courier who dropped the videotape in my mailbox on Grace Street "might have been a guy in bow tie"—a member of the NOI's impeccably dressed paramilitary wing, the Fruit of Islam. I'd taken it as a joke or a red herring, but it stuck with me. When I asked about that comment years later, one of the two claimed not to remember it or know what I was talking about. The other said only, "Might have been."

At the end of the prosecution's case, the questions Abdon and I had were, where the hell were all of these other witnesses, and what about those other videotapes? But the question defense attorney Sam Adam Jr. planted in jurors' minds had been the loudest. Where was the victim?

CHAPTER 11

THE DEFENSE AND THE VERDICT

Later in the evening of June 3, 2008, the day the prosecution rested its case in *The State of Illinois v. Robert Sylvester Kelly*, Abdon Pallasch and I had just finished comparing notes at his desk when city editor Don Hayner summoned me to a characterless, fluorescent-lit conference room in the paper's new home at 350 North Orleans Street. When Lord Conrad Black's newspaper empire began to crumble because of his securities fraud, his company sold the old, ugly but lovable barge-like building overlooking the Chicago River. We had all relocated to bland cubicles in rented space at the Apparel Mart, while the newest Trump Tower rose where the *Sun-Times* once stood.

I sat alone on one side of a conference table with several of the paper's top executives arrayed opposite me. Looking decidedly grim were Hayner, Hook and Crook (editor Michael Cooke and publisher John Cruickshank), entertainment editor John Barron, who'd been at my side when we handed the now-notorious video to police, and Barron's college buddy Jim McDonough, who'd been hired as the in-house lawyer for the corporate honchos. I'd been less tense walking into that room than the bosses appeared to be, assuming they had a solution to Judge Vincent Gaughan's increasingly angry demands that I appear on the stand. Then McDonough extended a hand from the tailored sleeve of a charcoal suit.

"To be clear, I am here to represent the newspaper, *not you*." After that, a cinder block between my chest and the pit of my stomach made breathing a chore.

My name first appeared on the witness list for the prosecution in 2004, during the interminable six-year-wait for Kelly's trial to begin. State's Attorney Dick Devine assured Hook and Crook that was strictly a formality, and I'd never be called to testify. I dropped off the prosecution list a few months later, but one day in early 2006, Abdon Pallasch tossed a document from the

Kelly camp on my desk. "Look at *this*." I had reappeared on the witness list for the defense. Abdon seemed jealous that they wanted to hear from me and not from him, but only one of us had gotten the tape that led to the star's indictment dropped anonymously in his mailbox. Lucky me.

"Don't worry about it, DeRo," Hayner said many times over the next two and a half years. "You'll never have to testify." Now, finally, everybody worried about it.

The phrase "reporter's privilege" refers to the concept as well as the patchwork of federal and state laws allegedly protecting reporters from being compelled to testify about confidential sources. Before my name began appearing on witness lists, I hadn't thought about it since I majored in journalism at NYU. *New York Times* reporter Myron Farber had visited one of my classes to talk about his role in the notorious "Dr. X" case. In 1966, surgeon Mario Jascalevich became the suspect in a series of suspicious deaths by curare poisoning at a hospital in New Jersey. The case lay dormant for a decade for lack of evidence, but after Farber received an anonymous letter citing as many as forty poisonings, the reporter began investigating. His story prompted prosecutors to revisit the cold case, and they eventually charged the man the *Times* called "Dr. X" with five murders.

During the trial, the defense subpoenaed Farber for his notes from 193 interviews. The judge allowed what the *Times* called "an unprecedented fishing expedition," and the paper refused to comply. Sentenced to six months in jail and fined five thousand dollars a day, Farber spent forty days behind bars, and the paper paid nearly a million dollars in legal fees and penalties. Jurors eventually acquitted the doctor, though he lost his license and died in disgrace. Governor Brendan Byrne pardoned Farber and ordered the return of the fines, but the episode hardly stood as a victory for the free press.

Conflicted about his ordeal, Farber hadn't been a particularly inspiring speaker, but in the heady days of journalism a decade or so after the Pentagon Papers and Watergate, my classmates romanticized his principled stand. Some of us even hoped we'd have a chance to do the same. In fact, the press generally avoided conflicts with the courts, wary of setting further precedent.

In the 1972 case of *Branzburg v. Hayes*, stemming from a Kentucky reporter's refusal to reveal his sources about the local drug trade, the Supreme Court split five to four, ruling the First Amendment does not exempt journalists from testifying. The majority couldn't find a reporter's privilege in the Constitution. Some scholars say there isn't one, while others believe that case simply didn't warrant it.

"The opinion is regarded today as a muddle; it does not make clear how much protection journalists deserve," Steve Coll, dean of the Columbia University Graduate School of Journalism, wrote in *The New Yorker*. Subsequent rulings by the lower courts were contradictory. In 1981, the Washington, D.C., Circuit Court of Appeals ruled that Michigan journalists did not have to testify about a Detroit mobster because their information also appeared on government tapes. But in 2003, the Court of Appeals for the Seventh Circuit in Chicago reaffirmed the majority in Branzburg in the case of *McKevitt v. Pallasch*. That's Pallasch as in my partner, Abdon.

Abdon had done stories interviewing an informant who infiltrated the Irish Republican Army. The court ordered him to turn over those tapes, and he vowed he'd never do it. "I've never had a reporter as eager to go to jail for the First Amendment as Abdon," Hayner told me. My buddy didn't deny that, but ultimately, he complied with the judge's order, turned over his tapes, and avoided being jailed for contempt of court.

Since my own charcoal suit was five years old, ill-fitting and not nearly as snazzy as the company lawyer's or even any of Abdon's when I got married in it in 2003, my wife, Carmél, convinced me to buy a new one. I'd have it for family weddings or funerals, she said, though hopefully I wouldn't have to wear it to court. We nevertheless cancelled the trip to Spain we'd been planning for years because the dates clashed with the start of the Kelly trial.

The concept of Reporter's Privilege had tarnished considerably when I began closely following cases in the news during the wait for Kelly's trial. In 2005, discredited *New York Times* reporter Judith Miller spent eighty-five days in jail for refusing to disclose the source who named CIA agent Valerie Plame after she exposed the fallacy of weapons of mass destruction in Iraq. The next year, two reporters from the *San Francisco Chronicle* drew a sentence of eighteen months after refusing to name the source of leaked grand jury testimony about a company providing illegal steroids to baseball players Barry Bonds and Jason Giambi. The reporters only avoided jail when their source, the company's former attorney, pleaded guilty to leaking, lying, and obstructing justice.

Protecting sources as ethically dubious as the lawyer for the steroids company and Scooter Libby, Vice President Dick Cheney's felonious chief of staff, didn't seem worthy of going to jail, but I would not compromise the people who had spoken to me off the record during my eight years of reporting about Kelly. They requested anonymity for the best reasons whistle-blowers ever do, because they feared a powerful man might hurt them if they spoke publicly. Still, I'd done enough reporting on conditions at the Hudson County Jail earlier in my career at the *Jersey Journal* to have lost any romantic illusions about being locked up, and that loomed as a very real possibility, given Judge Gaughan's notorious temper.

"Kelly's lawyers have figured out a new defense strategy: make sure the singer isn't the only one on trial," Jennifer Vineyard, one of the sharpest reporters covering the trial, wrote for MTV News. The defense painted Sparkle as an angry former employee seeking revenge by blackmailing Kelly. They hinted that ex-manager Barry Hankerson was the puppet master behind Sparkle and a conspiracy to destroy the singer, and they'd try to say I was part of it, too. They also would imply that I had "committed a crime by allegedly making and keeping a copy of the sex tape," Vineyard wrote. The irony didn't escape her, since another part of their strategy was to argue the tape wasn't child pornography at all.

"The logic of their motion escapes me," media attorney Damon Dunn told Vineyard in one of my two favorite quotes by him through all our years of working together. The other came after one of his several spirited arguments to quash my subpoena, when the defense said Kelly had a constitutional right to show that I had "written articles critical of Kelly." I was, after all, a music critic, but that didn't mean I was not a judiciously fair reporter. In any event, Dunn said, "Whether or not DeRogatis has a bias against pedophiles is of no importance to this case."

A soft-spoken, silver-haired, immaculately groomed Galahad to many journalists in Chicago, Damon Dunn had argued dozens of First Amendment and media-law cases for the *Sun-Times* and other news organizations in seven state supreme courts. More cynical in unguarded moments than the most grizzled reporter about how the system could be rigged, he nevertheless retained his idealism, and like city editor and law-school grad Don Hayner, he believed I would not have to take the stand. On May 30, early in the Kelly trial, the judge rule that, indeed, I would. Dunn continued to file motions to block the inevitable, and Gaughan got testier and testier as I failed to materialize in court, threatening to throw not only me in jail for contempt, but Dunn, too.

On June 2, Judge Gaughan announced that I'd be arrested if I did not appear before him at ten the next morning. That night, *Sun-Times* music editor Thomas Conner called my wife, Carmél, and told her she shouldn't answer our door at home for anyone, in case the judge jumped the gun and sent sheriff's officers to fetch me. When I didn't appear again on June 3, Gaughan really lost his temper, but Dunn protested I'd never personally been served with a subpoena. (I only finally got a copy from him in 2018.) "I'm going to give DeRogatis the benefit of the doubt," the judge reluctantly decided. Stifling his anger, he emphasized that if I didn't show up in court on June 4, he'd order Cook County Sheriff Tom Dart to arrest me. Which brought me to that conference room full of dour faces on the evening of June 3.

"You've got three options, DeRo," Hayner began. "One, you can testify— it's your choice as a citizen—but it would set a bad precedent for other reporters in Illinois, and maybe nationally. And you should know that you can't pick and choose which questions to answer. If you answer one, even your name, you'll have to answer them all, and if they ask you about your sources . . ." He trailed off and let the unspoken conclusion hang over the conference table: If I were asked about sources and I refused to name them, I'd be held in contempt.

I asked about the other options, trying to sound courageous, cinder block be damned.

"Well, you could go underground," Hayner said. My jaw dropped; that sounded so damn sixties! "Leave town, go to Michigan or Wisconsin, wherever, but don't tell us where you are, don't go online, and don't answer your phone. You can come back when the trial is over, but you should be aware that Judge Gaughan may still throw you in jail for contempt when you get back." I briefly considered the appeal of my in-laws' retreat in Indiana farm country, but I didn't like the odds of testing Gaughan's wrath. Plus, a true city kid, I've always gotten antsy without concrete underfoot.

Cooke piped up enthusiastically when I asked about the final option. "If you show up tomorrow and refuse to testify, you'll go directly to jail, but I think you should wait in the newsroom until the sheriff's officers come for you, and we'll put the story and the photos on the front page!"

Frantically brainstorming with a then–junior partner, Neil Rosenbaum, in search of any other option, Damon Dunn joined the meeting late on a tinny speakerphone from the Loop offices of Funkhouser Vegosen Liebman & Dunn. Unlike the company lawyer, he *was* representing me (as well as the paper), and I appreciated my bosses for paying his bills. "Jim, you don't have to decide now," he said. "Give us the night and we'll keep working on this."

When I got home, Carmél picked out a tie for me.

At 7 a.m. on June 4, after a long and sleepless night, I gathered in Cooke's office with Dunn, Rosenbaum, and Hayner. As promised, Dunn had stayed up all night and hit upon a solution he called "the nuclear defense." The law views child porn as such a radioactive crime, he said, that admitting I'd touched much less watched the videotape meant admitting I'd committed a felony. Though I would have to appear in court, I could plead the Fifth Amendment and decline to testify because I had the right not to incriminate myself, just like every mobster and crooked politician I'd covered in Jersey.

Dunn showed me an index card he'd prepared, which he said I should read in response to every question. That solution sounded good, but I said I intended to stress the First Amendment over my Fifth Amendment rights. "Gaughan has ruled on this, Jim, and if you do that, and keep doing it after he tells you to stop, he will hold you in contempt." I said I'd drawn my line in the sand. Hayner gave me a sort-of hug, a most un-Hayner-like gesture.

I reread the card several times as we drove to Twenty-Sixth and Cal, but I was too nervous to memorize it. A dozen photographers and TV cameras captured me walking into the courthouse. My legs felt rubbery, but I tried to appear confident instead of scared shitless. I hoped my suit and tie looked all right.

On the fifth floor, a sheriff's deputy ushered me into a closet-size room behind a door to the right of Judge Gaughan's towering rosewood bench. Later, he led me to the empty jury box so I could hear Dunn argue yet again with the judge about the reporter's privilege. Gaughan never hid his contempt for Dunn or the free press. "Speak up, or you'll say I'm having another secret hearing," he barked.

Ushered onto the witness stand, I scanned the press in the gallery, recognizing only a few of my fellow journalists. The legal and pop music beats don't usually overlap. I knew more of the photographers outside, since they also shot concerts. I saw Kelly at the defense table fifteen feet to my left, but I don't recall him looking at me.

Gaughan had made a decision about my testimony that managed to displease everyone involved: I would take the stand, and become part of the record, but not in front of the jury. Dunn and the *Sun-Times* didn't want me to be hauled into court because of the bad precedent it would set for other journalists. The defense wanted the jury to hear me take the Fifth, making me look guilty of *something,* fostering their hazy argument that I was part of a conspiracy to hurt their client. The judge pressured the prosecutors to give me immunity to say I'd handled the tape, and they saw the whole thing as a pointless waste of time. I certainly didn't want to be there; I didn't want to risk exposing sources I'd promised confidentiality.

By agreement with the defense, Dunn asked the first three questions after I took the oath and stated my full name for the record. "James Peter DeRogatis," like my mom used to say when she got angry. Dunn knew how I'd answer, but he wanted the questions in the record because he intended to file an appeal after the trial to prevent the precedent Gaughan was setting for a journalist being forced to testify. (He fought it all the way to the Illinois Supreme Court, which decided not to hear the case.) Dunn asked if I'd received a video showing Kelly with an underage girl, if I'd talked to sources who'd seen that video, and if I'd assured confidentiality to sources while reporting on Kelly. I could not answer then—instead I read my index card—but I can now. Yes, hell yes, and you bet your fucking ass I did.

The defense didn't sic one its bellicose big dogs on me. I got Marc Martin, who started by calmly asking, "What do you do for a living?" I read my index card, respectfully declining to answer blah, blah, blah, First and Fifth Amendments. This prompted yet another argument. "Saying what he does for a living would not incriminate him," Martin said. Dunn disagreed; it was all part of the chain. Gaughan sighed. "Mr. DeRogatis, right now I have to make a determination whether these privileges apply. You have the choice of either answering who you're employed by, or me holding you in direct contempt. Talk to Mr. Dunn." Damon nodded okay, so I gave my first and only full answer.

"Your Honor, I'm the pop music critic at the *Chicago Sun-Times* and the co-host of a show on Chicago Public Radio." Gaughan seemed pleased. The absurdity still strikes me.

The defense asked sixteen more questions about whether I'd written articles "critical of Mr. Kelly," received the videotape, given it to police, copied it, or made alterations to it. The index card got progressively soggier in my palm as I read it sixteen more times. I'm a lousy actor (that's my daughter's talent), but I did consciously perform, punching one word every time I read that card. That word was an outlet for all the frustration and disgust I'd lived with since the day I began looking into the fax. That word meant a lot to me. That word was "First."

"Each time he gets to the final sentence, DeRogatis pauses, then half-shouts—'the FIRST . . . and Fifth Amendments'—like a television sportscaster making sure we all notice his trademark catch phrase," Josh Levin wrote in Slate. "The tightly wound Gaughan, shockingly, doesn't seem to find this performative style annoying."

As a deputy ushered me out of court, defense attorney Ed Genson hobbled over, leaned on his cane, and said, "Thanks, you did exactly what we wanted you to do." Kelly sort-of thanked me too, in *Soulacoaster*. "The *Chicago Sun-Times* reporter, Jim DeRogatis, who broke the story and was the first to receive the supposed sex tape, took the Fifth and refused to testify." He left out the First Amendment, but then his book omits a lot of things.

Genson's words haunt me to this day, though Dunn assures me Judge Gaughan would not have allowed me to testify about anything I'd learned about Aaliyah, the girls who sued Kelly, or what the *Sun-Times* called a pattern of predatory behavior dating to 1991. The only testimony the judge would allow was about one girl on one videotape, and the jury never heard anything I said anyway.

My colleagues gave me a standing ovation when I returned to the newsroom, and Laura Emerick, who edited both me and Roger Ebert, handed me a note from the film critic, who called me "a hero." Battling cancer and no longer able to walk, speak, or eat solid foods, Ebert continued reviewing movies for the paper until the day he died in 2013. Nothing I'd done came close to that kind of heroism, much less the heroism of the girls who'd spoken to me despite fears the Kelly camp would retaliate. I remember feeling the way you do when you narrowly avoid a car wreck. I took off my tie and threw it in the trash can beside my desk.

R. Kelly's defense team started its case on June 5 and moved quickly. They called another three of Reshona Landfair's relatives and asked them if they recognized the girl on the tape. "No, I don't," said Leroy Edwards, her uncle and the manager of the vocal group 4 the Cause. "No, she definitely wasn't her," said Shonna Edwards, a cousin who sang with her in the group. Another of Reshona's aunts, Charlotte Edwards, said the girl in the video had bigger breasts than her niece. Ed Genson asked if she'd seen Reshona naked. "Yes, when I used to change her diapers."

Bringing some additional star power to the trial, the defense called Jack Palladino, a tough-talking Hollywood attorney and private investigator to the stars. His résumé included work for John DeLorean, Michael Jackson, Courtney Love, the Menendez brothers, and Bill Clinton, whose first presidential campaign tapped him to handle the infamous "bimbo eruptions." Hired by Kelly in the early 2000s, Palladino had questioned Demetrius Smith about the tape circulating on the streets, and Smith told him he didn't know anything about it. That did not come up in court (and Smith was never subpoenaed, either). Palladino testified that he'd interviewed Lisa Van Allen and her fiancé, Yul Brown, in early 2002 over dinner at Atlanta's Four Seasons Hotel. At that meeting, Palladino said Brown claimed the couple had a six-figure book deal to tell Van Allen's story.

"I didn't believe there was a book deal. The $300,000 deal was a coded way to get money from my client," Palladino said. On cross-examination, prosecutor Robert Heilingoetter noted that neither Brown nor Van Allen had asked Kelly for money. "I'm trying to figure out where this extortion is, except somewhere between your ears?" Palladino insisted the book deal meant the two would clam up if Kelly paid them. "There's little doubt about what that meant," the private detective said. Book equals blackmail? Heilingoetter was incredulous. "Nice work, detective," he cracked.

A month after the trial ended, Judge Gaughan shined a spotlight on how concerned the Kelly camp had been about Van Allen's testimony and the tape of her threesome with Kelly and Reshona. The judge unsealed a transcript from a closed hearing during the trial, the only one he ever made public. During that session, prosecutors said they were weighing charges against Kelly's manager Derrel McDavid for bribery and witness-tampering, Abdon reported. Van Allen gave sworn testimony that McDavid told her he should have "murked" her, gangster lingo for "beaten" or "killed." Instead, he paid her $100,000 over three meetings in his Oak Park office in return for her telling Kelly's attorneys she never had sex with the singer, prosecutors said. In her sworn statement, Van Allen said she'd done as instructed and lied because she was afraid of McDavid.

The fact that Van Allen had testified despite her fears struck Abdon and me as particularly brave. Yes, she'd taken money. She'd also had her reputation dragged through the mud by the defense on cross-examination. The FBI, the United States attorney, and the state's attorney declined to comment about McDavid. An investigator told Abdon they were looking into him, but authorities never brought any charges against him.

Wrapping up its case, the defense called its own video expert, Charles Palm, whose only hits on the Nexis news database come from the Kelly trial. Palm said the tape could have been faked. He called the spot on Kelly's back "video noise," not the mole seen in photos. On cross-examination, lead prosecutor Shauna Boliker got Palm to admit he couldn't detect any fakery; he simply couldn't rule it out. "Is it true that water or urination would be difficult to fake?" she asked, her discomfort obvious. "A lot of things would be possible to fake at this level," Palm said, though he granted that act might be especially challenging.

"People do not want to read about urination in their morning paper," *Sun-Times* Editor Michael Cooke had declared before our first story about the tape. By the end of the trial, news reports regularly mentioned the act, and Kelly's lawyers joked about it. One day, when a TV reporter asked Sam Adam Jr. about the brand of the cologne he had worn to court, the lawyer laughed. "Urine!"

Many people had come to call the video "the pee tape," focusing on that one act instead of the statutory rape depicted in graphic detail for almost half an hour. It wasn't the pee tape, it was the rape tape, but urination as a sexual fetish became the focus. That was what comedian Dave Chappelle had mocked in "(I Wanna) Pee on You," and that's all that stuck with many people who hadn't seen the whole horrifying video (Kelly later told *GQ* he had never heard of the Chappelle skit, but in 2019, the comedian and his friend and showrunner Neal Brennan told several media outlets that Kelly's crew menaced them and wanted to fight when they visited Chicago for a show by rapper Common. "Dave's goons intervened. [Kelly's] goons negotiated," and nobody got hurt, Brennan said.)

On June 10, Kelly stood before the bench and assured Judge Gaughan that he understood his rights, and after discussing the matter with his attorneys, "I decided not to testify." With that, the defense rested. The prosecution recalled one of its video experts to refute the expert for the defense, and Atlanta prosecutor Robert Wolf flew to Chicago to testify that Yul Brown had not been offered a deal on gun and drug charges there in exchange for his fiancée Lisa Van Allen's testimony at the Kelly trial. Two days later, on Thursday, June 12, both sides made their closing arguments.

Prosecutors once again showed the full video to the jury, the media, and the spectators who, as on opening day, filled the courtroom to capacity for the big finale. As it played, Robert Heilingoetter methodically cited each of the remaining fourteen counts from Kelly's indictment, one per key scene on the tape. "Adjustment of the camera; more production," and so on. At one point, Juror No. 61, the Romanian immigrant, looked away, disgusted even after so many viewings. Citing Sparkle's testimony that her niece had once been a happy-go-lucky "jolly" girl, Heilingoetter said that on the tape, "she had become something else. Sweet, nice, lovely people are not insulated from being victims."

"The world is watching," Adam Jr. said as he started closing arguments for the defense, clearly relishing his plum role. He'd brought his wife to court. "We're making a tape, but she's legal!" he said when introducing her to reporters. To find Kelly guilty, he bellowed at jurors, "You are going to have to call Reshona, fourteen times, individually and collectively, a whore. You're going to have to say this girl, before the world, is a whore! My momma used to tell me, if you ain't got nothing nice to say, don't say it at all."

Promptly forgetting that, Adam Jr. painted Sparkle and Van Allen as thieving liars. He mocked the duffel bag—"Like some kind of porno Santa Claus, he's running around with a bag of porno tapes wherever he goes"—and misquoted 2 Corinthians 11:14 to call Van Allen the devil. Most effectively, he questioned why prosecutors didn't call Reshona as a witness. "Why don't they bring her in? She's just down the street . . . She was placed under oath at the age of fifteen or sixteen, she saw that tape, and said, 'It's not me!'"

Judge Gaughan instructed the jury to disregard that comment. They were not supposed to hear about or consider what Reshona had told the grand jury.

Not one to slow down for a speed bump, Adam Jr. barreled ahead. "Look in the crowd right now. Is Reshona here or not?" Fully in his thrall, half the jury scanned the gallery. Sweat dripping from his face, he went on to show the photo of the mole juxtaposed with a frame from the video. "If that mole is gone, it's not Kelly." He brushed off family members who identified Reshona as the girl in the tape but who didn't take action against Kelly. "Any solid man in the family, any solid woman, would have gone over there and broken his legs! They would have beat the crap out of him!"

After quoting the Bible for the older churchgoers on the jury, Adam Jr. tossed in some pop-culture references for the younger members, name-dropping Janet Jackson, Dave Chappelle, and the tween phenom of the moment when he asked why Reshona hadn't talked to her friends about having sex with Kelly. "She is a thirteen-year-old-girl having raunchy, dirty, nasty sex . . . with a superstar who's won Grammy Awards and she tells no one? You couldn't keep a thirteen-year-old girl's mouth quiet about having Hannah Montana tickets!"

Press accounts agreed that Adam Jr. put on a hell of a show, while Boliker kept her closing rebuttal simple and direct. "You know what's on that tape. You know it's vile. You know it's disgusting. And you know it's Robert Kelly and Reshona Landfair." As for the victim, "How dare he call her a prostitute?" she asked, her sunny singsong cracking. "This is not a who-done-it. It is a he-did-it."

Jurors began deliberating at 2:30 p.m. on Thursday, June 12. An hour later, they requested transcripts from the entire trial, or at least the testimony of the "bombshell witness," Lisa Van Allen. They also asked for a copy of the videotape and the equipment to view it. Judge Gaughan denied their requests. They broke at 5:50 p.m., and the judge sent them to their hotel for the night. Two jurors signaled their unhappiness. One sent the judge a note complaining that his dinner arrived late, and shortly after deliberations began again at 8:30 Friday morning, another sent a letter asking, "How can I be removed and go home? I really need to." The point became moot when, at 1:30 the afternoon of Friday the thirteenth, the jury bell rang, signaling a verdict after a total of seven and a half hours of deliberations.

Conventional wisdom held that relatively brief deliberations after more than a month of testimony spelled doom for a defendant. Courthouse veterans whispered in the marble hallways that Kelly would spend the next fifteen years in prison. As Courtroom 500 filled to hear the verdict, a downcast Adam Jr. shook Kelly's hand and somberly told his client, "We did everything we could." Judge Gaughan threatened to cite anyone who disrupted the reading of the verdict for contempt, immediately sending them next door to Cook County Jail. "I don't want any outbursts."

Shortly before 2 p.m., the foreman read the verdict for the first of fourteen counts against R. Kelly for making child pornography. "Not guilty." Ignoring Gaughan's warning, Adam Jr. shouted, "Yes!" His client broke down in tears. Wiping his face with a baby-blue handkerchief, Kelly whispered, "Thank you,

Jesus." He repeated those three words thirteen times when the verdict came in for each of the remaining counts. After the final "not guilty," the singer slapped Adam Jr. on the back and hugged Ed Genson, resting his head on a grandfatherly shoulder and crying some more. Kelly's manager Derrel McDavid cried, too. The prosecution team looked stunned.

Minutes later, Kelly walked down the handicap ramp at his special entrance a free man. The Pied Piper patted his heart, smiled, and waved at the photographers, television crews, and a hundred supporters who finally thronged on the big day. "I love you!" one fan shouted as Kelly sped away in a black SUV. It went to Douglas Park on the West Side, where Kelly's tour bus waited with more of his entourage.

Both legal teams held brief press conferences on the street in front of the courthouse. Looking sullen, State's Attorney Dick Devine joined his underlings who'd done all the work. "As we must, we accept the verdict of the jury in this case. This prosecution is one we have no reservations about." Devine added that the case had been unusual because the victim denied she'd been victimized, but "if we acquire the same evidence today or tomorrow, we will bring that case." Lead prosecutor Shauna Boliker didn't regret not subpoenaing the victim. "We were not going to re-victimize her." She didn't answer questions about whether the now-twenty-three-year-old woman had perjured herself before the grand jury.

The state's witnesses had all been courageous, Boliker said. "It was a difficult thing for them to do. They care about her. If we did anything with this prosecution, it showed the world how difficult this crime is to prosecute." When a reporter asked if prosecutors thought Kelly would stop the behavior they tried him for, Devine said, "We hope people get a lesson from this and don't think this is free territory for them now."

"Robert said all along that he believed in our system and he believed in God," Kelly's crisis manager Allan Mayer said, "and that when all the facts came out in court, he would be cleared of these terrible charges. But he did not expect that it would take six and a half years. This has been a terrible ordeal for him and his family and at this point all he wants to do is move forward and put it behind him."

Six months after that statement, the star's divorce from Andrea became final, and Kelly saw even less of his family than he did before, his children later said.

R. Kelly "was found not guilty because he had the best jury that Cook County could produce," Adam Jr. declared. "Two things happened today: R. Kelly got his name back, and Reshona never had to lose hers." (The trial made Adam Jr.'s name, as his father had hoped it would.)

The Dean of Local Defense Attorneys Ed Genson cracked that he'd "graduated from late middle age to senior citizen on this case. Now I am going to get a little sleep." (In March 2019, in a deathbed interview with *Sun-Times* columnist Neil Steinberg, Genson said, "I've represented entertainers, represented people connected to organized crime, represented professional criminals. I've represented guilty people, I represent innocent people." Of Kelly, he declared, with punctuation and italics from Steinberg, "He *was* guilty as hell!")

Some of the jurors held a press conference, too, and they said that in their first poll, five members voted to convict Kelly. No one caved because they were just eager to go home, they said, though one of the alternate jurors later told me they'd all been agitated about the possibility of being sequestered over Father's Day weekend. The biggest factor was they never heard from Reshona. Juror No. 9, the black Christian man who disliked seeing porn at 7-Eleven, initially voted guilty. "I thought it was R. Kelly on the tape. I still think that. What held me back was Reshona. I was eighty-five percent sure it was her, but it wasn't one-hundred-percent, the way her childhood friends identified her."

"Neither side proved their case beyond a reasonable doubt, and that's why we had to go for not guilty," said Juror No. 21, the criminal justice student. No. 61, the Romanian immigrant, said he did not find the state's witnesses believable. (Years later, in *Surviving R. Kelly*, he explained. "I just didn't believe them, the women. I know it sounds ridiculous. The way they dress, the way they act—I didn't like them.") The jurors who spoke to the press seemed stunned when reporters told them about all of the evidence they hadn't heard: the civil lawsuits, Aaliyah, the other tapes, the Florida photos, the pattern of behavior reported by the *Sun-Times*. "If they had presented it, who knows what we would have done," one of them said in a tone that made clear they'd probably have voted to convict.

Judge Gaughan didn't speak to the press publicly, but in a bizarre footnote to the way he ran a trial he vowed wouldn't become a media circus, he threw a party at a local tavern a week later. His assistant Terry Sullivan emailed invitations to the defense, the prosecution, court personnel, and all of the reporters who covered the proceedings. "Dress is casual. Come and celebrate the trial's conclusion and everyone's hard work." My Chicago Public Radio colleague Natalie Moore told me, "It was a hoot. Everyone was loose and relaxed." Edward McClelland also went and described the scene in *Blender*. "Gaughan was in the center of the room, in a wide-lapel suit with an American Legion pin. The judge cracked jokes with a reporter he'd kicked out of his courtroom and hammed for a buddy shot with an NPR correspondent, who posted the photo on her Facebook page. Sam Adam Jr. made his way to the bar for a free drink. Boliker chatted with journalists, most of whom had predicted Kelly would go down. Everyone seemed relieved that the trial was finally over."

I didn't see what anyone had to celebrate. If the jury had acquitted a guilty man, the system failed and he might continue hurting young girls. If an innocent man escaped imprisonment, the state diverted resources desperately needed to prosecute other sex crimes while he'd been through hell for six years. At one point during the long wait, Boliker told Abdon, "I wish we could be done with this so we can get back to prosecuting real crimes." We knew what she meant—she saw no end to cases that were the worst of the worst—and we didn't think she minimized Kelly's victims.

The state expected the singer to take a plea deal—maybe a year or two in prison—count his blessings, and wise up. The defense and prominent members of the black community, including the Rev. Jesse Jackson and the Rev. James Meeks, according to my sources, told State's Attorney Dick Devine that Kelly would take a different deal. "They wanted probation on this," a member of the prosecution team told me, "and ultimately Devine made the decision that probation wouldn't be appropriate." In *Soulacoaster*, Kelly claims the defense urged him to accept a plea bargain for eight months in prison, worried that Van Allen's testimony would lead to his conviction. "I'm not copping to nothing," Kelly says he told his lawyers. "I got God with me . . . Just do the job I'm paying you to do."

The plea never came, the cash never stopped flowing to work the system, and God may or may not have intervened, but Abdon and I didn't think Kelly would stop now that he'd been acquitted. As Dr. Domeena Renshaw told us, "Pedophiles will risk four years back in jail for four minutes with another young girl." I felt sick to my stomach when I heard about Gaughan's party, but not as ill as I felt when I learned the verdict in the newsroom at the *Sun-Times*. Don Hayner didn't even have to say it when he hung up with reporter Eric Herman at the courthouse. I could tell by his look.

The editors wanted me to write a piece with context and commentary, but for the first time in my daily-newspaper career, the words failed to come. I never felt like journalism and criticism mattered less. The deadline loomed, and Cooke hovered. The deadline passed, and Hayner hovered. The extended deadline loomed, and Hayner and Cooke sent Abdon over to hover. Finally, Cooke slammed my desk like he'd slammed the table during the argument about urination in the morning paper. "Damn it, DeRo, we have to have you in the paper. Get it done!" I finally sent seven hundred and sixty-three words to the copy desk.

As any criminal-defense attorney will attest, "not guilty" doesn't mean "innocent," I wrote in a pathetically clichéd lede. I quoted Kelly, a line from "Been Around the World" on *Chocolate Factory*: "God gonna judge me / The same day He judge you." Cooke wanted me to comment about the future of Kelly's career, but I had nothing, so I quoted Kelefa Sanneh in the *New York Times*. "The sex scandal that threatened to derail his career in 2002 ended up doing the opposite. It made him more productive, more successful and, somehow—maybe because more people began paying attention to his excellent music—more respected than ever before." I still wrestle with that.

The day of the verdict, fifteen-year-old Jerhonda Johnson, one of the two regulars who attended the trial and called themselves "R. Kelly's biggest fans," talked to reporters. She gleefully jumped up and down on the street at Twenty-Sixth and Cal. "They can't call him a pedophile anymore," she said. "They can't say he likes little girls! They don't have proof of that, because he's innocent now, he's free!" She could not have been happier.

PART III

CHAPTER 12

"HOW OLD ARE WE TALKING?"

On September 15, 2008, R. Kelly sat in a Philadelphia hotel suite with Touré, a music journalist and critic who'd written for the *New York Times,* the *Village Voice,* and *Rolling Stone.* He now hosted a BET show called *The Black Carpet.* Kelly wanted to do the interview in Philly, his crisis manager Allan Mayer told me, because three months after having been acquitted on all charges of making child pornography, the singer felt like Rocky.

This was an important piece of media intended to relaunch Kelly's career, though his album and concert-ticket sales had never faltered after the state of Illinois indicted him in 2002. Mayer fretted. The Kelly camp had chosen an interviewer they believed would be friendly, and they'd set some boundaries for the questions, but they worried because Kelly hadn't prepared. The singer had spent the previous evening partying with his crew, and he brushed Mayer aside when the publicist wanted to work with him to rehearse talking points as they'd done before the Ed Gordon interview more than six years earlier. "No, I got this," Kelly said.

When the singer saw the cameras and lights the next day, he finally got serious. "Before the interview, he was so nervous he was shaking," Touré recalled. The star's handlers had asked to see the questions beforehand, "and it was clearly a condition of the interview." Touré had readied about ten questions, and he turned them over, though he intended to follow the interview wherever it went once the cameras rolled. "They had all the power, until we started. Once we started, the equation totally changed."

His beard and hair neatly trimmed, Kelly wore a black leather jacket over a black T-shirt with white lettering. Things started out well, with both men all smiles. "You had a long tribulation, you came out victorious, you've gotta be feeling like Ali, like 'I just won a big fight,'" Touré began. "Well, I just feel good, man, you know? Move on with my life," Kelly replied. "Your music is amazing," Touré told him, adding that Kelly was one of the geniuses of the era. "Like Marvin Gaye and Prince *only*, you're able to do the spiritual stuff and the sexual stuff, and it works. I'm like, how are you able to work both sides of the listener that way?"

Kelly took a second to ponder, as if considering this dichotomy for the first time. "I keep it real," he concluded. "I grew up in church, and I grew up in the streets as well, so I've kind of got a bit of both sides in me. Which I believe we all do, in one way or another."

The flattery continued. "Over the last six years," Touré said, "you've had this trial hanging over your head, but you've *still* been able to create great music." How had he been able to do that despite "this personal pressure"? Kelly drew inspiration from difficulties such as the death of his mother and the trial, he said, and he found strength in his fans and family. Then Touré tossed a curve ball. "Do you like underage girls?"

Mayer jumped in front of the camera. "No, no, no, you can't ask him that!" Once again, Kelly brushed Mayer aside. "No, man, I got this, it's cool. I wanna answer this." Mayer sat down again. "Okay, you're the client," he said, and the interview resumed. (The first question and Mayer's interruption would never air.)

The interviewer posed the question to forty-one-year-old Kelly a second time, with a slight change in the wording. Because of Kelly's reply, BET only aired the interview once. "The day after," Touré told me, "Kelly's people called and demanded it be shelved or they would sue. On what grounds? No idea, but BET shelved it." (The clip floats on the Net, until unseen forces remove it, and then someone posts it anew.)

"Let me ask you something real that millions of Americans are wondering about you," Touré began the second time. "Do you like teenage girls?"

Kelly, who'd been leaning to his left, sat up straight. "When you say teenage, how old are we talking?" The interviewer's face registered almost comic surprise. "Girls who are teenagers," Touré said. "Nineteen?" Kelly asked. Dumbfounded, Touré replied, "Nineteen and younger." Kelly took a moment to consider. "I have some nineteen-year-old friends. But I don't like anybody illegal, if that's what we're talking about, underage."

Touré tried one more time. "Some people think that you like underage girls. What do you say to them?" R. Kelly smiled. "Well, those people don't know Robert."

Growing up thirty-five miles west of Chicago in suburban Streamwood, Jerhonda Johnson had heard R. Kelly's music for as long as she remembered. He provided the soundtrack to her childhood, at birthday parties, backyard barbecues, even at church and in school. At age eleven in 2003, she became "a superfan," thanks to "Ignition (Remix)" and *Chocolate Factory.* "My family listened to his music, my friends listened to his music, everybody was just in love with the music. I literally had every single CD he had released. It was just his music that, like, *attracted* me, and then everywhere I'd go, people were playing his music, so it was like nonstop *Chocolate World.*" When she wasn't spinning Kelly's CDs, she told me she blasted Chicago's R&B radio powerhouse. "WGCI was the biggest supporter—they played him *all the time*—and it was my favorite radio station."

I first heard how Jerhonda met Kelly in January 2012, three and a half years after the verdict. Writing anonymously and in all caps, and noting that my father-in-law was a co-worker—the longer you live in Chicago, the more it becomes a very big small town—one of her relatives claimed to have "A GOOD STORY." Eventually, the correspondent gave me Jerhonda's contact info, and we traded a dozen emails and texts over the next five years before she trusted me to tell her story publicly for the first time.

Throughout the trial, Jerhonda had been one of the two supporters who attended Cook County Criminal Court several days a week. "R. Kelly's Biggest Fans," the media called them. "I had never experienced a trial in person, and they have this big R&B star whom I really like, and I just wanted to experience it." She told reporters she was eighteen, but she was really fifteen. Doe-eyed, with a slight build, chubby cheeks, long black hair, and a wide smile in her many photos at the time, I would have thought she was twelve.

Sheriff's deputies were supposed to card at the door of Courtroom 500, barring admittance to anyone under eighteen because the child pornography video would be shown as evidence. Jerhonda had a cheap and obviously fake ID that somehow passed muster. Cutting as many of her sophomore high-school classes as she attended, she took the Metra train to Chicago because she wanted to see Kelly and learn the truth about the things people were saying. "Did he really do it? I wanted to see everything for myself. At the time I was still, you know, pretty starstruck, so I was in disbelief. I thought, 'Well, maybe that's not the girl.'" Like everyone who followed the trial closely, she had an opinion about the verdict. "If she would have come forward, I think it would have made a huge difference."

Jerhonda met Kelly when he walked into the courthouse. "He seemed like a cool guy, and he would always speak to me when he saw me." One day, she even got Kelly's autograph. "He didn't have anything to sign, and neither did I, but my friend reached into her pocket and found an old bank slip, so I got his autograph on her bank slip." She showed me. She'd had it laminated.

In May 2009, eleven months after the trial ended, Jerhonda said a member of Kelly's crew sought out and friended her on Myspace. He invited her to a party at Kelly's home at One Maros Lane in Olympia Fields. The singer lived alone, now that his divorce from Andrea was final. The mansion boasted a soaring three-story atrium, five bedrooms, seven baths, half a dozen fireplaces, a home theater, a log-cabin room with a hot tub, and a large, Hawaiian-themed indoor pool. It sat on almost four acres of rolling green hills behind rock walls and iron gates, with a long, tree-lined driveway, a pond, a tennis/basketball court, and a six-car garage, all overlooking the fourteenth hole of the Olympia Fields Country Club's South Course. Jerhonda had never seen anything like it.

"I was a bit nervous. Even though I had already met him at his trial, I was, like, literally at his *house,* so it did not feel real." She had just turned sixteen, and she lied to her parents, telling them she'd be at a friend's place. During the party, Kelly called her over to the tiki bar in the pool room, saying he remembered her from court. He asked for her cell phone and entered his number. "At the time, I was still, you know, pretty starstruck, so I was in disbelief." She didn't tell him her age, and he didn't ask.

On June 5, Kelly invited Jerhonda to come back, and he sent one of his crew to pick her up in a black SUV. He told her to bring her bathing suit. "I really thought I was going to his house just to go swimming." This time, they were alone in the pool room. "He told me that he wanted me to undress for him, and walk back and forth like I was modeling. From the pool room, he took me into his game room, and he just laid me on the couch, and then we had oral sex back and forth. Then he took me into his sex room, which is a room full of mirrors. The entire room is, like, *mirrors*. We just talked for about thirty minutes, and that very first time, it was just oral sex between us."

Kelly also made Jerhonda write and sign letters stating she'd stolen jewelry and cash from him, and that her parents had set her up to blackmail him. He told her it was "insurance" so she wouldn't talk about their relationship. None of the charges were true, she said, but she did as he instructed.

On her third visit four days later, Kelly gave Jerhonda a strong but fruity drink he called Sex in the Kitchen, "like his song," and it hit her hard. "I was drunk, because I wasn't used to alcohol." They had intercourse, and Kelly took her virginity. "He thought that was exciting." They continued having sexual contact for the next seven months, and Kelly filmed many of their encounters. He never asked permission. He just did it.

"I had to call him 'Daddy,' and he would call me 'baby.' He wanted me to have two pigtails, and I had to go out and find little schoolgirl outfits," Jerhonda said. She began spending a lot of time at the mansion. "I noticed every time I brought up me going home, he would ask me, 'Well, what do you have to do?' And I was like, 'I just want to go home to get a change of clothes.' And he'd go, 'I could buy you some of those.' He never wanted me to leave."

If Kelly had previously been unaware of Jerhonda's age, she said she told him for certain that she was sixteen on July 17. "I gave him my state ID," the real one. She recalled Kelly saying it was fine, but she should tell anyone who asked she was nineteen, and act like she was twenty-five. "I asked him, like, 'Do you like your girls younger?' He said, 'Of course I do, because I can train them.' He said, 'Older women, they have too much knowledge. When they're young, I can train them and I can mold them to be who I want them to be.'"

When she spent weekends at the mansion, Jerhonda often lied to her parents and said she was staying with her seventeen-year-old friend Dominique Gardner, another thin and petite Kelly superfan one year her senior. They met on Myspace, too, and bonded in person when they both bought tickets for their favorite singer's concert at the United Center during the Double Up tour in December 2007. Jerhonda had problems at home, with sexual abuse in her past, and she liked staying with Dominique and her mother.

Jerhonda shared Kelly's phone number with Dominique, who began calling and texting the star. Dominique first met Kelly after watching him play basketball, then she started going to the mansion, too. While they were there, Jerhonda said they had to follow what Kelly called his "rules," dressing in baggy clothing, sometimes turning over their phones, and asking him permission to shower, eat, go to the bathroom, or leave the property. "I asked him, 'Okay, why are you taking my phone away?'" Jerhonda recalled. She hated giving it to him, and often hid it in her pocket. "He said, 'Because if people knew that we were dating, they would be jealous.' He said, 'Everybody would be jealous, and they would try to, you know, take you away from me. They wouldn't want me around you. They would want what you have, and I don't want them, I only want *you*.'"

If Jerhonda broke Kelly's "rules" or hesitated when he asked her to perform certain sex acts, she said he insulted and slapped her. "He had strap-ons. We'd have to do stuff like that. And he wanted me to engage in sexual activity with other people while he sat there and he watched. And it wasn't a comfortable situation." Nevertheless, she went along. "At the time, I didn't know what I liked, honestly. I just knew that I liked his music, so I was pretty much accepting of anything that came with him at the time."

On occasion, Jerhonda and Dominique were both at the mansion at the same time, but they knew it only if they'd broken Kelly's rules, kept their phones, and texted each other from the separate rooms where he sequestered them. "He had different girls in different rooms, and he would go room to room doing whatever he did with each girl," Jerhonda said. On June 14, 2009, two Olympia Fields police cars pulled up to the mansion in search of Dominique. Her family had called for a well-being check, concerned that the seventeen-year-old girl was with Kelly. Dominique wasn't there—she later told me she was at a cousin's house—but Jerhonda was watching *Transformers* in the mansion's home theater. Usually, Kelly only joined her to watch Bulls games—he once hit her because she was rooting for the Cleveland Cavaliers instead of his favorite team, she said—or *Toddlers & Tiaras*, a show she claims he loved. With the cops at the door, Kelly panicked, rushed into the theater room, and told Jerhonda to hide.

"'They're looking for a seventeen-year-old. You're not seventeen, because, like I said, you're nineteen,'" Jerhonda recalls Kelly telling her. She saw the cops at the door on the mansion's closed-circuit video system, and she heard Kelly call his attorney Ed Genson, who advised him he didn't have to let officers search his home if they didn't have a warrant.

Word spread on the Net of cops descending on Kelly's mansion after a frantic call about him preying on teens. Some even used the word "rape." By the summer of 2010, the fertile new field of online rumor and innuendo had already blossomed to the point where only an idiot believed a quarter of the stuff on gossip websites and fan groups, or on the still-new but exploding social-media platforms of Facebook and Twitter. (Instagram didn't launch until that October.)

In July, Lauren FitzPatrick of the *Southtown Star* got wind of the rumors online, started digging, and discovered that police had indeed visited the mansion. She couldn't find a police report (it only surfaced a decade later, thanks to a Freedom of Information Act request), and Chief Jeff Chudwin didn't tell her much. Police "were informed of a possible criminal matter. We investigated the issues, found there to be no crime, and the matters have been closed." Kelly's crisis manager Allan Mayer issued a statement on the PR Newswire in response to the rumors on the Net. "This is completely false. No police ever showed up at Kelly's house with a search warrant nor was his house ever searched. It is also not true, as the unsubstantiated report claimed, that any such girl ever stayed overnight in Kelly's house or that she had been there but left shortly before some mythical police search. Kelly's attorneys have informed the police that they will cooperate fully with any investigation."

When I first interviewed him for this book, reconnecting after the many times we spoke during the 2000s, Mayer told me he quit as Kelly's crisis manager the day after the Touré interview. A week later, I realized his statement about the police call came a year after that. "It's true that for a year or so beyond the Touré interview I continued at the request of Rob's lawyers to release some statements for him on minor matters," he said, "but as far as the major issues were concerned, I was done in September 2008, and I never spoke out on his behalf again." A spin doctor never stops spinning.

The Olympia Fields police had visited Kelly's mansion at least three times before. They conducted the well-being check on his wife, Andrea, as requested by her mother in 2003, and they investigated the complaint by Henry Vaughn, the king of the steppers, in 2006. With the help of a reporter at the *Chicago Tribune,* I also unearthed a heavily redacted file documenting a third visit.

The file began with an incident report for a criminal sexual assault on a twenty-three-year-old woman on January 27, 2008—five months before the verdict in Kelly's trial. Police took the woman's statement at nearby St. James Hospital, which collected a rape kit. The woman told police she'd been invited to a party at the mansion where about thirty people gathered. A man whose name was redacted sexually assaulted her in the studio, according to the police report, and when she protested, he told her, "You talk too much, got too much mouth, this is what I do around here." The file ended with the detective noting that on January 31, a lawyer representing the victim informed police she didn't want to press criminal charges, but would file a civil lawsuit. I didn't find a subsequent legal claim.

Michelle Kramer, Dominique Gardner's mother, blamed the Olympia Fields Police for turning a blind eye toward the happenings at the mansion. Kelly was the largest taxpayer in the village of 4,700, *Southtown Star* reporter Lauren FitzPatrick noted in a follow-up story about the 2009 police call to Maros Lane. His property taxes equaled a tenth of the police department's annual budget in 2008. "If they'd done their jobs, none of this would have happened," Kramer told me. Her daughter was one of Kelly's lovers for nine years, from 2009 until she finally broke with him in 2018.

Jerhonda told me she had sexual contact with Kelly more than fifty times when she was still sixteen. "He was a very sexual person." He asked her to engage in threesomes, and she once had sexual contact with him and a woman he called his "trainer," because she taught new girls "the rules." The trainer had been best friends since high school with Reshona Landfair, and Jerhonda saw Reshona herself at a party at the mansion one night. Jerhonda recognized Reshona from the half-dozen times she saw the videotape in court.

In January 2010, Jerhonda broke off contact with Kelly after the two had an argument when he caught her texting a friend. She was still only sixteen. Because she broke his rules, he demanded that she have a threesome with him and another man to prove her loyalty, she said, and she refused. He'd asked and she'd declined once before, and he slapped her then and lashed out again now, holding her against a wall and choking her, she said. "I didn't want to have sex with anybody else."

After Kelly slapped and choked her, Jerhonda said he ordered her to fellate him, and he spit in and ejaculated on her face. "It went all over my forehead, and it was nasty. I wiped it off and I kept his DNA, and I lied to get out of the house," saying she had to duck out to a nearby relative's place for fifteen minutes. She offered to show me the semen-stained blue T-shirt that she used to clean herself, and I declined. (In 2018, she gave it to the Olympia Fields Police Department, and although the statute of limitations had not expired, they did not immediately pursue a case. After DNA testing confirmed the presence of Kelly's semen, the T-shirt would be cited by the state's attorney as evidence in the new round of charges against the singer in February 2019.)

Jerhonda corroborated her story by giving me legal documents, phone logs, texts, emails, bank records, letters, and the results of a polygraph test. She broke a nondisclosure agreement with Kelly when we talked, three months before women did the same when speaking out about Harvey Weinstein in the *New York Times* and *The New Yorker*. She provided the NDA, and in seventeen years of reporting on Kelly, it was the first time I'd seen the actual legal tool he'd used to silence his victims.

> Except as may be required under compulsion of the law, the parties agree that they shall keep the terms and the existence of this Agreement and of the 2010 Settlement Agreement, strictly confidential and promise that neither they nor their representatives, agents, or attorneys will disclose, either directly or indirectly, any information concerning this Agreement (or the fact of settlement) to any other person or entity. . . . In the event that [Jerhonda] Johnson, her agents, attorneys, or any person or entity acting on their behalf,

breaches the confidentiality or non-disparagement provisions of this Agreement, Kelly's obligations hereunder to make any further payments from and after the breach shall cease. . . . The parties and their attorneys expressly stipulate and agree that confidentiality is imperative and is an essential term of this Agreement. . . . Any breach of this confidentiality provision would cause Kelly irreparable injury. . . . Kelly would be entitled to an injunction, in addition to any other legal remedies he may have.

A twenty-four-year-old mother of three when we first spoke on the record, Jerhonda was living in Virginia, happily married to her friend Dominique Gardner's cousin Joseph Pace. She broke down in tears a few times over the phone, but she'd taken more than five years to decide she wanted to tell her story. She mostly powered through with steely determination, only pausing at a few points to talk to one of her children. "You go play now, Mommy's busy." We returned to some of the incidents she described half a dozen times in subsequent interviews. Some things were hard to talk about the first time, and I had to do the job of the reporter, pressing for specifics, details, and dates. Almost as difficult as talking about the abuse was charting the long, twisted path of not one but two settlements with Kelly. Jerhonda felt she'd been victimized twice, once by him, and again by lawyers she trusted to help her.

Shortly after leaving Kelly's mansion for the last time in January 2010, Jerhonda called the office of Susan Loggans. "It was on their website that they had worked with a lot of women who went against Kelly, and I thought, 'Oh, that's a *good thing*.' I thought it would be okay, because they had experience with him, and they turned out to be a bunch of floozies." She was told the settlement would make her a millionaire, she said, and was dissuaded from going to the police. "They said if I was to get criminal charges, it would probably be like it was last time, where he wouldn't get convicted and it would just be I would be another girl that he did it to. If I wanted real justice, I would go ahead and I would do what I had to do and I would get money from him instead."

After the first three lawsuits Loggans filed against Kelly for Tiffany Hawkins, Tracy Sampson, and Patrice Jones, she followed a new tactic, she and several of her clients confirmed. When girls came to the office with complaints about Kelly, Loggans approached his attorneys with their charges directly; provided corroborating evidence—including submitting the girls to lie-detector tests—then struck settlements for payments in return for nondisclosure agreements, all without court records or publicity.

Loggans sent Jerhonda to take a lie detector test administered by a private detective agency in suburban Hinsdale. F. L. Hunter and Associates sent the seven-page results to the lawyer in a letter dated February 1, 2010. The document details the questions Hunter asked the victim, including whether she had intercourse with Kelly, if she told him she was only sixteen, and whether he slapped, choked, and spit on her during an argument. She answered yes to all the questions. "It is the opinion of this examiner, based upon an analysis of her polygraph records, that she is truthful in her answers," Hunter concluded.

As usual, Loggans would not comment, but Jerhonda said and documents confirmed that her attorney struck a $1.5 million settlement for her with Kelly in return for signing an NDA.

In 2012, Jerhonda complained to Loggans's office about late or missing payments from Kelly. She provided those emails and the responses, including some from Kelly's veteran manager Derrell McDavid and his new attorney, Chicagoan Linda Mensch.

By then, Kelly had serious financial problems. The singer had to pay substantial child support and alimony to Andrea; he owed the IRS nearly $5 million in unpaid taxes, and the mansion he purchased in 2002 had gone into foreclosure. (It had been appraised for as much as $5.2 million before the housing market crashed.) In March 2013, his lender on the property, JPMorgan Chase, bought it for the sole bid of $950,000, and a few months after that, Rudolph Isley, the eldest of the legendary Isley Brothers, wound up with the place at the bargain price of $587,000. Isley, whose brothers' career Kelly had revitalized in 1995, bought the sprawling estate so he and his wife could live closer to their grandchildren.

Jerhonda went to a second lawyer, but she fired him because he insisted on working with Loggans, who had all the files for the case. She didn't want her new lawyer to have anything to do with Loggans, she said, because that firm had never taken her seriously. "Well, I found me another attorney," she continued. "I was downtown on my way to meet Loggans, because I felt some type of way. I was boiling over with steam, so I was going down there to give Kim"—Loggans's assistant, Kim Jones—"a piece of my mind. And downtown, outside their building, I ran into a guy. I was eavesdropping, and I heard his conversation, and I saw he was an attorney. And that's when he got off his phone and I walked up and I said, 'I have a case for you.'"

Attorney number three, David Fish, filed suit for Jerhonda not only against Kelly, but against Loggans. That suit claimed the settlement with Kelly was "orchestrated so that they (but not Jerhonda) would be paid their $500,000 immediately. Jerhonda would have to wait for her money [and] ultimately, the man who abused Jerhonda defaulted on his payment obligations." Jerhonda only got $250,000 of the $1.5 million. (Loggans presumably got all of her $500,000, since Fish's lawsuit noted that Kelly's payments totaled $750,000 before he began defaulting.) Jerhonda settled the claim against Loggans for $27,000, and she settled her second claim against Kelly for $375,000, a fraction of the amount she was initially supposed to get. Things had gotten very complicated.

After reading about the foreclosure on Kelly's mansion, Jerhonda felt sorry for the singer she had once considered "a boyfriend." She began cashing his checks, putting the money in an envelope, and bringing it to Derrel McDavid's office in Oak Park, she said. She sheepishly told me she also hoped to rekindle her relationship with Kelly. She was still only nineteen at the time. "I was stupid; I was a kid." She sometimes sounded immature even as a twenty-four-year-old mother of three.

Although the NDA legally bound her from talking about her relationship with the star, Jerhonda had been hanging out with friends one day when she confided in them. They secretly recorded her on a cell phone and took the video to McDavid's office, seeking to get paid, Jerhonda said. Kelly's handlers threatened her for breaking her first NDA for the settlement struck by Loggans. Eventually, they agreed to pay her $375,000 in monthly installments of $5,000, and they got her to sign a second NDA. They believed this deal would finally keep her quiet. Indeed, her then-current attorney, David Fish, strongly advised her not to talk to me, warning that Kelly could retaliate.

How effective is an NDA? Attorney Damon Dunn pointed me to a ruling by the Appellate Court of Illinois in February 2005 in the case of a woman who sued Michael Jordan after she broke a nondisclosure agreement and talked about her paternity claim against the basketball legend. "We recognize that there are contracts for silence that are unenforceable," the court wrote. "For example, they may suppress information about harmful products or information about public safety, they may conceal criminal conduct, or they may constitute extortion or blackmail." Challenging the validity of NDAs to silence victims is now a prime consideration of the #MeToo movement, but the Kelly camp never retaliated against Jerhonda, or even contacted her.

The singer's handlers did give me a brief statement for the story I wrote about Jerhonda for BuzzFeed News. "The allegations against Mr. Kelly are false, and are being made by individuals known to be dishonest. It is clear these continuing stories are the result of the effort of those with personal agendas who are working in concert to interfere with and damage his career. Mr. Kelly again denies any and all wrongdoing and is taking appropriate legal action to protect himself from ongoing defamation."

"I know speaking out against Kelly, Kelly could sue me," Jerhonda said, "but I'm really not worried about it anymore. I feel like this is a healing process for me, because I've been holding this in for so many years, and to see that he always gets away with it, it's just not right." She also had another reason for telling her story. She worried about Dominique.

After years without communicating, Dominique messaged Jerhonda via Instagram in December 2016. "She had told me that she needed help and she was, you know, drinking a lot, and she was just really stressed out. And she was living downtown in a high-rise." After losing his mansion, Kelly rented a luxurious apartment in Trump Tower Chicago. Dominique didn't mention Kelly by name in her messages, Jerhonda said, "but she was just, like, giving me so many hints. 'You can't tell anybody it's him.' So everything she said, I knew who it was. She was like, 'You know, the guy we had in common.' She said it was really stressful on her, and she just wanted to get out."

For the first few years Dominique dated Kelly, she lived at home with her mother, Michelle Kramer. In 2015, she began living with Kelly, and her mother heard from her only via sporadic calls and texts. Kramer said some were "like prison calls," and they often ended abruptly. When we talked in 2018, her daughter was one of six women living with Kelly in what some of their families called his "cult." Kramer cried, and she had a message for Kelly. "Ain't nothing in your life going to go right until you let these girls go home and face your judge, your maker."

Jerhonda also cried when she talked to me about her friend, as well as the other girls living with Kelly and following his rules. "If I can speak out and I can help them get out of that situation, that's what I will do. I didn't have anybody to speak up on my behalf when I was going through what I was going through with him. He's brainwashed them really bad, and it kind of reminds me of Charles Manson. He needs to be stopped."

My friend and former *Chicago Reader* music critic Bill Wyman first wrote about R. Kelly when the then-rising star filmed the video for "Bump N' Grind" at the Vic Theatre on the North Side in 1993. Bill had been an occasional sounding board for years whenever I needed to decompress and try to connect the dots in my reporting. In early 2019, I told him I would never understand Kelly's Rasputin-like power to captivate young girls. Bill— echoing Jerhonda—said the better comparison might be Charles Manson. He recommended I reread the epic article David Felton and David Dalton wrote for *Rolling Stone* in 1970.

Like a lot of the alternative press at the time, the magazine had initially been skeptical of the accusations against Manson, suspecting zealous prosecutors of demonizing a culture they'd never comprehend. The accusations had just seemed too weird to be real. The reporters soon learned the truth, from digging into the story, and from talking to Manson himself. Charlie told them he sought out and liked having sex with a certain type, "girls who break down easier," and music was part of his lure, because "kids respond to music." Once Charlie picked a girl and went off into the woods with her, a member of the Family said, she was never the same when they came back, and she never left.

CHAPTER 13

"IT'S JUST MUSIC"

R. Kelly took the stage as the headliner on the third night of the ninth annual Pitchfork Music Festival in Union Park on Chicago's West Side on July 21, 2013, only a mile and a half from where I conducted an emotional interview in a source's living room thirteen years earlier. I watched Kelly sing from the dugout behind the temporary stage set up in a dusty baseball field. I'd seen him perform only once since the show with the threesome in a jail cell that opened the Best of Both Worlds tour in 2004. The other gig also came in the wait before the trial, during but not officially part of South by Southwest, spring break for music geeks, in 2006. Kelly performed at Bass Concert Hall on the campus of the University of Texas in Austin while fifteen protestors from a group called Feminists of Color United stood in the parking lot chanting, "We love R&B, not child pornography." They handed out leaflets detailing the charges against Kelly, as well as the horrifying statistics for all sexual assaults on women of color. Most fans heading inside ignored them. "Get a hobby," one shouted. "It's just music!"

The last words are the ones that made me want to scream. They always do.

No one protested Kelly's performance at Pitchfork seven years later. The pain he caused so many girls and the families he destroyed had largely been forgotten, even in the hometown where many of them lived, even before a crowd of twenty thousand college-age music lovers who considered themselves hip, green, and woke. Published at the cusp of the digital revolution, none of the stories Abdon Pallasch and I reported before or during the wait for Kelly's day in court could be accessed via the clunky website at the *Sun-Times*. It was as if our work had never existed. And even it *had* been easily accessible, it seemed as if many wouldn't have cared. There were always isolated pockets of loud, angry, often female voices like those women I met in Austin—two who always inspired me were Mikki Kendall in Chicago and Jamilah Lemieux in New York—but their voices were often ignored, marginalized, or mocked. Why did they want to bring the party down? Why did anyone keep bringing up all that unpleasantness? *It's just music.*

Though I'd never loved any job more, I left the *Sun-Times* as its pop music critic in May 2010 after fifteen years, when the paper had its third owner during my tenure, and its fifth since 1980. Chicago financier and civic activist James Tyree bought the tabloid in 2009 as it teetered on the brink of extinction after the conviction of Lord Conrad Black. Tyree believed in the importance of journalism and the necessity of the *Sun-Times* to provide an alternate voice to the *Tribune*, but the mantra in dead-tree media had long been "do more with less." Every newspaper lost revenue from classified advertising to Craigslist, display ads to online platforms, and paid circulation to free digital media. Extinction loomed.

"Disruption," the techie utopians call it. As a punk-rocker, I'm all for out with the old, in with the new. Maybe the new models will be better, but I've yet to see many offer the level of institutional support that allowed us to do the sort of stories we did about R. Kelly. In an effort to staunch the hemorrhaging, Tyree trimmed staff and imposed an across-the-board salary cut in 2010. He died the next year, and things at my old paper and journalism in general only got worse after that.

Every journalist I know has dark hours when she believes the profession is dying. Some think it's already dead. Many people I love, respect, and admire have left, including Don Hayner, who reluctantly retired, and Abdon, who went into law enforcement (sort of; he became spokesman for Cook County Sheriff Tom Dart) then politics (as director of communications for Illinois Comptroller Susana Mendoza, an unsuccessful candidate for mayor of Chicago in 2019). Mary Mitchell is still at it, still providing a vital voice for many who don't have one at a *Sun-Times* that somehow continues doing good journalism while on life support. I started teaching Reviewing the Arts as an adjunct at Columbia College Chicago, and when the English Department offered me a full-time position, I gratefully accepted. I continued doing music journalism and criticism with *Sound Opinions* and in a blog for the show's home base at public radio, WBEZ, but it was time to pay the rent with a primary gig elsewhere.

The thing about teaching, as a brilliant artist named Sheperd Paine taught me, is that it forces you to think deeply about what you've spent your life doing, so that you can articulate how others should do it, or at least how *you* do it. I define criticism in my classes as the attempt to convey your analysis of a work of art and your emotional reaction to it. Head and heart, you need both, always, per Lester Bangs and Roger Ebert. Everyone who cares about art should be a critic, because, *damn it*, nothing matters more. Politics, sex, religion, morality, social justice—any issue you can name is in the art, so we're never just writing about a play, a movie, a painting, a book, or whatnot. It's never *just* music. Especially not music, the most powerful and most emotionally resonant of the arts, at least for me.

The tools we have for this daunting task are insight, evidence, and context. What do *you* think the art is about, and how does it make *you* feel? Back up that analysis and emotional reaction with evidence, plenty of it. And, finally, know where the art came from and where it fits in our culture. Give context, because nothing exists in a vacuum. Nothing is *just* anything.

Criticism of Kelly's music after the first revelations about his predatory behavior had been, as my students would say, an epic fail. And it only got worse during the first nine years after his acquittal.

When R. Kelly walked out of the courthouse at Twenty-Sixth and Cal after hearing the words "not guilty" fourteen times, he had been a platinum-selling artist for almost two decades. Jive Records released his tenth album a year and a half later, in December 2009. *Untitled* became the first to fall short of a million copies sold. In fact, it didn't do half that, never even going gold, despite generally positive reviews. Writing in *SPIN*, Mikael Wood noted that it "contains no shortage of fresh raunch. 'Bangin' the Headboard and 'Pregnant' (as in 'You make me wanna get you . . .') are bawdy even by Kelly's considerable standards." That didn't bother him, and Wood gave the disc a rating of seven on the magazine's ten-point scale. It didn't unduly disturb Jon Pareles of the *New York Times*, either. "Call it focus, call it obsession, call it tunnel vision, call it formula: R. Kelly is consistent. Album after album he provides single-minded, slow-grinding songs about sex. . . . Still, even a routine R. Kelly song outshines much of the competition."

The fans seemed to be growing tired of Kelly's horny club grooves, how-ever, or at least less accepting of them from a relentless, aging player now forty-two years old. Always adept at reading the market and the moment, Kelly shifted gears into a more mature, retro-soul mode on his next album in late 2010. On the cover of *Love Letter*, he donned a tuxedo, sported shades, and struck a Stevie Wonder pose, just like he'd done at the Kenwood Acad-emy talent show in 1982. The album went gold, Kelly served as honorary grand marshal of the South Side's Bud Billiken Parade, and critics once again applauded.

"His decision to ditch the club and retreat to a more conventionally romantic setting allows him to let his voice take center stage, which is where it should have been all along," Maura Johnston wrote in *SPIN*. In the *New York Times*, Jon Caramanica heard Kelly channeling Frankie Lymon, Jackie Wilson, and James Ingram. (I'd have cited instead his longtime favorite Donny Hathaway.) "Never less than impressive, in places, it's phenomenal, with Mr. Kelly singing as vigorously as ever, on songs that are some of the most elegant of his career. And *Love Letter* is notable for what's largely absent: Mr. Kelly's id, which has otherwise gone untamed—on record, at least—for the better part of the last two decades."

Kelly's biggest booster and benefactor during those two decades had been Jive founder Clive Calder, but in 2002, the South African music exec sold the label he launched during the New Wave era to the German media group Bertelsmann for $2.74 billion. Disruption hit the old-school music biz as hard as it did journalism. Consolidation ran rampant as what had long been "the big six" major labels became "the big three," Universal, Warner Music, and Sony BMG, where Kelly became part of RCA/Sony Music.

In 2011, digital downloads topped the sale of CDs for the first time, and within the next five years, both would yield to streaming, and record companies would become less important than ever. (Marketers and publi-cists are a different story.) At the same time, the global concert giant Live Nation gobbled up Pac-Man-like the independent promoters that had been doing big business regionally since the sixties. The new shareholder-driven monopolies had no problem grabbing a piece of the revenue generated by Kelly. After all, he'd been acquitted.

Few mourned the loss of Jive Records. In addition to enabling Kelly for most of his career, the label had given another of its most profitable partners cover to commit myriad crimes. In a 2007 exposé for *Vanity Fair,* journalist Bryan Burrough reported that "until he fled the country in January, accused of embezzling more than $300 million, Lou Pearlman was famous as the impresario behind the Backstreet Boys and *NSYNC. Turns out his investors weren't the only victims, colleagues reveal: Pearlman's passion for boy bands was also a passion for boys." Prosecuted for fraud, though not the sexual molestation charges documented by Burrough, Pearlman died in prison in 2016. Jive had also presided over the hypersexualized marketing of Britney Spears since she signed to the label at age sixteen, and it kept profiting from her throughout her long, sad, and very public meltdown.

In 2012, a year and a half after *Love Letter,* Kelly released his first album for RCA/Sony Music, *Write Me Back*, an uninspired sequel that continued in the retro-soul mold. It didn't sell in any format—few albums did anymore by then—and it signaled to me an aging artist in decline and devoid of new ideas. Other critics disagreed. "It's slightly less drenched in retro tropes, but it's no less of an enjoyable listen," Maura Johnston wrote in the *Village Voice,* but she added that where Kelly really delivered was onstage. The concert she'd seen a year earlier during the Love Letter tour had been "one of the most impressive live spectacles I've been witness to in my two-plus decades of attending big arena shows."

Johnston and Kelefa Sanneh, both of whose work I often admired, were leading lights in a new wave of music critics who called themselves "popists." I'll spare you the internecine debate, but it's important to understand that many (though not all) critics in the first two decades of the new millennium thought like that editor with whom I'd strongly disagreed at the *Sun-Times,* the one who didn't want to upset Michael Jackson fans by mentioning the accusations that had been made against him. *It's just music.* Try to listen from the perspective of the fans who love it, these critics contend. Just write about the music, and go easy on the cultural context.

Kelly released more than just music in these years. June 2012 saw the publication of *Soulacoaster: The Diary of Me.* The cover depicts its hero standing in his shades and retro-soul tux, striking a Christ-like pose while surrounded by dozens of microphones, symbolizing both his crucifixion by the media and the act of recording the music he offered like a sacrament. Publisher SmileyBooks was part of the media empire started by the entrepreneurial PBS television personality Tavis Smiley, who first trumpeted the book in a press release years earlier, noting his excitement about Kelly joining a roster of authors that included Dr. Cornel West and Henry Louis Gates Jr. "We are thrilled to be the conduit through which R. Kelly will tell his own story," Smiley said.

The press release also quoted Kelly. "I'm writing this book as Robert, not R. Kelly. I'm tired of being misunderstood. I will show you the tears, fears, and sweat. I will open my heart and reveal the good in my life as well as all the drama. I want to tell it like it is."

SmileyBooks delayed *Soulacoaster* several times, apparently because of legal challenges. In late 2017, Smiley became embroiled in his own sexual harassment scandal, leading to his termination by PBS, which had distributed his nightly talk show.

Like his albums, Kelly's book garnered embarrassingly positive press, despite the many troubling aspects of the singer's actions it never addressed. "A tell-all, this is not," Jesse Washington wrote in a review for the Associated Press. "Instead, *Soulacoaster: The Diary of Me* recounts the creative and family life of a once-in-a-generation performer and musician." Despite the omissions, Washington concluded the book charts "an entertaining journey that reveals much about the musical engine of a true artist."

One line in *Soulacoaster* resonated with me through 2013, the most notable year of Kelly's post-trial career. After he'd tapped the retro-soul well dry, he returned to unleashing his id, and the sexual Superfreak reached out to a new, younger, mostly white audience. In his book, Kelly brags about the especially cartoonish sex songs on *Double Up* becoming "a big hit with indie-rockers." Now, his manager, Derrel McDavid, worked with Jonathan Azu of Red Light Management, whose other clients included Phish and the Alabama Shakes, to boost Kelly with the jam-band and indie-rock crowds during a series of high-profile festival appearances.

In April 2013, Kelly made two "surprise" cameos with the French dance-pop band Phoenix, joining its members to sing "Ignition (Remix)" during their headlining slots on two consecutive weekends at the Coachella Valley Music & Arts Festival in Indio, California. In June, he appeared as a headliner at the Bonnaroo Music & Arts Festival in Manchester, Tennessee. And in July, the singer performed as the closing act at Pitchfork.

Meanwhile, cable's IFC showed *Trapped in the Closet*, now with ten new chapters, in heavy rotation, and Kelly continued to write for, produce, and collaborate with other artists, none seemingly troubled by the years of accusations about his sexual predation. His long-anticipated pairing with Whitney Houston finally came with the 2009 duet "I Look to You," and Kelly appeared with Houston again on the soundtrack for the 2012 film *Sparkle* (a remake of a 1976 movie about a girl group, not the singer who'd testified at his trial). In February 2012, he sang "I Look to You" at Houston's funeral. At first hesitant to embrace him, attendees responded with thunderous applause when Kelly finished the moving ballad on the altar.

During the nine years after the trial and before his next major scandals, Kelly also collaborated with R&B singers Jhené Aiko, Kelly Rowland, Jordin Sparks, and Chris Brown (years after Brown made his own headlines for assaulting pop star Rihanna); rappers Young Jeezy, Migos, Ty Dolla $ign, and fellow Chicago superstars Kanye West and Chance the Rapper; indie-rock and alt-country darling Will Oldham (for whom Kelly was, according to a profile by Kelefa Sanneh, "a living hero"), and pop stars Robin Thicke (whose hit "Blurred Lines" some critics excoriated as a paean to date rape) and Justin Bieber. Hardest to fathom, Lady Gaga scored a Top Ten hit with Kelly on "Do What U Want" in October 2013.

"You can't have my heart and you won't use my mind / But do what you want with my body," Gaga sang when she performed the duet with Kelly on *Saturday Night Live* and at the American Music Awards. For the latter, he portrayed President Clinton pursuing her Monica Lewinsky in the oval office. In her own video for the song, Gaga appeared on an examination table while Kelly played doctor, then she posed nude for fashion photographer Terry Richardson, who directed the clip and appeared in it as himself. Shortly after its release, Gaga pulled the video, because Richardson too had been accused of sexual harassment and an obsession with underage girls. Many in the music industry found it hard to believe that the whip-smart diva, a sexual assault survivor herself and a supporter of female and gay empowerment, did not know Kelly's history. Was she just pushing transgressive buttons like her role model Madonna? Did she just not care? I got no response to several requests for comment to her management.

"I have always been an R. Kelly fan and actually it is like an epic pastime in the Haus of Gaga that we just get fucked-up and play R. Kelly," Lady Gaga told MTV News circa the single's release. She added that she thought, " 'This is a real R&B song and I have to call the king of R&B. I need his blessing.' It was a mutual love. He's a very, very, very talented man. I'm so excited to be on this album with him."

R. Kelly's big year ended with one more triumph. More than any album since *Chocolate Factory*, critics enthusiastically embraced *Black Panties*, released in December 2013. On the cover, he appeared in a bandit mask while a woman naked except for the aforementioned undies sat on his lap. He bowed her like a cello. Jezebel, the ostensibly feminist Gawker sister site, hailed the disc as "a magnificent ode to pussy." Wrote critic Isha Aran, "Be prepared to be bombarded with some super-sexy R. Kelly sex. Like, more than usual. There's 'Crazy Sex,' there's sex in 'Every Position,' there's some 'Physical' sex, there's sex with the 'Lights On' . . . [and there's] a marriage proposal to a pussy."

"Kelly allows himself to be more human than the rest of us," Jordan Sargent wrote in Pitchfork. "It is not ridiculous that he wants to marry a pussy—that level of carnality exists somewhere in all of us, male or female. His brilliance is in routinely bringing out into the open the things that—with good reason!—stay in the darkest corners of our minds. In disrupting the social order, maybe his music helps preserve it as well."

Behind the scenes, Kelly faced some disruption of his own. The first blot on his big year came with an acrimonious split from manager Derrel McDavid, who had quietly steered the singer's career since Barry Hankerson left in 2000. McDavid "knew where the bodies were and he had the keys to the vault," said Cheryl Mack, one of the singer's former personal assistants. "I mean, he *really* had video. He had paperwork. He just had a baby, though, and he was done."

McDavid had partnered with many other music-biz heavyweights to drive Kelly's continued success, including Jonathan Azu of Red Light during the year of indie outreach, but the star always hated to share credit or profits. Before Azu, Kelly and McDavid worked with tough-talking Jeff Kwatinetz of the high-powered West Coast management company the Firm, whose other clients included the Backstreet Boys, Jennifer Lopez, Kelly Clarkson, and Snoop Dogg. In 2011, Kwatinetz sued Kelly for $1 million, claiming he'd been stiffed on his 15 percent commission "because the monies were needed for payments to avoid lawsuits and adverse publicity resulting from Kelly's alleged [sexual misconduct]," according to TMZ. Kelly ended that lawsuit, like so many others, with an out-of-court settlement.

The business relationship and friendship between Kelly and McDavid dated to the Public Announcement days. McDavid had also gone to Kenwood Academy, and although he was only six years older than Kelly, he looked at the singer "like a son." He didn't like his name appearing in the news. "During the trial, [McDavid] was a fixture in the courtroom," Edward McClelland wrote in *Blender*. "At the time, no one could figure out what he did. Asked his function, McDavid said, 'I don't exist.'" But for years, McDavid was there, just a step behind Kelly, at court or on the red carpet.

Six months after their split, McDavid sued Kelly for missing the $40,000 monthly payments on the $1.3 million settlement that ended their partnership, according to a story by Michelle Manchir in the *Chicago Tribune*. "McDavid has suffered significant harm as a proximate result of Kelly's breach of the settlement agreement, and is entitled to recover from Kelly the full amount owed," the lawsuit claimed in August 2014. I wrote about it for my blog at WBEZ.org, noting that the then-fifty-three-year-old manager had stood by Kelly as his staunchest defender through the singer's darkest days. McDavid read and seemed to appreciate that, and he wrote me via Facebook Messenger. "It's been a long time. You got it right this time. Thanks." I responded that I always tried to get it right, and McDavid replied, "You still covered by whatever amendment? Talk tomorrow, maybe we can meet."

We never met. I believe McDavid, inspired as ever by gangster movies, shared that exchange with the Kelly camp and used it as leverage to get his money, something along the lines of, pay up, or I'll talk to that fat fuck DeRogatis. Shortly thereafter, Kelly settled the lawsuit with McDavid. The terms and amount were not disclosed.

Before Kelly headlined Pitchfork in 2013, a booking that made McDavid especially proud, I worked with colleagues at WBEZ to post an exhaustive timeline of the singer's story from the beginning. I tried to grapple as a critic (and now a professor) with the big questions posed by Kelly's continued success. Can the ideal of separating the art from the artist apply to him, given the long list of disturbing accusations? And *should* it?

In a six-part video series called "The Kelly Conversations," I talked with fellow critics, academics, mental-health professionals, activists, and fans to wrestle with the issue. Take the most extreme examples you care to name: a clown-face painting by John Wayne Gacy, or the album Charles Manson recorded. I can't condemn you if you find beauty or pleasure in either in a vacuum, but if you know the context, and you embrace those works *because* of that context, well, you're a sick fuck and I want nothing to do with you.

Things get a lot more complicated with, say, Pablo Picasso, Woody Allen, or Bill Cosby. Like many Chicagoans, I'm proud of the sculpture in Daley Plaza; I know Picasso's history with women, but I do not see it reflected in that work of art. As a history geek, a Francophile, and a fan of Ernest Hemingway and Salvador Dalí, I love *Midnight in Paris*, but I can never watch *Manhattan* again in the wake of abuse accusations by Allen's daughter Dylan Farrow, seeing as how the movie depicts a forty-two-year-old comedy writer dating a seventeen-year-old girl. *Fat Albert* was a favorite childhood cartoon, and I still relate to the title character, but *The Cosby Show* now seems like a hypocritical lie, the perfect family it portrays serving as a jarring contrast to the star's decades-long pattern of sexual predation. And the music of R. Kelly? Well, you have your answer, and I have mine.

That's where we all wound up at the end of "The Kelly Conversations." It had been a game attempt, perhaps, but I think it ultimately failed to grasp at least one element of Kelly's appeal. Consciously or not, some people love him and his music *because of,* not *despite* his predatory behavior. After my series ran, my friend Mikki Kendall wrote a series of tweets (she's @Karnythia) hashtagged "mandingo."

"Mandingo is the myth that black people are hypersexual," Kendall further schooled me via DM. "Mandingo warrior = black men who are always ready to have sex. Black women are unrapeable . . . because of the trope that we always want sex." It's all, Kendall wrote, "a huge fetish subculture." Bigger, even, than urination.

Some of the concertgoers bounce-bounce-bouncing to "Ignition (Remix)" at Coachella, Bonnaroo, and Pitchfork in 2013 wore diapers when "I Believe I Can Fly" powered *Space Jam*. Most weren't even born yet. The only context many had for Kelly's behavior came from Dave Chappelle in reruns on Comedy Central, or maybe a then-current bit by comedian Aziz Ansari. After introducing Kelly as "a brilliant R&B singer/crazy person," Ansari went on portray a sexual Superfreak with an unquenchable libido, yet again masking a pattern predation by making us laugh. Yet if concertgoers in 2013 could claim ignorance or a lack of understanding, the promoters who booked Kelly couldn't, and those at Pitchfork bothered me most.

I'd had an at-times contentious relationship with the brain trust behind one of the most dominant voices in music criticism since the heyday of *Rolling Stone*. Pitchfork founder Ryan Schreiber and his business partner Chris Kaskie stopped talking to me after I made one too many swipes at their lack of consciousness and ethics. I gathered they were genuine, unquestioning fans of Kelly's music, thrilled to host him under their umbrella, and blithely unconcerned about his predatory behavior. Festival booker Mike Reed, a well-respected drummer on Chicago's avant-jazz scene, did the hard work of actually staging the festival, with help from volunteers in the local underground music community. Those included many of my close friends, among them former intern Anders Lindall, with whom I saw the Best of Both Worlds concert. Some had problems with Schreiber, Kaskie, and Reed "co-signing" Kelly, as the hipsters say, but Pitchfork booked him anyway.

I reviewed the 2013 Pitchfork Music Festival for my blog as usual, and I had transcendent experiences that weekend with two of my all-time favorite bands, veteran art-punks Wire and the female quartet Savages, both among the many tattooed on my arms. Then Kelly capped the weekend on Sunday night. The set found the singer Rated PG-13, with no sign of the giant bed or threesome in a cell. The Pied Piper played all or part of thirty hits, and the crowd reveled in bumping and grinding to "Sex in the Kitchen," "Flirt," and "Ignition (Remix)." For the big finale, Kelly sang "I Believe I Can Fly" and released hundreds of white dove-shaped balloons into the night sky. Then he left the stage as "Trapped in the Closet" provided a taped soundtrack for fans to file out and head home.

Irony fueled the appreciation of Kelly by some of the paying customers at Pitchfork, I concluded. The merch for sale onsite testified to that, including five-dollar bumper stickers with the singer's face and the slogans, "After Sex, I Beat My Chest Like I'm King Kong" and "Do You Mind if I Strip for You?" The very mundanity of Kelly's performance led to my second, sadder conclusion, that Schreiber, Kaskie, and who knows how many others in that dusty baseball field just didn't think what happened onstage mattered in the "real world." It was all just entertainment product to consume. *It's just music.*

As often happened, I caught shit for being moralistic, out of touch, and too fat and old to enjoy music in the summer heat anyway. Typical was a snide piece in Vice's Noisey. "DeRogatis's assessment . . . indicated a fundamental disconnect between the way he perceives music and the way we consume it today," Drew Millard wrote. "Music fans listen to R. Kelly with the same genuine enjoyment they listen to Wire. . . . Pitchfork booking R. Kelly had more to do with iconography than irony, and that's a good thing. . . . R. Kelly's life's work is to bring joy to people."

I said it then, and I'll say it again now. Fuck him. I could take pride in the derision of anyone connected to misogynistic bro-central Vice, but some tweets by fellow Chicago critic, former fanzine editor, and ardent feminist Jessica Hopper got under even my elephantine skin. Hopper and I had our critical spats over the years, but no serious music fan should respect any critic with whom they don't occasionally disagree. I welcomed any conversation about why Kelly's history shouldn't impede us from enjoying his bedroom jams. We began an email dialog that led to a lengthy in-person interview that she posted on the *Village Voice* website in late December 2013. According to editor Brian McManus, it became the most-clicked piece the vaunted alt-weekly ever published online, and the quote Jessica noted at the end of her introduction went viral. It was just me using my megaphone (one I'm privileged to have) to amplify what many black girls told me for years.

"I was one of those people who challenged DeRogatis and was even flip about his judgment, something I quickly came to regret," Hopper wrote. "DeRogatis and I have tangled—even feuded on air—over the years; yet amid the Twitter barbs, he approached me offline and told me about how one of Kelly's victims called him in the middle of the night after his Pitchfork review came out, to thank him for caring when no one else did. He told me of mothers crying on his shoulder, seeing the scars of a suicide attempt on a girl's wrists, the fear in their eyes. He detailed an aftermath that the public has never had to bear witness to. DeRogatis offered to give me access to every file and transcript he has collected in reporting this story—as he has to other reporters and journalists, none of whom has ever looked into the matter, thus relegating it to one man's personal crusade. I thought that last fact merited a public conversation about why. . . . [H]e says, ultimately, 'The saddest fact I've learned is nobody matters less to our society than young black women. *Nobody.*'"

Almost three years later, a mother in Georgia read that quote when someone tweeted it. The tweet led to Jessica's interview, which led the mother to Google my name. She read every other word I'd reported on R. Kelly that she could find online. Then she emailed me.

By 2015, R. Kelly spent only half his time in the city he called "the center of my universe." When he was in his hometown, he could often be found in the latest Chocolate Factory—after his hit album, he called every studio where he worked "the Chocolate Factory"—in a rented warehouse on North Justine Street. It stood a block away from the West Side's Union Park, site of the annual Pitchfork Music Festival. I have always been struck by how Kelly returns to the same handful of key places in his life again and again—the house at 107th and Parnell, the former YMCA building in the South Loop, the Rock 'N' Roll McDonald's. Now, he also rented an apartment in Trump Tower Chicago, which rose on North Wabash Avenue at the river in 2005, after the Trump Organization bought and demolished the old, ugly but lovable *Sun-Times* headquarters. He lived part-time at the location where I'd gotten the fax, started my reporting with Abdon Palasch, and watched the Reshona Landfair videotape with Sparkle. Did he know that?

Like a lot of aging, wealthy Chicago snowbirds, Kelly now wintered in the south. He rented a luxurious seven-bedroom French-style mansion on Old Homestead Trail in Johns Creek, a suburb thirty miles northeast of Atlanta. He also leased a four-bedroom, four-bath single-family home two miles away on Creek Wind Court. Cheryl Mack, the latest in a long and constantly revolving line of personal assistants, began working for Kelly in mid-2013, and she found both of his Georgia rental properties. She and many others told me he called the smaller home the "guest house." Mack was one of several sources Jonjelyn Savage, who goes by J., led me to when we began talking after she first emailed me.

"Hi, I am a mom of a young adult daughter who is caught up as a victim by Mr. Kelly," J. wrote on the morning of November 2, 2016. Her email arrived as I worked at home, grading papers for my Reviewing the Arts class at Columbia College Chicago. "I spoke with another parent recently, who I believe has or will be contacting you soon from Florida. I reside in Atlanta. If you can give me a contact # and a time to reach you later this evening, my husband & I will call u together with more information. This is not easy for us and we are not looking for any exposure or seeking money. I never thought my daughter would end up dealing with someone like this. He is still up to his same tactics, he just makes sure they are over 17 or 18. Kind Regards, J."

Unlike the fax, I didn't sleep on the email, and my first long conversation with J. and her husband, Tim Savage, a few hours later led to many more.

According to the Savages, the first of fourteen sources who told me the same story, six women who slept with Kelly in Georgia moved between the guest house and the Johns Creek mansion. The star denied the women, all legal age, any contact with friends and family, my sources said. He controlled every aspect of their lives, dictating what they ate, how they dressed, when they bathed, when they slept, and how they pleasured him in sexual encounters that he recorded. Kelly punished the women physically and mentally, my sources added, if they broke "his rules."

The first journalistic colleague I approached after my earliest conversations with the Savages looked at me quizzically. She didn't see a story. Tim and J.'s eldest daughter, Joycelyn (who goes by Joy) was twenty-one, over the age of consent in both Georgia and Illinois. Pop-star kinks and polyamorous behavior weren't new and weren't news, and people chose to live in a lot of alternative or nonconventional arrangements. "Have you heard of *Fifty Shades of Grey*?" my colleague asked.

I thought this was different. Perhaps because I knew Kelly, at least through years of reporting and hundreds of interviews with people who'd worked with, closely observed, and been hurt by him. I spent the next nine months reporting a story that made the case that these women might be in peril. Five news organizations passed on it before BuzzFeed News, the news organization that broke the Trump dossier, finally published it in July 2017.

Tim and J. Savage started dating in junior year of high school in Memphis, and they fell in love over burgers at a restaurant where R. Kelly's music played in the background. They went to different colleges but married before heading off to school, and on one of their weekends together, J. got pregnant with their first daughter, Joy. In time, Joy had two younger sisters, Jailynn (called Jai) and little Jori. The oldest girls sang in church. After Joy and Jai impressed the judges of an *American Idol*–like talent contest at a local shopping mall, they made it to the next round in California. The Savages scraped together a thousand dollars in entry fees and drove the whole family thirty-four hours west. "They wanted us to move there," Tim said. Instead, the dedicated but cash-strapped stage parents relocated to Atlanta, hoping to forward their girls' careers in the vibrant music scene there. The city music fans call "Hotlanta" had a lower cost of living, Tim said, and extended family lived nearby.

Tim sold cars at a Ford dealership while J. ran a small boutique in College Park, not far from Hartsfield-Jackson Atlanta International Airport. They paid for Joy to record with a producer named T.O.N.E., sent her demos to record labels, and ferried her to auditions. "Me or him would travel with Joy so she was never . . . ," J. said, and Tim completed her sentence: ". . . alone by herself." After two decades of marriage, the couple often spoke as one in a quick rush of thoughts. Tim was more focused and matter-of-fact, J. talked fast and jumped from topic to topic, and both were very emotional. We spent hours talking, but eventually I politely asked to speak to one at a time. It was just too hard keeping up with both of them on speakerphone.

While J. worked at her store, she frequently played her daughter Joy's demos, and in April 2015, a woman liked what she heard while shopping. The woman said she knew someone in R. Kelly's inner circle, and she took J.'s contact info. Excited, Tim took the call from a man who said he was Kelly's road manager. "Send me some pictures. Send me the songs." The proud father did, and that resulted in an invitation to see Kelly perform at the Atlanta Funk Fest at the Wolf Creek Amphitheater on May 15, 2015, complete with three VIP passes backstage.

J. kept a close eye on her two eldest daughters as they snacked at the backstage buffet. The watchful mom did not see one of Kelly's crew press the singer's phone number into the palms of her daughters' hands. Jai, midway through high school, threw away the tiny balled-up piece of paper. Joy, about to enter her first year of college, kept it.

A few days later, J. and Joy got another invitation, to fly to California to see Kelly perform at the Fantasy Springs Resort Casino in Indio on May 23. "When we got to go backstage with R. Kelly, we stayed there over two hours," J. told me. "One-on-one with just me and my daughter and him. We went back to talk about the music. He listened to her CD. He was going to help her with her CD, and I was really impressed with him at first, because I have always been an R. Kelly fan."

J. had heard about the accusations in Kelly's past, but he genuinely seemed to want to help her daughter pursue her love of music. "I knew the history for the teenage girls who were sixteen, fifteen, fourteen, but I think in the back of our minds, we were thinking Joy could be around him if I was with her. It didn't really hit home. Even with the Aaliyah situation, now that I think about it, 'Age Ain't Nothing but a Number,' but you don't think about that. You grew up with the song, and you like the song. I didn't think about how he is really a pedophile who married a fifteen-year-old."

After the second visit in California, Joy secretly began talking with Kelly on her cell phone. "As far as I know, we weren't talking to him anymore. Or at least *I* wasn't talking to him anymore," J. said. She paid her daughter's phone bill, and she showed me the call logs. Joy had taken a year off after graduating from Dutchtown High School in Hampton near the Savages' home in the Atlanta suburb of Smyrna. She spent that year concentrating on her music and working at a Domino's Pizza franchise, but in the late spring of 2015, Joy decided to go back to school. One weekend, according to her parents, Joy lied and told them she was making a visit to a nearby college under consideration. Instead, she flew to Oklahoma City on a trip arranged by Kelly's personal assistant, Cheryl Mack.

Joy had sex with Kelly for the first time after he performed in Oklahoma at the Cox Convention Center on June 4, 2015, she later told her parents, her college roommate, and T.O.N.E., her friend and producer. Short and thin, with high cheekbones and long, flowing black hair, Joy was naïve, a trusting, optimistic, bubbly girl who was "young for her years" at twenty-one, my sources said.

Uncertain whether Kelly believed in her talent or just wanted sex, Joy came home from Oklahoma City and asked T.O.N.E. to record her on the phone with the star. "She told me she was nervous every time she talked to him, so she wanted to put me on three-way with them so I could hear the conversation to determine what he was really about, as in wanting to help her music-wise or sexually," T.O.N.E. said. "Of course, the conversation turned sexual." Recording third-party conversations without consent is legal in Georgia, and T.O.N.E. and the Savages shared that recording, which they said showed the predator at work. I'd never heard the singer in seduction mode, and it was as troubling as some of the videos I'd seen.

"I miss my baby," Kelly said only hours after he and Joy first had sex. She chuckled. "I miss you, too."

"What do you have on right now?"

"*Um*, the clothes I had. Well, now I've changed, actually. Some pants and a shirt. I'm comfortable here."

"I want to know what kind of panties you got on."

"*Huh*?"

"I want you to get in the habit of telling me what color panties you got on every day."

"*Okay* . . . You want to know the color of my panties that I have on every day?"

"Yeah. Absolutely."

"I know you like the black," Joy said, chuckling at her allusion to the *Black Panties* album.

"You know, any panties would look good on you," Kelly said. "I'm going to teach you how to flex them little titties. It's going to be on. You seen how much came out of my dick?"

"Yeah, I did."

"You made me come so hard."

Joy tried several times to bring up her music. "I want to work with you on that song. *Hello*?" she finally said.

"Yeah, uh-huh. I will listen to that song and I will let you know. I'm more interested in developing *you*. New songs are not an issue. I always do hit songs. I always do great songs."

"Right."

"First things first. Gotta keep that character up if you're turned out."

Several of the girls I'd interviewed over the years, including Jerhonda, said Kelly used the phrase "turned out" with them, too. It can be heard as street slang for transforming a girl or young woman with minimal sexual experience into one who's much more experienced, or a pimp controlling a prostitute.

Joy did not object to the phrase. "You know I'm on it." Then Kelly scolded her for taking pictures of him on her cell phone, and made her promise she'd deleted them.

The Savages provided documentation of Joy's travels to be with Kelly, some of it sent to them by his assistant Cheryl Mack, but they had no pictures of Kelly and Joy together after their first meeting backstage in Atlanta. Taking pictures broke his "rules."

Joy enrolled at Georgia Gwinett College in Lawrenceville and started summer classes in 2016, rooming in the dorms with Torie Savode, then an eighteen-year-old nursing student. The two became fast friends. At first, Torie didn't believe Joy knew R. Kelly, she told me, but Joy started putting him on speakerphone while the two flirted and had phone sex. Joy often visited Kelly at his two houses in Johns Creek, twelve miles from college, and she sometimes traveled with him to Chicago, Torie said. During the first few weeks, Joy always returned for her classes on Tuesdays and Thursdays, but by the end of the fall semester, she stopped coming back to the dorms. Torie said Joy missed all her classes and did not take her finals. The college confirmed Joy had dropped out.

The relationship had warning signs even before Joy left school, Torie said. Joy told her roommate she was one of six women Kelly housed and slept with, and the others called her "a prude" and picked on her. "Once, I left for the weekend, but I came back early to surprise her, and she was crying. I was like, 'What the hell is going on?' That's when she told me everything." Kelly had sent a cab to pick up the girls at his guest house and bring them to an Atlanta nightclub. Joy laughed when the male driver told a joke, and one of the other girls texted Kelly to report this violation of his rules. When Joy arrived, Kelly "bent her over and he whupped her behind."

That wasn't the only time Kelly got physical, Joy told Torie. "She told me that Kells beats them. I was like, 'Excuse me?' She was like, 'He spanks us. You don't know what a spanking is?' She's twenty-one! I was like, 'Why is he spanking you?' I said, 'Has your father ever laid a hand on you?' She said no. But when they go out, they're not allowed to talk to any males. They're not allowed to speak to anybody, or they get whupped."

Kelly took the cell phone Joy's mother paid for and "threw it into the lake," Joy told her friend, replacing it with one for his use only. "She says that at night, watching TV, she has to ask if she can go to bed," Torie said, growing more upset, and eventually breaking down in tears. "That does not make sense! They have to ask to go to the bathroom, when they want to go to bed, when they want to eat." Joy's appearance started to change; she began losing weight, and she cropped her long, flowing hair short, permed what was left, and dyed it blonde. She looked like a young male prison inmate. "I was like, 'Why do you do that to your hair?' And she said, 'Kells likes it.'"

Almost fifty years old in 2016, Kelly ordered the women he housed to perform sexual acts for him, Joy told Torie. "There were threesomes multiple, multiple times—a lot of times. He makes them do stuff with each other, even if he's not involved, and she told me he's into that kinky stuff. He's really into butt plugs, that kind of weird stuff. She doesn't like it, but she's doing it. She was crying when she told me. She doesn't like it, but she won't listen about leaving him. She won't leave. It's like she's a robot. It's like she's brainwashed."

Georgia Gwinnett College was thirty-five miles from the Savages' home in Smyrna, and through the fall semester, Tim and J. only had sporadic contact with their daughter. Joy was busy, she was in school, she was making new friends, and it was all good, her parents thought. Then Joy stopped calling, stopped taking their calls, and stopped coming home to visit and do her laundry. Eventually she missed birthday parties, holiday dinners, her sister Jai's high-school graduation, and even family funerals.

R. Kelly had followed *Black Panties* with a lackluster sequel in 2015, *The Buffet*. His latest album—and, as it would turn out, his last for RCA/Sony Music—had been *12 Nights of Christmas*, released in time for the 2016 holidays. He appeared on *The Tonight Show Starring Jimmy Fallon* on December 23, 2016, garnering a bro hug from the host who also tussled Donald Trump's hair. Independent publicist Carise Yatter hyped the album by cheerfully quoting Kelly. "How am I spending my Christmas holidays? I'm going with the traditional, you know? I like to spend the Christmas holidays with my family and friends." That December 25, Joy sent her parents a one-sentence text. "I hate Christmas has to be this way this year." It's one of the last times they heard from her directly.

J. closed her store and became a relentless amateur private detective. She reached out to everyone in her daughter's life and Kelly's former circle, and one person led to another, each adding pieces of the puzzle. The Savages also filed a missing person report with the Georgia Gwinnett College campus police, but I got the same response they did: The school couldn't do anything because Joy's parents knew where she was, and she was of legal age to go where and do what she pleased. A lawyer told the Savages he couldn't help, either; they had no standing to sue Kelly.

J. and Tim also called police in Georgia and Chicago and asked for well-being checks on Joy at Kelly's addresses. "DOOR OPEN/HOUSE CLR/NO ONE THERE," Officer Michael Carter wrote in the Georgia police report, two days after Christmas, 2016. Police never returned to the guest house to follow up. A few weeks later, shortly before noon on January 30, 2017, three officers visited Kelly's recording studio on North Justine Street in Chicago. Led by Sergeant Dion Trotter, head of the Child Protection Response Unit for the Cook County Sheriff's Office and an instructor in its human-trafficking program, they surveyed the perimeter of the two-story brick industrial building, noting the iron bars on the windows and the video cameras lining the exterior. One of Kelly's assistants came to the door when they rang the buzzer, then he summoned Joy to speak to the officers.

"JOYCELYN SAVAGE RELATED THAT SHE WAS FINE AND DID NOT WANT TO BE BOTHERED WITH HER PARENTS," Sergeant Trotter wrote in his report. (Cops universally love all-caps.) "JOYCELYN SAVAGE FURTHER RELATED THAT SHE KEEPS IN CONTACT WITH HER MATERNAL GRANDMOTHER." The Chicago sheriff's deputies took no further action. "I'm gravely concerned about her," Joy's grandmother told my editor at BuzzFeed News, Marisa Carroll.

The last time the Savages saw their daughter, a few weeks before that text on Christmas Day, 2016, they attempted what they called an "intervention." She'd told them she needed some things from home, and the whole family as well as Joy's friend and college roommate Torie had gathered in the Savages' kitchen when she arrived. Her hair shorn and dyed blonde, Joy looked like a boy in baggy gray sweatpants and a hoodie, but she smiled and dismissed everyone's concerns. "It was as if she was brainwashed," J. said. "Joy looked like a prisoner; it was horrible. I hugged her and hugged her, but she just kept saying she's in love and he is the one who cares for her. I don't know what to do. I hope that if I get her back, I can get her treatment for victims of cults, they can reprogram her, but I wish I could have stopped it from happening."

When I wrote the first drafts of my story, I struggled with the words to describe the situation. "Cult" and "brainwashed" seemed bizarre, even melodramatic, but those were the words my sources used, and they were repeated by Georgia and Chicago police in the reports about their cursory well-being checks. I only realized months later that "brainwashed" had been the word Gerri Cruz had used fourteen years earlier, when she told *Sun-Times* columnist Mary Mitchell she thought R. Kelly "controlled" her daughter Andrea.

Tim Savage said he and his wife decided to go public with their story because nothing else seemed to help, and they felt as if they had nowhere else to turn. "It's not about my daughter per se, it's about all the girls," Tim said. "The abuse that my daughter is actually enduring, nobody should go through."

A few weeks after I began talking to the Savages, I also started speaking with the parents in Florida who J. mentioned in her first email. By then, the story Angelo and Alice Clary told me about their daughter seemed eerily familiar. Curly-haired, cherubic, and tiny, Azriel had the voice of an angel at age seventeen, many people told me, and when I watched her home videos singing opera as well as pop songs on YouTube, I had to agree. Music gave her strength and provided an outlet, but it wasn't always enough. She suffered from depression, and in the spring of 2015, she tried to hurt herself.

The Clarys lived in Polk County, not far from Disney World. A construction manager who grew up tough on the streets, Angelo Clary, like Tim Savage, seethed with anger but stayed focused during our interviews. Like J. Savage, Alice Clary was excitable, but less scattered, and more hesitant to talk at first. Angelo decided to speak on the record right away, but Alice took a few weeks to reach the same decision. They disagreed a lot about how to handle the situation with their daughter. Both had some troubles with the law in their past, but their love for each other and their children was obvious, and nothing they told me failed to check out or lacked corroboration. Both used the words "so stupid" when they talked about how they felt about believing Kelly when he first told them he'd make their daughter a star.

"My thing was, I *trusted*," Alice said. "I have never been in the music industry before, ever, and he is a lyrical genius. He is R. Kelly! And the fact is, he went to court, he was never found guilty, he was acquitted, and we were led to believe there was no truth in it."

The Clarys bought three tickets to see Kelly perform at Funk Fest in Orlando during the Black Panties tour on April 18, 2015. They had promised to take their oldest daughter, A'lceis, but they didn't want to leave Azriel home alone in her fragile state, so they took her instead. "During the show, they were pulling people out of the audience," Alice recalled. "A guy said, 'Oh yeah, *her*.' He pulled her up onstage." After the show, a member of Kelly's crew passed Azriel the singer's phone number. Her parents didn't believe it was really Kelly's number, and they got no answer when they called. "Then I guess he must have got back later on or texted her later on," Alice said.

The relationship between Kelly and Azriel developed over phone calls and texts she kept secret from her parents. "And then one day we were looking for her because she should've been coming home from school," Alice told me. "Finally, we get a text message saying that she's okay, that she had met up with R. Kelly in his hotel, and I'm like, 'You met up with R. Kelly at his *hotel*?'" The Clarys rushed to the hotel and called Orlando police, who told them to deal with hotel security. They did, and their daughter finally came down to the lobby, but Kelly refused to talk to them. Angelo and Alice took Azriel home.

"After that, she was only talking to him when one of us was around," Alice said. Like the Savages, the Clarys believed Kelly would help Azriel find a career pursuing her love of music. They vowed to be more careful. "We needed to make sure it was about music, because he was going to mentor her," Alice said. "And then from there he wanted her to travel with him so she could see how the music game really was. We thought it could be an opportunity and that she was going to be with a guardian, a female guardian that would keep an eye on her." The Clarys trusted that the guardian, one of Kelly's handlers in the inner circle, would look out for their daughter. "So stupid," Angelo said.

"We allowed her to go, but we were kind of nervous about her situation," Alice continued. "And that's the messed-up part. She had been lying to us the whole time, and a relationship that was supposed to be about music had turned sexual." The Clarys told me Azriel admitted she began having sex with Kelly in 2015, when she was seventeen, a year below the age of consent in Florida. "It's a situation of this guy is very good at what he does," Alice said, "and what he does is seduce people into being abused." Azriel never came home from her travels with the singer, and the sources I developed said she became his "favorite" among the six women he housed in Atlanta and Chicago, "his number-one-girl."

The Clarys tried to intervene to bring Azriel home the first time in late August 2015. They sent their oldest daughter, A'lceis, to Chicago, believing the Kelly camp would be more likely to trust her than two angry parents. A'lceis went to his recording studio on Ohio Street downtown; Kelly had not yet moved the Chocolate Factory to North Justine Street. She got into a loud argument when she started fighting with the star and his crew, demanding to see her sister. "You need to shut the hell up with all this noise. I don't do drama. You're making a scene," Alice heard Kelly tell A'lceis when her older daughter held her cell phone up during the fight. Alice called the police. When CPD arrived at the front door, Azriel was no longer there. A'lceis came home alone.

The Clarys later filed a police report in Chicago, when a lawyer advised them that could help. CPD took no action. The Clarys said they also got nowhere when they tried to get Florida police to investigate Kelly's relationship with Azriel, which began when she was underage. Polk County officers investigated but also took no action. After the Savages met for hours with FBI Agent Kelly Jo Strickler in Georgia, the Clarys talked to her at length, too. She wouldn't talk to me and referred me to an FBI spokesman, who would neither confirm nor deny an investigation.

Like Joy Savage, Azriel Clary felt more comfortable talking to her father than to her mother, and he got a few calls after she began living with Kelly.

In July 2017, Azriel said Kelly wanted to invite him to a concert in Indiana, where the two of them could talk "man to man." Wary of Kelly's motives, Angelo did not accept the invitation. Then Azriel told her dad some news: Kelly had recently paid for her to have breast enhancement surgery. The Savages later learned that Joy had the surgery, too.

"I am beyond furious," Angelo told me. "I said to her, 'How could you *do* this? What the *hell* were you thinking? What if you died on the operating table?' I don't even know what we can do anymore. I just know we got to get her home." He paused and took a deep breath. "I'm filled with anger and rage," Angelo continued, in a tone that convinced me I wouldn't want to be on the receiving end of those emotions. "I do believe she has been brainwashed. She's starstruck and believes he will help her do the things she's dreamed about. But she's not doing anything, not singing, *nothing*, and I just don't know what we can do."

For a long time, Alice didn't want to act rashly. "I have read some tried to kill themselves because he no longer deals with them," she said of Kelly's girlfriends. "I desperately want my daughter back, but what will the repercussions be if she doesn't come willingly? These girls think this man loves them." She broke down in tears. "We've had deaths in the family, birthdays, and I haven't heard from her and she hasn't been here for any of it. I didn't even hear from her on Mother's Day [in 2017]. All I want to do is bring her home."

The Clarys themselves tried again to bring Azriel home in May 2018. They flew to Chicago, rented a car, and drove to Kelly's new studio on North Justine Street. There, they argued with two of his omnipresent security guards, who called Chicago police. The cops threatened to arrest the Clarys for causing a disturbance, they told me, and the officers would not take a police report or conduct a well-being check. Angelo said the responding officers seemed to know and were friendly with Kelly's security. "This has got to end. They're all in his pocket and nobody's doing anything."

CPD's top spokesman told me off-duty officers are not required to report who they work for part-time, although they carry their badge and service sidearm. For years, activists for police reform have called this a recipe for conflicts of interest, and and it's one of the rare criticisms in which they're joined by CPD brass. Chicago's powerful police union fights to keep the policy in place. I'd long heard some officers in Chicago and Olympia Fields worked security for Kelly, and department rules didn't stop them from doing it or require them to tell anyone about it.

A few hours after their visit to North Justine Street, Azriel called her parents via FaceTime. She said she was fine and just wanted to be left alone. It was almost the same language Joy Savage used when she made a YouTube video telling her parents to leave her and Kelly alone. "Like they was following a script," Tim said. "Yep," Angelo agreed. In the FaceTime chat, Azriel said Kelly was the only person who really loved and cared about her. Then she wished Alice a happy Mother's Day and hung up.

Three other key sources contributed to my first story about what a police report had called "THE R. KELLY CULT." The singer's former personal assistant Cheryl Mack told me a lot about her time working for Kelly and how she saw him mistreat the women he housed. Two of those women, Asante McGee and Kitti Jones, spoke to me for the first time about what they experienced while living with what they had also come to call the "cult." All of them said they believed Kelly had a problem, and he had to stop.

Girls initially think, "This is R. Kelly, I'm going to live a lavish lifestyle," Cheryl Mack said. "No. You have to ask for food. You have to ask to go use the bathroom. . . . He is a master at mind control. . . . He is a puppet master." Kelly ordered the women he housed to dress in jogging suits because "he doesn't want their figures to be exposed; he doesn't want them to look appealing" to anyone else, she said. When other men entered the room, "he made the girls turn around and face the wall in their jogging suits because he doesn't want them to be looked at by anyone else."

A Tennessee native who juggled corporate jobs with freelance artist management, Mack met Kelly at the 2004 MTV Video Music Awards in Miami. Three artists she represented wound up having sexual relationships with the star over the next decade, she said. The first was an artist in her thirties. The second was a seventeen-year-old singer from Chicago's West Side then living in Atlanta. Mack said Kelly took the young singer's virginity, and when her relationship with him ended a year later, "she tried to slit her wrists on several occasions, and she drove her car in the middle of traffic in Chicago." Other sources confirmed that story.

The young singer and her mother approached Susan Loggans. Citing attorney-client privilege, the lawyer who'd made a specialty of settling complaints by underage girls with Kelly declined as usual to comment, but Mack said Kelly's attorney Ed Genson and manager Derrel McDavid "worked their magic to get [the singer] and her mother paid off, $750,000. This is what Robert told me. At the time, he was such a big hit for that FIFA Cup, he didn't want the publicity, so he settled."

After Kelly's first trip to South Africa in 2009, he returned the next year to perform at the opening ceremony of the 2010 World Cup. "I see the light at the end of the tunnel," he sang in "Sign of a Victory," his newest anthemic single. "And I can feel heaven in its place."

At Kelly's suggestion, Mack paired the young singer she represented with a nineteen-year-old songwriter she met at an Atlanta club called the Twelve. "She looked like an Aaliyah. She had a beautiful voice and her potential in terms of being a writer was amazing." The star began a sexual relationship with the songwriter after Mack began to represent her, Mack said, and the songwriter also became a member of the cult. "She looks awful. He dresses her up in sweats, threw her in a room, and threw away the key. She doesn't write anymore. She doesn't record any music. She does absolutely nothing. She's a servant to Robert. It's so sad."

Though Mack said Kelly's behavior troubled her, she accepted his offer in mid-2013 to serve as his personal assistant. Like many before her, she thought she could change him. "I really, honestly, *did* want to help him. I felt like I was the one who was going to." Though some of the women in the cult were in their twenties or thirties, Mack used the word "girls" because "Robert makes all of them dress up like little girls, just all kinds of little-girl outfits, barrettes and scrunchies and things like that." He orchestrated threesomes and sometimes demanded the girls have sex with him in front of others. During one of those scenes, Mack said he told the young singer she represented, " 'If you want to learn and engage an audience, you have to learn it right *here*.' "

After a year and a half and a credit on the *Black Panties* album, Mack split from the singer in the summer of 2015. "I felt like I had enough. He was saying things like, 'Cheryl was in control of my whole life.' He did the same thing he did with Derrel [McDavid] and everybody else. 'She was taking my money.'" Mack denied that allegation. She'd signed a nondisclosure agreement with Kelly, but she initially said she was not afraid to talk to me. She also sent me a copy of what she called her "book," a five-page narrative PDF with names, dates, and incidents, almost all of which I corroborated.

"Maybe I should be scared, but I fear more for the girls," Mack told me. Then, after several on-the-record conversations and a lot of forwarded documentation, she said she'd changed her mind about telling her story. She threatened to sue if I used her name in any story I reported. BuzzFeed's media lawyers told her it didn't work that way, and the story ran with the information she had freely shared with me on the record. As of this writing, Mack has not spoken publicly about Kelly again, but before she went silent, she confirmed that two other women had been a part of the cult. I connected with them after they, too, first spoke to J. Savage.

Thirty-seven when we first talked, Asante McGee grew up in New Orleans but had lived in Atlanta for a decade when she met R. Kelly and started a year-long sexual relationship with him that ended in the summer of 2016. A member of the star's entourage invited her backstage during the Black Panties tour, and she and Kelly began exchanging text messages and phone calls. Early on, "he asked me if I was sure I wanted to be in his world, because his world is not like any other world. I was like, 'Yes, I'm sure,'" she told me. She believed he loved her, and she loved him. "I used to travel and go to different shows and stuff, and he actually introduced me to the other girls" in the cult, including the woman he called his "trainer." She was the same woman Jerhonda Johnson had met.

The trainer bragged of starting her sexual relationship with Kelly when she was fifteen, and of being friends in high school with Reshona Landfair. McGee watched Kelly having sex with the trainer, who was thirty at the time. "She entered one of the doors—you have to knock; you need his permission—and he told her to come in. He called her a b[itch]. He said, 'B[itch], get down on your knees.' She came in the room butt-naked, and she got on her knees in a dog position and he was just asking her questions like, 'How long have you been with me? How many shows have you gone to?' He was asking those questions and she was answering, and then he was like, 'Okay, b[itch], get up,' and he told her to suck his, *you know*."

McGee never saw Kelly hit any of the girls he called his "babies," but she did witness what she called other kinds of abuse for breaking his rules. "He left Azriel on the bus for like three days, and she was not allowed to come out." He criticized her for not doing her homework, even though Azriel wasn't in school. Kelly did not physically abuse McGee, but she said she did experience "mental abuse and sexual abuse. He would try to make me believe these things. He would try to feed your head with a lot of things . . . You want to satisfy him so bad and wanted his approval that you were willing to go to any level."

Kelly took video of their sexual encounters, which surprised McGee at first. "When I saw the light flashing, it took me by surprise, and I was like, 'What?' He would put it on his phone, iPad, whatever is near, and he'd show his friends." She said he orchestrated threesomes with her and another of the girls, and he demanded acts of "sexual humiliation that I didn't approve of . . . I don't care about your sexual preferences, but for you wanting me to do these things to you, I just couldn't get with it. It bothered me."

Those acts and the realization that her housemate Azriel Clary was only seventeen prompted McGee to begin rethinking her relationship with Kelly. "I have a seventeen-year-old daughter myself, and I think that was the biggest wake-up call. When I saw Azriel with him, it took me back. This could be *my* daughter. I just knew that it was not right, and I just couldn't understand what a man almost fifty is doing having sex with someone the same age as his daughter. That's when I realized it was more of a mind-control thing. He likes when you talk like a little girl. When Azriel was doing sexual stuff with him, he wanted her to sound like a little girl, so the whole voice would have to change."

"Everything was building up," McGee said. The end came after Kelly berated her for wearing shorts and a tank top instead of a jogging suit on a one-hundred-and-two-degree summer day. "In my head then, I'm *gone*."

Echoing what Kelly's friend Kim Dulaney had written years earlier in her book *Star Struck*, McGee concluded Robert was the sweetest person you could meet, but R. Kelly "was a monster."

Kitti Jones told a similar story, but she said Kelly did hit her during a relationship that lasted from 2011 to 2013. "I was in a situation where I felt trapped. I gave up everything for that, and it wasn't worth it." As a radio personality with 97.9-FM The Beat in Dallas, she met the singer when the Love Letter tour played the Verizon Theatre in Grand Prairie, Texas, on June 19, 2011. Kelly gave her his number and they began talking and texting. Eventually, she quit her job to join him, lured by his offer to dance onstage as part of the threesome in the cell. Thirty-five at the time, she said she looked twenty-two. "That's what attracted him, because he was really shocked when he found out I was a little older than I looked."

Over time, Kelly introduced Jones to the other women in what she also called the cult. The first woman she met, who was then nearing age thirty, was Reshona Landfair. As in the past, when approached in 2017, Reshona declined to speak to me in advance of the BuzzFeed News article. "I asked him, 'How long have you known 'Shona?'" Jones told me. "He said, 'I don't like people asking me my business, but I raised her.' Those were his words." Jones later sought out and watched the infamous video for which Kelly was tried and acquitted. "It registered to me at that moment what I was watching. *That* was the girl he introduced me to. She never stopped coming around the whole time that I was living in Chicago."

Several incidents prompted Jones to leave in September 2013. "I got tired of the abuse and I got tired of feeling like I was just there whenever he needed sex. I had to put up with all of these things," including sex acts that made her uncomfortable. "I was too afraid to share these things with friends and family that cared about me. I was really going through hell." Kelly made her perform in threesomes with the other girls, she said, and he filmed their sexual activities. Then, in the spring of 2013, she and several of the girls ate with him at a Subway restaurant down the block from the Ohio Street recording studio. Jones claimed Kelly took offense when she chatted with the male cashier, dragged her outside, threw her against a tree, and kicked, choked, and slapped her.

"I couldn't believe that he was bold enough to do that in open broad daylight in front of people. Sure, somebody out here knew it was R. Kelly, but maybe they didn't think it was, because who would be that bold to do that if you're someone people can recognize?" Jones endured other alleged incidents of physical abuse. She initially spoke to me off the record, only deciding to let me use her name not long before BuzzFeed News published the story.

Despite months of reporting with fourteen sources on the record and extensive corroborating documentation, the story about Kelly's cult proved more difficult to publish than any in my career. That period provides a case study of the troubled state of journalism circa 2017. I worked at length with three news organizations, all of which provided additional reporting help, and I got far down the line with editing, fact-checking, and legal vetting at each before executives above the level of the editors I worked with decided not to publish. Desperate to bring their daughters Joy and Azriel home, the Savages and the Clarys contacted me several times a week throughout that long wait. They started to give up hope that the media would amplify their frustrated pleas for help. At times, so did I.

I spent a month doing my initial reporting after J. Savage first emailed me on November 2, 2016. Then I contacted Jessica Hopper, who'd interviewed me about R. Kelly's troubled history for the *Village Voice*. She had become executive editor at MTV News, and on December 6, she agreed to publish the story once we finished it. The broadcast channel had long since replaced music videos with reality-TV trash such as *The Real World* and *16 and Pregnant*, but one of its rotating corporate regimes had decided to create a forum for long-form cultural journalism and criticism online. Eventually, Hopper hit roadblocks with the corporate overlords at Viacom Media Networks. They wanted to break the story in a half-hour documentary, and the legal department balked at indemnifying a freelance reporter.

"Every part of it had hit a snag that I wasn't positive I could untangle," Hopper later told me. "That's when I said, 'Go ahead and walk with it.' I felt horrible." She left MTV four months later.

Editor Jake Malooley had been asking me to contribute to the *Chicago Reader*, and his deputy Robin Amer had been a colleague at WBEZ. The alt-weekly had recently published a long investigative story about sexual harassment at the vaunted Profiles Theatre, shaking the Chicago theater scene. The *Reader* was owned at the time by Michael Ferro, a digital entrepreneur with a short attention span and grandiose visions who'd purchased the *Sun-Times* after James Tyree died in 2011. Publisher and editor in chief Jim Kirk, a veteran of the *Chicago Tribune*, oversaw both papers, and the *Sun-Times* had of course published all of the original reporting about Kelly that I did with Abdon Pallasch. I met with Amer, Malooley, and Kirk in the same conference room at the new *Sun-Times* offices at 350 North Orleans where I'd been told I had three options the night before I appeared in court during the trial.

I worked on the story with Amer from mid-February 2017 until early May. Maya Dukmasova contributed additional reporting, and the piece was vetted by that silver-haired legal Galahad, Damon Dunn. Then Kirk decided not to publish. "We felt at the time the story as turned in needed more sourcing," he later told me. He left the papers a few months later, not long before Ferro bought the *Tribune* as the controlling owner of a corporation he renamed tronc, then he sold both the *Sun-Times* and the *Reader*. Those deals loomed in the background; my story was controversial, and controversy is bad for corporate dealings. Eventually, Ferro lost control of tronc and the *Trib* and put those up for sale, too, after sexual harassment allegations surfaced about him in March 2018.

From May through mid-July 2017, I worked with my colleagues at WBEZ to post the cult story on the website that hosted my blog of music news and criticism. Chicago Public Radio has a long, proud tradition of hard-hitting audio journalism—local stories as well as pieces for *This American Life*, which originated at the station—but it had never run a textual story so long, controversial, and complicated. Three editors worked with me through several more drafts, and Dunn vetted the story again. Early on July 11, Michael Lansu, as dogged a reporter as my old pal Abdon, made the necessary calls seeking comment from Kelly's label, RCA/Sony Music, and his current lawyer, Chicago attorney Linda Mensch. We did not want them to know I was the primary reporter—yet. Lansu outlined the damning allegations in the piece, set to post at noon on July 12. Executives at RCA/Sony Music declined to comment, but Mensch gave us a statement.

> We can only wonder why folks would persist in defaming a great artist who loves his fans, works 24/7, and takes care of all of the people in his life. He works hard to become the best person and artist he can be. It is interesting that stories and tales debunked many years ago turn up when his goal is to stop the violence; put down the guns; and embrace peace and love. I suppose that is the price of fame. Like all of us, Mr. Kelly deserves a personal life. Please respect that.

Ultimately, Chicago Public Radio CEO Goli Sheikholeslami, whom I respect and admire, decided not to publish the story on WBEZ.org. "My recollection is we needed more time to further fact-check the story," she later told me, "but we were sensitive to your desire to publish swiftly based on concerns that you'd be scooped when some of your exclusive sources held a press conference. At that point, we mutually agreed that you would approach other media outlets with the piece. Once BuzzFeed agreed to work on the story, we were all glad it was able to get in front of a national audience."

Frustrated, as I was, with the difficulties of publishing the story after nine months of reporting, the Savages planned to call every news organization in Atlanta and camp out in front of the guest house in Johns Creek if that's what it took to get people to pay attention to their efforts to bring Joy home. I did not care about getting scooped. My immediate problem that Wednesday afternoon was that the Kelly camp knew what the story contained and that it would be published soon (I hoped). I worried that Joy and Azriel or their parents could face retaliation. I made two calls to editors I knew at the *Chicago Tribune* and the *Los Angeles Times*, both of whom said their papers could not move quickly with the piece, if at all.

I generally avoided the typical celebrity fluff and shallow clickbait of BuzzFeed's home page, but BuzzFeed News had been doing some of the most impressive journalism of the Trump era. Editor Shani Hilton and I had never talked, but I appreciated a story she and Aylin Zafar posted on the site in 2013 under the headline "R. Kelly's Alleged Sexual Assaults and Why No One's Talking About It." We connected Thursday morning, and BuzzFeed News wanted the story. I worked nonstop on final fact-checking and editing for the next four days with a brilliant editor, Marisa Carroll, and the same legal team that had worked on the site's blockbuster story about Christopher Steele's Trump-Russia dossier in January 2017. The story finally posted under the headline "Inside the Pied Piper of R&B's 'Cult' " at 7:02 a.m. on Monday, July 17.

As always, there is context. "Call it the Gawker effect," *Washington Post* media columnist Margaret Sullivan wrote a week after my story posted.

British journalist and digital entrepreneur Nick Denton had launched Gawker in 2002 as "the source for daily Manhattan media news and gossip," and he built a new-media empire as famous for its snark as its scoops. The company crashed in mid-2016 after a $140 million judgment in a suit brought by wrestler Hulk Hogan (real name Terry Bollea) when Gawker posted video of him having sex with a woman married to his friend Todd Clem, a radio host known as Bubba the Love Sponge. Silicon Valley billionaire Peter Thiel, a major donor to the campaign of a new president who'd bragged that his celebrity allowed him to "grab them by the pussy," bankrolled Hogan's legal action, allegedly aggrieved because one of Gawker's sister sites had mentioned his homosexuality. Absent malice in intentionally publishing a story a news organization knows to be untrue, American law makes it very difficult to libel public figures, but the new verdict from the federal court in Florida set a precedent that even household names can successfully sue for "an unreasonable invasion of privacy," a nebulous and dangerous new standard.

"Plenty of people were disgusted by Gawker's airing of the Hulk Hogan sex tape," Margaret Sullivan wrote in the *Post*, "and, as a result, not unhappy to see the site go out of business. But some of them would be less pleased to know that a story like the R. Kelly reporting—or many others that we don't know about—might never see the light of day. [Fear] can result in self-censorship at any stage of a story's development, maybe before it ever gets out of a reporter's notebook, or in the hour before planned publication."

My first BuzzFeed story did not name Joy Savage or Azriel Clary, because we considered them victims of sexual abuse, and it did not name their parents, because naming them would identify their daughters. Numerous sources confirmed the identities of the four other women who until recently had been living with Kelly, but we did not name them, either. We described the other members of the cult only as a nineteen-year-old model; a thirty-one-year-old "den mother" who "trained" newcomers on Kelly's rules and how he liked to be pleasured sexually; a twenty-five-year-old woman who had been part of the singer's circle for seven years—Dominique Gardner would later go public—and an Atlanta songwriter, the woman whom Cheryl Mack had represented and introduced to Kelly.

Later the day the story published, Tim and J. Savage spoke to the media outside one of the two homes Kelly rented in Johns Creek. Asante McGee joined them; she *had* been named in the story, along with Kitti Jones and Mack. Angelo and Alice Clary did not go public until several months later.

In stark contrast to the first Kelly story that Abdon Pallasch and I published in the dead-tree *Sun-Times* in December 2000—a dramatically different era—the cult story instantly spread far and wide thanks to social media. BuzzFeed charted more than six hundred "media pick-ups," online and in print, and I did more than forty print and broadcast interviews in the first week after publication. I kept talking because I wanted people to care about Joy and Azriel.

As I prepared to go live with Canadian public broadcasting from a studio at WBEZ two days after the story ran, my phone rang. My stepfather, Harry Reynolds, the man who gave me his set of Slingerland drums and who encouraged me to always carry a handkerchief, had been struggling with Alzheimer's in a specialized care facility. He died shortly before the scheduled start of my interview with CBC Radio. I thought about canceling it and all the others scheduled for the next two days, but I'd made Harry's arrangements in advance. My brother called our mom, and my wife and daughter sat with her until I finally got there that evening.

My stepdad had spent the last thirty years of his career working with students just a little younger than Joy and Azriel in the public schools of some of the poorest neighborhoods in Jersey City. He had been the kind of teacher who'd take off his tie and give it to a boy to wear to the science fair, and who'd pass his lunch to a girl who didn't have one. The pain Kelly had caused so many girls for so long had grabbed the spotlight. I thought that talking about it was exactly what Harry would have wanted me to do, and I hoped I did him proud.

I also kept reporting. Six weeks later, BuzzFeed News published my story about Jerhonda Pace, née Johnson. The next spring, Lizzette Martinez spoke publicly to me for the first time about her underage relationship with Kelly and the miscarriage she endured alone in a Chicago hotel room when she was a teenager. That story also quoted Chicagoan Michelle Kramer. She said her daughter had been part of Kelly's cult since she and her best friend, Jerhonda, partied at his mansion in 2009. We did not name Kramer's daughter Dominique Gardner, but her mother later did. "Being silent is not the answer, so I said, 'It's time,'" Kramer told me. "I want my child home. I don't know what hold he has on her, but her last words to me was, 'Don't ever give up on me.'"

Although they often felt isolated and ignored, activists had never given up on protesting Kelly's predatory behavior. Launched in the summer of 2017 by Kenyette Tisha Barnes and Oronike Odeleye, a new crusade called #MuteRKelly succeeded in forcing the cancellation of eleven of his concerts over its first fifteen months. Their goal was to stop Kelly from hurting women by shutting down the income that had enabled him, stopping his ability to record or perform. In May 2018, Time's Up, the movement formed by Hollywood celebrities to fight sexual harassment in the wake of allegations about Harvey Weinstein, joined Barnes and Odeleye to release a strongly worded statement supported by, among others, directors Ava DuVernay and Shonda Rhimes, musicians John Legend and Questlove, and Tarana Burke, who had founded #MeToo in 2006.

"As women of color within Time's Up, we recognize that we have a responsibility to help right this wrong," the women in the organization wrote, and they demanded action by industry enablers such as RCA/Sony Music, Live Nation/Ticketmaster, Spotify, and Apple Music. They also called for criminal investigations.

"Kelly's music is a part of American and African-American culture that should never—and will never—be silenced," Kelly's camp fired back. No one working for the star put their name to the statement; his latest spokeswoman, Trevian Kutti, had recently resigned. "Since America was born, black men and women have been lynched for having sex or for being accused of it. We will vigorously resist this attempted public lynching of a black man who has made extraordinary contributions to our culture."

Some close to Kelly whispered to reporters that the girls he housed were runaways eager to escape difficult home lives, and the singer simply took pity on them. Those who left and spoke out against him were either jealous or looking for a payoff. I'd heard these arguments on occasion since late 2000, and it was impossible to believe that so many women had been lying about so many things for so much time. Kelly's critics certainly didn't buy that.

"It's going to take the black community to fully embrace the idea of R. Kelly being a predator, and to understand that even if the girls are now twenty-one or eighteen, it's still predatory behavior and that he shouldn't be celebrated in our community," Tarana Burke told me for another piece I wrote for BuzzFeed News in the spring of 2018. The problem, Kenyette Tisha Barnes added, is that people "don't give a damn about black girls," the majority of Kelly's alleged victims. "The bottom line is that R. Kelly . . . is the greatest example of a predator in that he went after the most vulnerable that no one cares about."

By the end of 2018, the FBI and local law enforcement agencies in suburban Atlanta, Chicago, Olympia Fields, and Polk County, Florida, still hadn't acted, despite hours of interviews with the parents and others in my stories, and seven complaints the Savages, the Clarys, and Jerhonda had filed against Kelly since 2016. Joy Savage released a second video through the Kelly camp's favorite pipeline, TMZ, once again claiming she was fine. This time, Dominique Gardner appeared at her side. Dominique would not go public about her nine years in what everyone now calls "the cult" until March 2019, the same time Azriel Clary first spoke publicly in an interview with Gayle King on CBS *This Morning*.

After the BuzzFeed News story, I received many inquiries about working with proposed documentaries; all of them wanted to be the next *Making a*

Murderer or *The Jinx*. The producers of Lifetime's *Surviving R. Kelly*, Bunim/ Murray, pursued me the most aggressively, but I declined for two reasons. BuzzFeed wanted to make a film, and given the support the organization had shown me, I didn't want to work with anyone else at the time. Bunim/ Murray also were the schlockmeisters behind *The Real World* and *Keeping Up with the Kardashians,* and I saw the blurring of reality and entertainment and the pursuit of celebrity *über alles* as part of the cultural disease that enabled Kelly. dream hampton was not yet connected with the project, and I had no confidence Bunim/Murray would do journalism, not sensationalism.

In the end, dream and her team contributed something enormously important with *Surviving R. Kelly*, which ran during the first week of a new year, 2019, and which broke viewership records for Lifetime. For nearly two decades, I had talked with women who told me how Kelly had abused them, and I'd interviewed most of the people who appeared in the series (including the former Kelly assistant shown in silhouette with an altered voice, one of two who held that position after Cheryl Mack). Thanks to dream, for six hours, viewers saw and heard these women speaking directly to them, and it made a difference.

When I was writing the first *Sun-Times* story in December 2000, the recent issue of *Vibe* magazine with dream's cover story about Kelly sat on my desk. About two months earlier, she'd spent several days in Chicago with the singer, waiting in and around the recording studio for him to grant her an interview. Talking to Jessica Goldstein of ThinkProgress in 2019, dream said she hadn't thought about the ages of the young women she saw hovering around Kelly until a month or two later, when the first *Sun-Times* story came out. "Not only did I immediately realize, 'Wow, I missed the whole story,' it's like being at Jeffrey Dahmer's house and being like, 'Fuck, I should've opened this fridge.'" In early 2019, more people than ever finally opened the door.

CHAPTER 15

RECKONING

During the reporting that led to this book, I learned the names of forty-eight women whose lives R. Kelly has significantly damaged and sometimes destroyed. They include Tiffany Hawkins, Jovante Cunningham, Aaliyah Haughton, Lizzette Martinez, Andrea Kelly (née Lee), Tracy Sampson, Patrice Jones, Maxine Daniels, Deleon Richards, Montina Woods, Reshona Landfair, Lisa Van Allen, Jerhonda Pace (née Johnson), Dominique Gardner, Kitti Jones, Asante McGee, Halle Calhoun, Azriel Clary, Joy Savage, Faith Rodgers, and others whose names have never become public. There's good reason to believe there are many more.

Just as disturbing, I put the number of people who knew about or witnessed that damage in the thousands. Among them are the employees of record labels, recording studios, independent publicity firms, concert promotion companies, music venues, rehearsal studios, radio stations, video outlets, magazines, websites, and newspapers. Many of these people were on his personal payroll: musicians, deejays, personal assistants, lawyers, accountants, spokespeople, tour managers, roadies, drivers, and security guards. Then there were the workers at Kelly's favorite hotels, restaurants, high-end gyms, and nightclubs, and the artists he produced, wrote for, and recorded with, as well as the directors of his videos and the many members of their crews.

Many of them knew, and many allowed him to continue, because he was a musical genius, an artist, and (perhaps most important) a lucrative hitmaker. Some actively enabled him, passing phone numbers to girls so their parents wouldn't see, arranging airplane tickets and hotel rooms, drafting nondisclosure agreements, and making payoffs. A handful cheered him on. Some even joined him.

Blame greed; no one wanted to shut down the cash machine. Blame celebrity; it's the most addictive drug of our times. Blame a lack of empathy and morality almost as sickening as Kelly's—or blame all that. Many knew, and few did anything to stop him.

Geoff Edgers, an investigative reporter and cultural critic with the *Washington Post*, spent five months working on a story that ran in May 2018 under the headline "The star treatment: As R. Kelly's career flourished, an industry overlooked allegations of abusive behavior toward young women." The nut graf of that piece, the central thesis of a story assigned by Christine Ledbetter, one of my former entertainment editors at the *Chicago Sun-Times*, read, "For more than two decades, the recording industry turned a blind eye to Kelly's behavior as his career continued to thrive and he was afforded every luxury of a chart-topping superstar."

No company profited from Kelly more than Jive Records—a source close to Kelly in the position to know told me the label earned a billion dollars from sales of his recordings—and Edgers succeeded in speaking to label heads Clive Calder and Barry Weiss, both of whom had long dodged my calls. "Calder, who is rarely interviewed, was reached at his home in the Cayman Islands," Edgers wrote. "He said he regrets not trying harder to get help for Kelly. 'But I'm not a psychiatrist, and this guy is a troubled guy. Clearly, we missed something.'" The retired mogul added that Kelly's Los Angeles attorney, Gerald Margolis, who died in 2008, told him the women who sued the singer were not credible, and were just shaking down the star for cash. "He said to me, 'There's this guy, Jim DeRogatis, at the paper in Chicago that's got an ax to grind for Rob,'" Calder told Edgers. "'They're looking to sort of stir up shit . . .' and that was it."

Barry Weiss, Jive's chief executive from 1991 to 2011, didn't even admit that much. He claimed he knew nothing of Kelly's behavior, even though the label he ran had been named as a party in several of the lawsuits filed by young girls against one of their biggest stars, dating all the way back to the first claim by Tiffany Hawkins in 1996. "I was a record company putting out R. Kelly's records," Weiss told Edgers. "That was all I knew. I wasn't involved in his criminal cases. We were a record company, for God's sakes."

"Robert destroys families, but everybody allowed Robert to do whatever he wanted to do, and he got lost in that," Kelly's friend and former tour manager Demetrius Smith told me—*two decades ago*. "He's R. Kelly, he made it, and he believes he's a god. When he made it, he turned into a monster. Barry Hankerson, Derrel McDavid, Jive Records—all of them could have helped Robert by not allowing him to have his way." Of course, Smith could have helped, too. He did bring Tiffany Hawkins to a lawyer, and Tiffany stands as the first person who tried to stop Kelly. But talking to Edgers in 2018, Smith confessed that no one asked the ages of the girls in Kelly's orbit, "because their mamas let them stay out all night." He's not wrong. Some of the parents of Kelly's victims need to be added to the list of enablers, too.

As testimony during Kelly's 2008 trial made clear, Greg and Valerie Landfair knew about the relationship between the star and their teenage daughter Reshona. Aside from the video itself, which I will never be able to unsee, the image that haunts me comes from the sworn testimony at the trial by the singer's personal assistant Lindsey Perryman, who saw Reshona, accompanied by her parents, bring a pillow and an overnight bag to the recording studio so she could spend the night.

Greg, Valerie, and Reshona did not speak to me for this book, and they've refused to speak publicly to anyone since 2000. If Reshona's parents were paid by Kelly, as many sources believe, the benefits were fleeting. Greg and Valerie Landfair have filed for bankruptcy three times, the first in August 2007, almost a year before the trial began. The court eventually discharged debts of nearly $450,000. The second time they filed for bankruptcy, the judge dismissed the filing because the required eight years between bankruptcy claims had not yet passed. The third time, in December 2016, the court provided debt relief of $100,000.

I spoke to several parents of the girls who received cash settlements in exchange for signing nondisclosure agreements. None of them were perfect— show me a parent who is—but none had reason to suspect their daughter would be seduced by a wealthy celebrity whose music she loved after meeting him in, say, Lena McLin's choir class, or at a radio station's "Expo for Today's Black Woman," at Evergreen Plaza or Aventura Mall, or at the Rock 'N' Roll McDonald's after her prom. Many of these girls had never had a real romantic relationship. Some had never had sex. They were young, not just in age, but in maturity. They didn't have the experience to suspect Kelly's professions of love as a tool of a predator—one who I believe will come to stand as the worst in the history of popular music, which, given the art form's often despicable history, is a particularly sickening distinction.

Kelly became expert at separating young girls from their parents, families, and friends, sources say, especially if they were from underprivileged neighborhoods. "He's really good with people who don't have material things," the former associate told me—again, *two decades ago*. "If you ever read about a pedophile, their whole life revolves around how to gain confidence for their sexual desires. Robert geared his whole life and career around this. He was attacking families."

Jerhonda Pace, née Johnson, heard the accusations against her musical idol, and she saw the video many times in Courtroom 500, but she wanted to believe Kelly was innocent, and the jury's verdict gave her permission to do that. She also compared Kelly to Charles Manson, and while that charismatic power may be difficult for some to understand, it cannot be denied. It worked even on mature women such as Asante McGee and Kitti Jones. Plus, there was the music—always the music. "Robert will sit in front of that piano," Demetrius Smith had said, and "make women melt."

Having spent many hours interviewing the Clarys and the Savages, I understand how they could say they knew but didn't *know*, and how they thought things would be different for their daughters. They wanted to believe Kelly would make their daughter a star like Aaliyah, and the doting stage parents thought nothing would happen if they stayed by their girl's side. "I knew the history," J. Savage said, but "it didn't really hit home." Added Alice Clary, "He was never found guilty, he was acquitted."

Obviously, the legal system failed, and so did law enforcement, for almost seventeen years after the the Youth Division of the Special Investigations Unit at CPD and the Polk County, Florida, Sheriff's Office arrested Kelly in 2002. Since none of the original charges stuck for making child pornography, maybe the police and prosecutors who followed just didn't want the trouble. Or maybe they thought anyone that rich or famous would just get off again. It had happened with his acquittal in 2008, and it had taken a big toll on everyone in law enforcement who worked on that case. It took years for me to convince some of them to talk about it again.

I can't discount journalism's epic failure. Yes, it also took years for the media to expose Bill Cosby and Harvey Weinstein, not to mention Woody Allen, Kevin Spacey, Les Moonves, James Levine, Brett Ratner, Louis C.K., Bryan Singer, Jeffrey Epstein—hell, the list is seemingly endless—but once the first reporters did, the floodgates opened. Almost two decades passed before other journalists began to follow a fat music critic and an impish legal affairs reporter who started digging in public files and ringing doorbells, and a tireless columnist, Mary Mitchell, who wouldn't stop shouting that her community needed to recognize the predator in its midst.

Because my first love is music criticism, I'm especially disappointed with my peers in that benighted field. In an essay she wrote when accepting the Pulitzer Prize for Criticism in 2014, *Philadelphia Inquirer* architecture critic Inga Saffron maintained that her early days as a reporter in New Jersey "covering small-town zoning battles and urban renewal fiascos" were "fundamental to my development as a critic. . . . I jokingly began thinking of myself as an investigative critic."

I love the idea of investigative criticism, and I don't think it's a joke. We need it more than ever when assessing any art in the wake of Black Lives Matter, #MeToo, and the Trumpian assault on decency, democracy, and truth, at least if you believe as I do that everyone *should be* a critic. Why? Because art matters, damn it! It changes the world because it changes *us*. We all need to be investigative critics, to think about whether the art we embrace lives up to the ideals by which we live, and to call it out when it doesn't. Or so says the fifty-four-year-old white cis male music critic and professor who, like young Jenny in my favorite Velvet Underground song, still believes in a life saved by rock 'n' roll.

In the program for a 1968 exhibition of his work in Stockholm, Andy Warhol presciently predicted everyone would have their fifteen minutes of fame, which presumes everyone *wants* it. Maybe he's right. In the months after my first BuzzFeed News stories, some of my sources, including a few who'd initially been reluctant to talk on the record for months or years, embraced the spotlight, appearing in *Surviving R. Kelly* and other documentaries, on radio, and on television talk shows such as *The View*, *Megyn Kelly TODAY*, and *The Dr. Oz Show*. Some started websites, posted YouTube videos, opened Twitter and Instagram accounts, and made Facebook Public Figure pages. A few hired celebrity lawyers and publicists to field interview requests.

The singer's second wife, Andrea, has yet to publish the book she promised in 2012, *Under the Red Carpet*, but she did make a "video memoir" that she posted online as a pay-per-view, and she screens it before speaking engagements. Kitti Jones self-published a book, *I Was Somebody Before This*, and she sold the film rights. Jerhonda Pace née Johnson wrote and published *A Life Beyond Abuse*, and she's working on a sequel. Lisa Van Allen wrote *Surviving the Pied Piper: The Untold Story*, and Amazon is selling *No Longer Trapped in the Closet: The Asante McGee Story*. You can also add *Sex Me: Confessions of Daddy's Little Freak* to your cart. That anonymous tome reads as such tawdry porn that I initially thought it was sick "fan fiction," but one of my sources claims to have spoken to its author, who swears she lived with the cult for a time.

It must feel liberating for these women, after years of keeping their stories and their hurt bottled up, to finally have the support of a sympathetic audience. It took extraordinary courage for them to speak out, and I'm sure it's emboldening to feel that our culture has reached a tipping point. Bravo to them. I am not shaming or judging anyone who's finding some mix of recompense and catharsis after being hurt by Kelly, and these stories needed to be told. Sadly, some of the women who summoned the courage to tell them have suffered. Lizzette Martinez lost her corporate job at a national restaurant chain after my story first published her name in May 2018. She appeared in—but did not watch—*Surviving R. Kelly*. "I need a break from all of this. This is a big mess in my eyes," she said. "I'm struggling bad. I lost my job at Benihana months ago, and things are not so good, but I'm trying to stay upbeat."

The thought of Lizzette still struggling after all these years saddens me, and so does the way some of the people in this story have turned on one another, after first being brought together by that intrepid amateur detective, J. Savage. Some resent the Savages' tendency to spread any scrap of information far and wide. Some are pursuing additional lawsuits against Kelly. Faith Rodgers, a Dallas woman in her early twenties who claims Kelly gave her herpes, was initially represented by renowned civil rights attorney S. Lee Merritt, but in early 2019, she, her mother, and Dominique Gardner's mother, Michelle Kramer, appeared at a press conference with celebrity lawyer Gloria Allred. The Clarys preferred to work quietly behind the scenes, until they announced that another celebrity attorney, Michael Avenatti, was representing them in early 2019. All of them hope the civil and criminal courts will finally give them some measure of justice, and the Clarys and the Savages are still desperate to bring their daughters home.

As of this writing, Joy Savage and Azriel Clary have not spoken to their parents in person for, respectively, two and a half and four years. What is life like for Tim's daughter Joy, now twenty-three, and Azriel Clary, now twenty-one? I can only imagine, but I did glean some understanding from one woman who spent several years with the cult, and whom I came to know in some small way.

Dominique Gardner first emailed me on July 6, 2018, a few weeks after she left R. Kelly, writing with all caps in the subject line, "PRIVACY IS EVERY- THING!" We met in person, then traded texts, emails, and phone calls for nine months before meeting again on March 7, 2019. She'd decided it was time to speak publicly, to "give my truth." She was twenty-seven, and she had been one of Kelly's lovers for nine years.

Dominique and Kelly first became intimate when she was seventeen, the age of consent in Illinois, starting in 2009, not long after her friend Jer- honda passed along the singer's phone number. In 2015, she became one of six women living with the singer. The others included Joy Savage and Azriel Clary, and Dominique said she was especially close to the girl she called "Az." The most dramatic scenes in *Surviving R. Kelly* showed Dominique's mother, Michelle Kramer, tracking her down to a Los Angeles hotel room and con- vincing her to leave the "cult." Dominique rejected that word, as well as the word "brainwashing," and she told me she hadn't watched the documentary.

"What's the point of seeing it when I lived it? People are using it as entertainment, when it wasn't entertainment for me, you know?"

After graduating from Hillcrest High School in Chicago's Southwest suburbs in 2009, Dominque began studying to become a dental hygienist, per her mother's wishes. She wanted to be a poet and a writer. "I only went because my mother gave me an ultimatum: 'You either stay with me and go to school, or get kicked out.'" She was close to her family, and even though they didn't approve of her dating an older man, she saw Kelly often for several years while still living at home. The sexual relationship began after she watched him play basketball at a West Side gym. "I was never starstruck with him, because I didn't see the R. Kelly side, I saw the Robert side. I was never with him for the fame, for his money." Why had she wanted to meet him? I asked. "I was in love with him before I even met him, and when I met him, it was like, *wow*."

Dominique frequently visited the mansion in Olympia Fields. After Kelly rented his getaway properties in the Atlanta suburb of Johns Creek, she began living with him there, as well as at Trump Tower Chicago and the recording studio on North Justine Street. "Atlanta is where he changed. It was like something switched," she said. Before that, "I used to go home on a regular basis. I was able to call my family. Then, all of a sudden, it was '*no*.'"

We first met in July 2018 at a bar she chose in Rogers Park on the North Side, a cozy pub with dark wood tables, uncomfortable stools, lame alternative rock blaring on the sound system, and a dozen craft beers on tap. Dominique was startlingly underweight, and she spoke haltingly while looking out the big plate-glass windows, watching for any black SUV that might stop and linger. "I wouldn't put it past him to have his guys following me," she said.

When the two of us met again to talk for my recorder, at a different bar in the same neighborhood nine months later, she looked much healthier, spoke more freely, and laughed more. She no longer worriedly scanned the street outside the windows. We started by chatting about music—we both agreed Kendrick Lamar is brilliant—and our tattoos. She admired that I'm "all tatted up." Only one of her tattoos, a lion's head on the back of her right hand, could readily be seen, protruding from the sleeve of her hoodie. I asked if she had others, and she said she does, two images of Kelly's face, one on her left leg and another on her rib cage—a particularly painful place to get a tattoo, she noted, especially when you're as thin as she is. I agreed it helps to have plenty of flesh in the areas you get inked, and she laughed.

Two weeks before our second meeting, on February 22, 2019, the state of Illinois had indicted R. Kelly for the second time, on ten counts of criminal sexual abuse involving four victims, three of them minors. One was Dominique's friend Jerhonda, and prosecutors said they confirmed the presence of Kelly's DNA on a T-shirt she gave police. Kelly's latest attorney, Steve Greenberg, maintained his client's innocence. "He's a rock star. He doesn't have to have nonconsensual sex." The star spent that night and the next two in Cook County Jail before a woman identified in court papers as "a friend" posted his $100,000 bond, a dramatic contrast to when he paid seven hundred and fifty hundred-dollar bills for his bail in 2002. Greenberg said his client had serious financial problems. "I'm a broke-ass legend," the star himself sang in "I Admit."

Two nights before Dominique and I met that second time, on Tuesday, March 5, Gayle King sat with Kelly for an eighty-minute interview at Trump Tower. The interview aired over the next three days on *CBS This Morning*, as well as in a primetime special Friday night. King also interviewed Joy and Azriel. They defended the man they said they loved and insisted they were living where they chose to live, but they also appeared scripted and defensive on camera. King later described how Kelly hovered in the background and coughed loudly at times, as if to remind the two women he was within earshot.

During his interview, Kelly became histrionic, crying, standing up, and directly addressing the cameras. It prompted an avalanche of Internet memes and a cold-open skit on *Saturday Night Live*. He maintained he was innocent of all the charges and accusations, and he branded all the women speaking out against him as liars. "I don't even know what a cult is. But I know I don't have one," Kelly told King. "I'm not Lucifer. I'm a man. I make mistakes, but I'm not a devil. And by no means am I a monster."

Dominique did not see all of the interview—she was avoiding most media, she said—but she saw that snippet. "That's not genuine. That's the devil talking. Talking about 'I'm not Lucifer.' Yes, you are." Yet she was clearly conflicted about the man she said she still loved. "He is a giver, because when everything between me and him was good—oh, my God, it was, like, *perfect*. But, as soon as he gets mad, he turns into a person like, oh, what up, *the new Rob*."

The desire to convey her complex feelings about Kelly is what prompted Dominique to start talking to me. People don't really understand, she insisted, at least not the way she does. Every time we talked, I asked her if she was in therapy. She was initially reluctant, but when we finally spoke on the record, she'd had her first session with a counselor just a few days earlier. "At the end of the day, I am not playing victim. I done did some shit," she said, including sleeping with two other men in Kelly's inner circle while she was one of his girlfriends. "Maybe he did hurt. Maybe he was in love with me. But I never gave him a fair chance."

I asked if she regretted spending a third of her life with Kelly. She didn't. "I loved him to death, you know what I'm sayin'? But he needs help. Who doesn't need help?" She struggled to find a way to describe the situation, since she didn't like the words people used. "I wouldn't even say 'mind games.' It was just the fact that he tried to break me. I couldn't be broken. He wanted that control over me, and I wouldn't give him that power. So, he figured, like, If I don't give her food, she'll come around. Nope. I'd rather die than come around and give you my soul."

Dominique had heard about other women saying they had to follow Kelly's "rules," but she didn't use that term, either, and she said some of what the singer's accusers have said was wrong. For example, she was allowed to watch television and connect to the Internet. There were "no locks on no doors . . . If them two other girls, Joy and Azriel, wanna walk out, they can do that." However, she said Kelly did take away his girlfriends' phones, replacing them with new ones to be used only with him; he did not allow them to contact their parents, family members, or friends; he decreed that they should all wear baggy gym clothes, so other men could not admire their bodies; he did not want them to look at or speak to other men, and they had to ask for his permission to eat or go to the bathroom.

"I couldn't even have a drink without his permission. I'm a grown-ass woman, and I've gotta ask you if I want a drink? Everything you do, you have to ask him. That's not living, that's not normal. I've got to ask to use the fucking bathroom? Are you serious? I'm about to pee on myself if I can't get in contact with you. What the fuck is this?"

Dominique said she was the "tomboy" among Kelly's live-in lovers, and the most rebellious. She often disobeyed him, and she suffered what she called "consequences," including spankings, slapping, beatings, and being hit with an extension cord. Once, after she threw a piece of a Keurig coffeemaker at Kelly, "he grabbed me and he pulled my hair out, and I had, like, patches torn from my hair." That's when she decided to cut her hair super-short, she added.

The "consequences" came when Kelly felt as if "we disrespected him or disobeyed him. It's like a parent when your children go against your word. When your children go against your word—'No, you can't go to that party'—I'm gonna sneak out the window anyway. You get caught, what you parents gonna do? They gonna punish you, right? But we're grown women. You can't do that. 'Cause now, it's like, that's abuse, sorry to say."

Still, Dominique said, "I'm not gonna sit here and act like I'm innocent . . . one time, I did hit him back. He's like, 'Are you crazy that you just hit me?' Like, yeah! Me and him had like an Ike and Tina moment, like they had in the limousine . . . I wasn't afraid of him."

After being reunited with her mother in May 2018, in the scenes captured in *Surviving R. Kelly*, Dominique returned to Kelly's side three days later. She stayed with him for about two more weeks, until she finally walked away for good. She did not do it face-to-face; that would have been too hard, she said. "He went to sleep, and I just wrote him a letter: 'You are a great man. No hard feelings, I am just over it. I am growing. This is not working.' And I left, and I never looked back."

When we met, Dominique was living with her mother again, working and saving money until she could afford a studio apartment of her own. "I would probably still be there if he would have let me go to my little brother's graduation. I'd still be there, but, when he told me no . . . I'm, like, 'What is *wrong* with you?' You don't let people see their families, I guess, because we might realize how much freedom and happiness we have out there with our families. . . . When you go home and actually see your family, you're like, damn, I am actually missing out on a lot."

Every time we talked, I asked Dominique why she stayed with Kelly for so long, and what she believes is the source of his hold over the women who live with him. Finally, she called up an image of the star on her new cell phone—his most recent mug shot. "It's, like, I know them eyes. Every time I looked in his eyes, I knew he was sorry. Like, when he hit us, hit me, he was, like, he apologized. Like, he said, 'I done did some things, and I apologize for it.' I'm, like, you did, you did! But enough was enough. Yes, you did say, 'I'm sorry, I'm sorry.' Okay. But, then again, you do it again when shit don't go your way."

Kelly often discussed the sexual abuse he claims he suffered, as well as his difficulties reading and writing. "At the end of the day, he's a victim, too, because he went through some shit, and people—they don't understand." Dominique had been contacted by both state and federal investigators, but at that point, she had avoided talking to them. "I'm just, *whatever*. I'm not talking to you guys." She was stung by criticism from some, including the Savages and the Clarys, that she should have spoken out against Kelly sooner, and that she should be talking to the authorities. "I just want to heal. I just want my privacy," she said. "People may disagree or hate me for what I'm saying. That's the reason why I never wanted to come out. Because I'm not trying to defend him and what he has done, but, at the end of the day, you don't understand what he's been through, as a child."

Many police officers have told me it's not uncommon for them to respond to a domestic-violence call and find one partner, battered and bleeding, standing beside the other, insisting the call had been a mistake, that it was all just a big misunderstanding, and they really love each other. Psychologists use the term "cognitive dissonance." Once again, I sought the perspective of Dr. Charmaine Jake-Matthews, who has spent much of her life counseling victims of sexual and domestic abuse in Chicago, since the years when she sang beside Kelly in the Kenwood Academy choir. "Simply put, this is the psychological tension that is caused when there is a mismatch between your actions and/or situation and your beliefs and thoughts. When such a mismatch occurs, the person seeks (even if at an unconscious level) to relieve it. . . . The victim is often unable to change the situation. Thus they must change the way they think about the situation to alleviate the dissonance," the good doctor wrote me. "If you trusted someone, got into a relationship with them, and then realized that the relationship was not good for you,

you would leave. However, if that person has all of the power and control in the situation, you cannot simply leave. The only way to alleviate cognitive dissonance is to convince yourself that this person is good to you and that you want to be in the situation. Of course, most victims do not do this consciously, but it occurs nonetheless."

When Dominique and I met in February 2019, Kelly was in Cook County Jail for the second time in two weeks, this time for failure to pay $161,000 in back child-support payments. He spent another three nights in a segregated cell, away from the general population, before another anonymous patron paid the court and he was released. Dominique felt sorry for him and thought it was unfair that he was being deprived of his livelihood and his lifeline—his music. "I feel like he should be on house arrest in a studio, because, like I said, his music makes him get through the situations, what's he going through. Jail time, no. He needs to have a twenty-four-hour therapist at his house."

She added, however, that Kelly at long last needs to be honest about his behavior. She leaned down and spoke directly into my recorder, as if talking to the man she said she still loves. "You can stop the cycle," she said. "Just be honest. People don't want you in jail."

As an atheist who rejected religion during freshman year at Hudson Catholic Regional School for Boys, I may be underplaying the role of faith in R. Kelly's story. The struggle by some to square his inspiring spiritual anthems with his hot 'n' horny bedroom jams is one I will never fully understand; I assume the former are a con and the latter are perhaps unwitting confessions of predatory behavior. The motivations of the singer's pastors and spiritual advisors leave me baffled, but then so does the way the Catholic Church has covered up for predatory priests for so long.

The churches that proliferate on Chicago's South and West Sides are centers of spirituality and community, but they are also political power bases, and few are bigger or more powerful than Salem Baptist Church in the South Side's Pullman neighborhood. Founded by the Rev. James Meeks in 1985, Salem Baptist drew more than nine thousand congregants to its weekly services in 2008, the year Kelly finally went to trial. By then, Meeks had added politician to a résumé including preacher, pastor, and superstar spiritual advisor. "There is nothing on earth that God does not do," the reverend told his flock, "but God has to have some people to do it through."

Meeks served three terms in the Illinois Senate, representing the 15th District from 2003 to 2013. For two years, he caucused as a Democrat in the state capital of Springfield with Barack Obama at the end his three terms representing the 13th District of Chicago's Hyde Park. Meeks was always flexible in his politics, however. He is the rare Illinois Dem who's proudly and stridently anti-gay, and in 2017, union-busting, hard-right Republican Gov. Bruce Rauner appointed him chairman of the State Board of Education.

Through the early 2000s, Meeks was often mentioned as the successor to the Rev. Jesse Jackson as leader of the Rainbow/PUSH Coalition, Chicago's long-running and most powerful black activist group. Some criticized his then-pending anointment, and it has yet to happen, since Jackson has yet to step down. In 2002, John B. Koss reported in the *Times of Northwest Indiana* that "Derrick Mosley, founder and president of the Brothers and Sisters in Coalition Bringing About Reform, maintained that Meeks, pastor of Salem Baptist Church of Chicago, is tainted with 'controversy and poor discretion,' and that putting him in charge of the organization is a mistake." That was before Mosley was convicted of using a videotape of Kelly and gospel singer Deleon Richards to extort her husband, New York Yankees outfielder Gary Sheffield. "Mosley said he was particularly bothered by Meeks's spiritual counseling of prominent people accused of sexual offenses, such as musician R. Kelly and former U.S. congressman Mel Reynolds, who was given the job of managing various church-related projects earlier this year."

Whether it was because he became mindful of the optics, or because Kelly stopped donating to his causes, as Mary Mitchell and several of my sources suggested, Meeks began to distance himself from the singer even before the trial started. By 2008, the reverend had stopped appearing beside Kelly in television interviews, and he no longer brought a yellow bus full of grammar-school children wearing "Free R. Kelly" T-shirts to Twenty-Sixth and Cal. He refused to be interviewed for this book, as did Reverend Jackson, who had urged readers of the *Sun-Times* to "avoid a rush to judgement" the day of Kelly's indictment, saying "there are other greater issues in the world."

Nevertheless, sources told me Chicago's Baptist pastors and politicians topped the list of prominent members of the black community who urged State's Attorney Dick Devine to dismiss the charges against Kelly with a plea deal that would have given him only probation.

"For all have sinned and fall short of the glory of God"—Romans 3:23. "God will bring into judgment both the righteous and the wicked"—Ecclesiastes 3:17. There are some good lines in that Good Book, if you bother to read them.

People believe many things, and I will not judge them. Demetrius Smith, Kelly's old friend and former road manager, had fallen on hard times when we reconnected in 2019, after talking many times in the early 2000s. Bitter, alienated from his children, and struggling to support himself, he relied on his own faith to sustain him after many villainized him for his comments in *Surviving R. Kelly.* In the series as in his book, *The Man Behind the Man*, Smith admits to securing the falsified marriage certificate for Kelly and Aaliyah, and some see him as one of Kelly's most sinister enablers. "I never want to talk to that piece of shit again," one of the show's creators told me. He may be flawed, but nothing Smith ever told me proved untrue.

"Robert don't know love," Smith said when I asked, for this book, about Kelly's relationship with his mother. Then he changed topics. "Did you read in my book where I talked about the demon?" I told him I'd read his book many times, and that passage always struck me. In 1996, Smith had split from Kelly, but the singer wanted him to come back, saying he desperately needed his old friend's help after the settlement with Tiffany Hawkins. They went to the East Bank Club in the West Loop near the Chicago River, a 450,000-square-foot fitness club with thousands of members and hundreds of employees. After Kelly played basketball, he sat in the fancy gym's restaurant at a table full of girls. Then the singer beckoned Smith into the men's room.

Smith picked up the narrative from his book when we talked, repeating parts of the scene word for word. "That actually happened, you see. I went in the bathroom with Robert, man, and he said, 'The spirit of the Lord is on me,' and I started prayin' and prayin', and he started prayin'. We started talking in tongues, and then that beast came, and I heard that demon. I am talkin' 'bout"—and here Smith lapsed into loud, angry, garbled noises like Mercedes McCambridge providing the voice of Linda Blair's possessed teenager in *The Exorcist*.

"I got scared, man. We was in what should have been a crowded bathroom downtown, and nobody came in that bathroom for about forty minutes. We was just talkin' the talk, and then that beast came up. He stepped back in the stall and that door closed, like somebody slammed it—*bam!*—and then . . ." And here he channeled the *Exorcist* voice again.

"Robert stepped out of that bathroom and he ain't never been the same, man. It's a beast in that boy, I am telling you, DeRo. This thing is spiritual. It's a spiritual beast in that man, and he need to be set down with that beast, so he can battle with him. That beast, it's a sex demon. *It's a sex demon!* Robert was molested and he survived it. He survived his molestation, you see, and now they trying to put him in jail, DeRo. They can't do that, man. That's the root, DeRo. It's a demon in that boy."

Smith noticed my silence. What the hell *do* you say to that? "It ain't real enough for you, huh?" he asked. I noted that Robert had had many chances for redemption. Hadn't the first lawsuit filed by Tiffany Hawkins in 1996 been enough to make him stop, to convince him to get help?

"If a demon got you possessed," Smith said, "you ain't gonna listen to nobody. 'Cause you possessed, and it's a *strong* demon. You know, Robert know God, but he got a strong demon on him. Anytime he can walk away from Ms. McLin and not listen to her, it's a demon in that boy, man. After his momma died . . . that's all I am sayin'. I would hate to see him get put away. His preference to young girls is because of his illiteracy, and I felt like . . . when he done pissed on that girl and that video came out, it shouldn'ta been no more girls. It shouldn'ta been no more girls under age. *It should not have been.* And if they are, he has to answer to them."

One thing I have always wanted to answer is the path the videotape took from R. Kelly's gym bag to my mailbox on Grace Street on the first day of February 2002. In early 2019, as I struggled to pull together all the details from nearly two decades of reporting for this book, a few final pieces of information came to me as fortuitously as the fax in 2000, this time via Twitter. The first shed some light on the connection to the Nation of Islam.

Founded in Detroit in 1930, the NOI is a religious and political movement whose goal is to "teach the downtrodden and defenseless Black people a thorough Knowledge of God and of themselves." At its peak, under the leadership of Elijah Muhammad, it numbered about three hundred thousand so-called black Muslims, including Muhammad Ali, according to the Southern Poverty Law Center, which considers it a "deeply racist, antisemitic, anti-LGBT" extremist group. Malcolm X remains its most celebrated member, but he split from Elijah Muhammad in 1964 over differences about philosophy and politics. He also charged his former mentor with having adulterous affairs with young female acolytes. Malcolm X was assassinated a year after he broke from the group.

Today, by most estimates, Minister Louis Farrakhan leads between twenty and fifty thousand followers from the NOI's headquarters at Mosque Maryam in the Stony Island neighborhood on Chicago's South Side. October 14, 2018, was a Holy Day of Atonement for the group, as well as the twenty-third anniversary of the Million Man March. Members gathered at the five-thousand-capacity Aretha Franklin Amphitheatre in Detroit, and Farrakhan spoke for nearly three hours. A tweet steered me to videos on YouTube and the NOI's website, pointing out a short part of that talk of special interest to me.

Fifteen months after my BuzzFeed News article about Kelly's cult and three months before Lifetime aired *Surviving R. Kelly*, Farrakhan spoke about the biggest R&B star of a generation. "I had a four-hour talk with R. Kelly," he began. The crowd booed and grumbled. Many wore street clothes, a striking contrast to the sea of suits and white habits seen in photos of Malcolm X addressing packed rallies during the NOI's heyday. They had been in the minister's thrall, until he mentioned Kelly. His followers clearly weren't fans.

"No, no, no," Farrakhan said with a smile, shushing the voices of dissent. "*No, no, no.* He came to our home with six of his friends, and I told him, 'R., I have had a message in my heart for you for over twenty years, and I'm so glad for the opportunity to share it with you.' He was managed by a friend of mine. What's that brother's name?"

Farrakhan turned to the men sitting behind him onstage. "Barry Hankerson," one said. Then the minister faced the crowd again. "Barry Hankerson," he said. "And Barry told me, 'I'm gonna get *rid* of him.'" The crowd gasped. Like me, they heard "get rid of" as "kill."

"I said, 'Barry, be patient,'" Farrakhan continued in a rolling cadence. "That boy is deeply spiritual. A man can't write no songs like that and not have God all up in him. But he's got to be *cleansed*. Do you understand what I'm saying?" The minister's voice grew louder with every word, and now the crowd cheered him on. "All of you in here have done something wrong, but you are not *evil* people. Somebody's gotta reach into you and bring out the God that's in you and clear you of your evil!"

With that, Farrakhan got a standing ovation and moved on to other subjects.

Was any of the talk of violence serious, or was it all just talk? In *Star Struck,* the book Kelly's former lover and confidante Kim Dulaney called a "thinly fictionalized account" of their friendship, the R&B star "Ben" says of the aunt of a girl trying to destroy him with a videotape, "I need her *done*. You know what I mean?" A member of Kelly's crew made the menacing comment that if Hankerson tried to testify at the trial, "he probably wouldn't have made it to Chicago." In one of the few transcripts of a closed hearing that Judge Vincent Gaughan unsealed, prosecutors said they were considering pressing charges based on a sworn statement by Lisa Van Allen that Derrel McDavid said he should have "murked" her. Now Farrakhan claimed Hankerson said of Kelly, "I'm gonna get *rid* of him."

Was any of that true? I wasn't eager to find out, but nobody ever got murked, as far as I know. I asked Hankerson in early 2019 about Farrakhan's comments, and he gave me a rare response via text. "The Minister prays for the worst of the worst; that's why he's the Minister. However, he has guided me well. ASA." That's "ASA" as in "as-salāmu ʿalaykum." Peace be upon you.

The number of times Hankerson has spoken publicly since he split from Kelly in 2000 can be counted on one hand. He and his son Jomo continue to oversee the recorded legacy of Aaliyah, whose large following remains intensely loyal, though her status is nowhere near that of many departed musical greats. "[You] won't find most of her music online," Stephen Witt wrote in a long and well-reported article for *Complex* in late 2016. "Aaliyah's most popular, most important works—the albums *One in a Million* and *Aaliyah,* and late-career singles like 'Are You That Somebody?'—aren't available for streaming or sale on Spotify, iTunes, Amazon, or any other online music service." Ironically, the only record that *is* available is the one produced by Kelly, *Age Ain't Nothing but a Number*, the one the Hankersons don't control. "Only her uncle, mysterious music industry exec Barry Hankerson, knows why."

Hankerson did not talk to Witt, but in mid-2018, he did speak briefly to Geoff Edgers of the *Washington Post*. "Hankerson said he was 'legally' prohibited from discussing Kelly," Edgers wrote. "When asked if he had regrets, Hankerson grew emotional. 'Let me tell you something. I'm a Muslim,' he said. 'I do my prayers every day, and I lost my niece in a plane crash, and please excuse my language, but I don't really give a fuck about none of them people you're talking about.'"

None of Aaliyah's other family members ever talk about her to the media, and most remained silent even after *Surviving R. Kelly* prompted renewed interest in their daughter's relationship with the singer. Her mother, Diane Haughton, did curtly deny that Aaliyah ever had sex with Kelly. But the most illuminating comment by anyone close to Kelly's most successful protégé came from Damon Dash, her boyfriend at the time of the plane crash. Broken up about her death and angry at his friend Jay-Z, Dash left the label he cofounded, Roc-A-Fella Records, soon after Aaliyah's accident. He stopped talking to Jay-Z because he thought the rapper should have publicly condemned Kelly instead of heading out with him on the Best of Both Worlds tour.

In early 2019, Dash recalled what Aaliyah shared about her relationship with Kelly, in an interview with Hip Hop Motivation. "I remember Aaliyah trying to talk about it, and she couldn't. She would just leave it at, 'That dude was a bad man.' And I didn't really wanna know what he did, to the extent that I might feel the need to deal with it, just 'cause that's what a man does. But it was just so much hurt for her to revisit it. It was like, I wouldn't even want to revisit it without a professional. Whatever got done was terrible."

During the trial and in the press, Kelly, his lawyers, and his handlers said they believed Hankerson and Sparkle were behind the video making its way to me, the *Sun-Times*, and thus the police. I understood why many in the black community, troubled by someone's actions and wanting to stop him, might turn to a journalist before an officer of the law. "Growing up in the 'hood, the number-one rule was don't snitch," Kelly himself says in *Soulacoaster*. While I still don't know if the Hankerson/Sparkle theory about the 2002 case is true, I did learn more about that videotape, and that was thanks to Twitter, too.

After my friend and public-radio colleague Peter Sagal tweeted a flattering compliment about my work, a Chicago attorney named Ian Alexander DM'ed me. He and Peter's brother Roger went to law school together, they're close friends, and their kids attend Hebrew school together in the suburbs.

When Demetrius Smith was on the outs with Kelly in the fall of 1996, around the time he heard his old friend speak in the voice of the demon, Smith felt sorry for one of the high school girls Kelly had sexual contact with, Tiffany Hawkins. Smith brought Tiffany to the law firm of Susan E. Loggans & Associates. It advertised a lot, Loggans did a lot of radio and television interviews, and she seemed to get results.

After passing the bar, Ian Alexander took his first job as a lawyer at Loggans's firm. He was twenty-five, and he loved music. (He told me he always read my reviews and listened to *Sound Opinions*.) When Smith brought Tiffany to the office, Loggans didn't want the case. "Who's R. Kelly? It's not like he's Frank Sinatra," she said. Alexander insisted the singer was a big deal. Loggans took the case, and the young music-loving lawyer did all the work on the first legal claim accusing Kelly of having sex with underage girls. Loggans never even met Tiffany, she admitted, and she didn't think highly of Alexander. "I thought he was a schmuck," she told me.

The ill will was mutual. "I was definitely a schmuck by virtue of the fact that I worked for her and let her sell out these poor girls," Alexander said. "That's something that I'll have to live with."

Alexander is haunted by yielding to pressure from Loggans to settle the case as soon as Kelly's lawyers, Gerald Margolis and John M. Touhy, made their first offer of $250,000 in exchange for an NDA the day after Tiffany's "hair-raising" seven-and-a-half-hour deposition. Abdon Pallasch and I had never thought to call any other attorney working for Loggans, though Alexander's name appears on many of the 235 pages in Tiffany's legal file. We kick ourselves for missing that step now, though Alexander says he couldn't have talked to us anyway, because of attorney-client confidentiality. He was still reluctant to address Tiffany's case in 2019, but he did say one thing about his former client that shocked me.

Tiffany initially wanted to press criminal charges. On her behalf, Alexander contacted the office of the Illinois state's attorney at the time, Jack O'Malley, but they chose not to pursue the case. Tiffany only filed her civil claim after law enforcement declined to act. More than two decades of predatory behavior might have been stopped there, in 1996.

Ethical concerns didn't apply to the other surprising story Alexander told me, because he never represented anyone connected with it.

When I started reporting in late 2000, graphic Kelly videotapes were already floating around "on the streets." They began showing up for sale as bootlegs in mid-2001. The first tapes and DVDs featured dancer Montina Woods and the girl Abdon and I never identified. The crew Kelly played basketball with at the time included someone my sources alternately described as "a thug," "a guy from the street," and "this dude originally from Philly." In his book and in interviews with me, Smith said the man's name was Generaall. I failed to learn anything else about him, much less contact him.

Smith said Generaall stole the tape with Reshona from Kelly's gym bag one night when the singer left it on the sidelines during a game at Hoops. "It passed from the hands of a thief, through the hands of street chiefs, gang leaders," Kim Dulaney wrote in *Star Struck*. When copies of the tape with Reshona began to circulate among Kelly's hangers-on in late 2001, some were titillated. Others were disgusted. Tapes of Kelly with legal-age women were one thing. The tape of him violating a fourteen-year-old was something else.

Sparkle told me she first heard about the tape on Friday, December 14, 2001, when two friends told her they'd seen it. On Tuesday, December 18, a man visited her claiming to have been sent by a lawyer named Buddy Meyers. He showed her the tape, which disgusted and infuriated her. She told me and said in her sworn testimony at the trial that she didn't know the man, and he left with the tape, though he gave her a business card.

The card was from the firm of Meyers, Alexander & Kosner. That's Alexander as in Ian Alexander. He had quit Susan E. Loggans & Associates and started his own practice with two new partners, one of them Buddy Meyers.

On Monday or Tuesday, December 17 or 18, two men visited Alexander at his new firm's offices. They occupied part of a floor at 640 North LaSalle Drive, a block from the Rock 'N' Roll McDonald's. The two men knew Alexander had represented Tiffany Hawkins. He understood how Kelly operated, he did right by Tiffany, and they wanted to talk to him.

Alexander had met Demetrius Smith, and he knew the names of several members of Kelly's crew, because he had worked on Tiffany's lawsuit for nearly two years. He didn't recognize the men who came to his office, and he said he didn't know and cannot remember their names. The men had a videotape they wanted to show him. The office didn't have a VCR, so Alexander and the two men went down the hall to Act One Studios, a now-defunct performing arts school that rented space on the same floor.

The tape the men showed Alexander included footage of Kelly with two different partners. The first, the men told him, was a girl named Reshona. The second, they said, was gospel singer Deleon Richards, who'd married New York Yankees outfielder Gary Sheffield.

Alexander wanted nothing to do with the video of Richards and Kelly. "I told the guys who brought it that I would not be a part of what seemed like a scheme to extort/blackmail Kelly regarding a consensual sexual relationship," Alexander wrote via email, one of many such exchanges and interviews. "I said if they did anything with that, they'd probably go to jail. That's the last time I ever thought about the second part of the tape."

When we first spoke, Alexander didn't know the rest of the story about the tape of Kelly with Richards, but I suggested he look it up. Derrick Mosley, "the poor man's Jesse Jackson," later used a copy of that video in an attempt to grab $20,000 from Sheffield. Convicted of extortion, Mosley spent two years in prison. Alexander found the stories about Mosley, Richards, Sheffield, and extortion online. He also found Mosley's photos on the Web. Mosley looked familiar. "Here is what I think," Alexander wrote. "Derrick Mosley and his partner in crime brought that tape to me. I honestly have no idea who the other guy was." Mosley would not talk to me for this book.

As it would most people of conscience, the tape of Kelly and Reshona sickened Alexander. He told the two men who visited him that he would be willing to help the teenager if she wanted to file a lawsuit or press criminal charges against Kelly. They wanted Alexander to hold on to the tape, but he refused to keep child pornography in his office. They left with it, but said they would return with Reshona and her family. Alexander scheduled the meeting.

On Wednesday, December 19, 2001, Sparkle called the state's attorney's office and talked to Robert Heilingoetter. She called DCFS, child protective services, and talked to a woman named Kim. Then she called me. She mentioned the name Buddy Meyers—the one on the business card left by the man who visited her—in all three calls. Meyers had been vague when we spoke on December 20. "I have no idea why they threw my name around . . . I've heard some scuttlebutt, but that's all I'm at liberty to say." Soon after Sparkle made her cold call to the state's attorney's office, investigators visited Meyers, Alexander & Kosner. Alexander told them he didn't have a tape; they'd have to get a warrant if they wanted to search for a tape; no judge would grant a warrant to search a law office, and anyway, he was not representing anyone in connection to a tape—yet.

Alexander had the meeting on his calendar, and he believed Reshona and one or more of her family members were driving to his office—he thinks he ordered a car service to bring them from Oak Park—when Kelly's attorney Ed Genson "intercepted" them. Either Genson knew about the tape because the two men told Kelly they had it, or Sparkle called Kelly and gave him holy hell after she saw the tape of him and her niece. (Sparkle would not talk to me again for this book.) I don't know what Kelly and Genson did next. Kelly certainly hasn't spoken to me, and Genson, who is retired and ailing, did not respond to my calls, emails, or letters.

While they were running around with the tape, the two men may also have talked to some of the bootleggers who provided the knockoff VHS tapes, DVDs, and CDs for sale on street corners. The first Kelly sex videos with Montina Woods and the girl Abdon and I never identified had done good business. The new one would grab even more attention.

I had talked to a vendor at the Maxwell Street Market in 1998 for a story about bootlegging, and I asked where he got his counterfeit goods. He looked at me as if I had two heads. It was as simple as setting up a few machines, and hitting play on one and record on the others. Bigger operators either sold wholesale to vendors or left their wares on consignment. You get a better deal on consignment, he advised—he had heard music critics got a lot of advance CDs—but you had to trust the guy who peddled your product to deliver your cut.

Genson and Alexander were friendly. Chicago is a very big small town, and the legal scene is even smaller. Genson called to apologize for "hijacking" the meeting Alexander thought he'd scheduled with Reshona and her family. It was just business, no hard feelings. This was about six weeks before the tape arrived in my mailbox. Did that only happen because someone's original plan got derailed? Had one or more members of the Landfair family intended to sue, press criminal charges, or both?

Ultimately, Reshona and her parents, Greg and Valerie, remained loyal to Kelly and never spoke to anyone, media or investigators. Alexander never saw the two men with the tape again, and he never spoke to the Landfairs or Sparkle. He followed every word about the case against R. Kelly in the papers through the six-year wait for the trial and once the proceedings started. His name didn't come up once, and he was glad it didn't.

In the early spring of 2002, bootlegged copies of the tape appeared for sale on the streets, not only in Chicago but in other big cities, as officials said at the press conference announcing Kelly's indictment. It was child porn, they noted, and they advised anyone who had a copy to destroy it.

While I've long wondered about the path of the copy I got, what's important is that it was out there at all. The videotape was a dirty bomb, a radioactive weapon ready to be used against Kelly by someone out for a big payday, sickened by his treatment of young girls, or set on revenge for the damage he'd caused.

Hankerson's niece Aaliyah had been hurt by Kelly. "What really pushed Barry over the edge about really wanting to destroy Rob was that Aaliyah died, and the guilt he felt," one of Kelly's handlers told me in early 2019. Reshona was having sex with Kelly, and the teenager's parents weren't stopping it. Sparkle is still furious. "I have a vendetta against him because of what he did to my niece," she told NBC's *Dateline* on January 18, 2019. Kelly's handlers claimed Sparkle and Hankerson were angry because their business dealings with the star had soured. That may be true as well. But can anyone blame them or the hundreds of loved ones of girls Kelly hurt for hating him for any number of reasons?

Sparkle told me several times during the six weeks between when she first saw the tape and when we watched it together in the *Sun-Times* video closet that she was frustrated that the state's attorney's office and DCFS weren't acting. Why couldn't they just go arrest Kelly already? she asked every time we spoke. No one seemed to be doing anything.

Both Sparkle and Hankerson denied they personally dropped the tape in my mailbox. Did either of them ask someone—"a guy in a bow tie," a member of the NOI's Fruit of Islam, perhaps—to drop a copy in my mailbox to speed things up? They never said.

Given that the tape began to appear for sale on the streets shortly after the *Sun-Times* revealed its existence, it was only a matter of time before it made its way to the media, law enforcement, or both. The tape was out there, and the story had been out there long before the tape. I just got both first.

While the tale of the tape is fascinating for what it says about the people around Kelly—opportunistic, disgusted, out for retribution, all of that and more—it doesn't really matter. What matters is what was on the tape. Here was seemingly irrefutable evidence of Kelly hurting an underage girl, one of many for almost three decades. The defense did refute it, however, and a jury of the singer's peers acquitted him. And so a pattern of predatory behavior that started in 1991 continued.

R. Kelly has a lot to answer for, as his old friend Demetrius Smith said, and maybe someday he will. I've certainly posed many questions, via his lawyers, managers, publicists, "crisis managers," and record-company overseers, dating back to November 2000.

After my BuzzFeed News articles in the summer of 2017, Kelly suffered a new round of defections from his latest inner circle, including his musical accompanist, DJ Phantom, and his lawyer, Linda Mensch, who'd given the memorable quote about how Kelly just wanted everyone to "put down the guns and embrace peace and love." Mensch emailed that Kelly is "a brilliant artist, with unlimited talent. But . . ." I pressed her several times on what exactly she meant by that "but" followed by an ellipsis, but she told me the partners at her law firm advised her not to talk to me. Phantom had no problem speaking his mind about Kelly. "He's a shitbag," he told me.

Three of the six members of Kelly's "cult" also left; those are women I've never named publicly. Dominique stayed for a while longer, and Joy and Azriel are still there as of this writing.

Kelly's career began to flounder after the year of indie outreach in 2013, when he split with his longest-serving manager, Derrel McDavid. I tried to talk to him in 2017, too, and he Facebook messaged me. "I'd appreciate it if you'd just let me sit this one out. Thanks. You've pretty much destroyed him." By the spring of 2018, Kelly had a new manager, Henry James Mason, an unknown in the music business who just went by "Mason." He had a flair for the dramatic and, like so many around Kelly, occasionally talked like a movie gangster.

In March 2018, I sat in a hall at the Austin Convention Center during the South by Southwest Music Conference & Festival, listening to a keynote address by Lyor Cohen, co-founder of Def Jam Recordings, now Global Head of Music at YouTube and Google. I was glad I'd set the ringer on my iPhone to silent, because it vibrated with five calls in rapid succession. Whoever was trying to reach me clearly wasn't going to stop, so I stepped out to return the call. It was Mason.

Kelly's then-manager wanted me to "clear the air" with his client, he said, and Robert would very much like to meet with me. I seriously doubted that, but I told Mason I'd be happy to sit with Kelly for an on-the-record interview, no holds barred, preferably on video. (I called my editor at BuzzFeed, Marisa Carroll, saying I might need the biggest, beefiest camera crew she could provide, and I asked if I could expense a Kevlar vest, size 3X.) There were two conditions, Mason said: He'd like to see copies of all the lawsuits I kept writing about, and he'd need a list of my questions. I told him the lawsuits are public record at Cook County Circuit Court—though good luck finding them in that black hole—but I agreed to email him a list of questions, and after Marisa edited them and BuzzFeed media lawyer Matt Schafer vetted them, I did.

I kept the list relatively succinct, limiting it to questions about Joy Savage, Azriel Clary, Dominique Gardner, Jerhonda Pace, and Reshona Landfair; the other women who told me about the cult; the books by Demetrius Smith and Kim Dulaney; the settlements for the lawsuits filed by Patrice Jones, the underage girl from the Rock 'N' Roll McDonald's; Montina Woods, the legal-age dancer on a videotape with Kelly; Tracy Sampson, the underage girl he met at the "Expo for Today's Black Woman"; and Tiffany Hawkins, the first underage girl who sued him after they met in Ms. McLin's classroom. Finally, I asked, what really happened with Aaliyah?

Mason never mentioned the interview with Kelly again.

The manager and I did continue talking, and a month later, Mason made another offer, saying he'd like me to speak with Joy Savage. Once again, he asked me to provide my questions, and once again, I did. That interview didn't happen either. In January 2019, Mason surrendered to the Henry County Sheriff's Office in Georgia on an outstanding warrant from the summer of 2018, when Tim Savage charged that he threatened to kill him and hurt his family because they wouldn't stop trying to bring Joy home. Mason posted $10,000 bail and called the felony charge of terroristic threats a "miscarriage of justice." By then, he'd resigned as Kelly's manager and been replaced by Don Russell, another unknown in the music world. Russell claimed he'd been a friend of Kelly's for thirty years, but former members of his crew told me they'd never met or heard of him.

In early 2019, Kelly hired a new Chicago-based defense attorney. "Steve Greenberg has made a career out of representing what many consider the lowest of the low," read the subhed of a profile by Lisa Bertagnoli in *Crain's Chicago Business.* "'The greatest rush in the business is when you know someone is guilty and you win the case,' he says." Acting as Kelly's spokesman, Greenberg vehemently denied all the accusations against his client and branded all the women accusing him as liars. Many final attempts to get Kelly to comment for this book were directed to him. Greenberg acknowledged receiving my messages, but he ignored them.

Kelly seems to think he can spin his way out of trouble, and he'd already made many of the arguments he offered in the March 2019 interview with

Gayle King months earlier, in "I Admit," an epic, nineteen-minute song in the mock-operatic mode of "I Believe I Can Fly (Remix)" and "Trapped in the Closet." At a point where RCA/Sony Music was reluctant to release his new music, the star floated it on SoundCloud on July 23, 2018.

"I admit I done made some mistakes," the Pied Piper begins, "and I have some imperfect ways." He proceeds to try to evoke sympathy for his inability to read or write, as well as for the sexual abuse he says he suffered as a child. As in "Heaven, I Need a Hug," he condemns friends who betrayed him, managers who robbed him, and women who lied about him, all seeking one thing. "Where the fuck is my money?"

"Only God can mute me," Kelly sings, and he never admits any of his actions were wrong. "I admit I fuck with all the ladies, that's both older and young ladies / But tell me how they call it pedophile because of that / Shit is crazy." The song goes on (and on and on). "I got some girls that love me to pull they hair," he sings. "Some like me to spank 'em." Ultimately, he blames their parents. "Don't push your daughter in my face / And tell me that it's OK / 'Cause your agenda is to get paid / And get mad when it don't go your way."

The singer poses some questions, too. "What's the definition of a cult? / What's the definition of a sex slave? / Go to the dictionary, look it up / Let me know, I'll be here waiting." Genius, the website that posts and annotates pop music lyrics, helpfully answered. It defined the characteristics of a cult, including "authoritarian leadership, isolationism, and opposition to independent thinking." Genius concluded, "While it may not be a literal 'cult,' what Kelly is doing certainly has the features of one."

"I Admit" also gives me a shout-out. "To Jim DeRogatis, whatever your name is / You been tryin' to destroy me for twenty-five whole years / Writin' the same stories over and over again / Off my name, you done went and made yourself a career / But guess what? I pray for you and your family, and all my other enemies."

I really didn't need the prayers, but I appreciated the sentiment, even if it was coupled with the dig that I've done nothing else in my career. (My Lester Bangs book was pretty good, and some of my students like me; there's *Sound Opinions*, and I'm not a bad punk-rock drummer.) Ultimately, I found the math the most interesting thing about that verse. When Kelly released the song, I'd been "writing the same stories" for a little less than eighteen years, but it had been about twenty-five since Kelly ended his sexual contact with Tiffany Hawkins and began with Aaliyah, neither of which he's publicly admitted.

As the financial pressures mounted in 2018, property owners evicted Kelly from the mansion and the guest house in Johns Creek, Georgia, for $30,000 in back rent and fees, not long after a former member of his crew allegedly robbed all the furniture from those homes because he hadn't been paid. The star also owed $170,000 in back rent for the recording studio on North Justine Street in Chicago, on top of fines levied by Cook County Judge Patrice Ball-Reed for illegally using a building zoned for manufacturing as a living space. City building inspectors visited the studio in mid-January 2019, and their photographs, which documented sixty-seven code violations and also showed a massage table, were quickly leaked. On January 23, the judge surveyed the photos. Stopping at one picture, she barked, "Christmas is over. This tree needs to go!"

When Chicago decides to fuck with you, you are well and truly fucked.

Ironically, the last major-label album of seventeen during Kelly's career was *12 Nights of Christmas*, released in late 2016. Although executives refused to comment, in early 2019, RCA/Sony Music dropped Kelly from its roster, with two albums left on his contract. Listeners greeted "I Admit" as a bizarre curiosity. "Born to My Music," a jaunty stepping song bragging about all the children conceived to his grooves, also fell flat when Kelly self-released it on New Year's Day, 2019. And that was only the start of a very bad year for him.

After the six hours of accusations in *Surviving R. Kelly* began airing on Lifetime on January 3, the singer's own children publicly condemned him. He was fighting lawsuits by Faith Rodgers, the Dallas woman, and a Mississippi sheriff's deputy who charged that Kelly seduced his wife and gave her a venereal disease. More legal threats loomed from celebrity lawyers Michael Avenatti and Gloria Allred, who both got plenty of air time criticizing him. The #MuteRKelly movement was shutting down almost every concert he booked, and Spotify, after much criticism, had rolled out a feature that allowed users to tell the service "don't play this artist" (a literal "mute R. Kelly" button, though they didn't call it that). After ignoring requests to comment for the last year and a half, artists such as Lady Gaga, Phoenix, Chance the

Rapper, Céline Dion, Ciara, Nick Cannon, and Syleena Johnson released statements criticizing Kelly. Some also pulled their collaborations with him from streaming services, the iTunes Store, and Amazon.

On January 8, 2019, Cook County State's Attorney Kim Foxx held a press conference asking for witnesses hurt by the singer to come forward. Foxx, a black, forty-six-year-old former sex-crimes prosecutor with the office, had been elected to replace Dick Devine in November 2016. She said she'd watched all of *Surviving R. Kelly*, which had finished its first airing three days earlier. "I was sickened by the allegations. I was sickened as a survivor, I was sickened as a mother, I was sickened as a prosecutor. I worked in this office for a number of years, including in 2008, so the allegations were not new to me." Foxx vowed to hold the star accountable.

Kelly did not seem concerned. That night, he celebrated his fifty-second birthday at a party at a South Side nightclub called V75, and he performed his 1994 hit "Bump N' Grind" to a taped backing track. The crowd sang along, and some of the women actually shouted, "Abduct me!"

I learned on February 13 that Foxx's office had convened a grand jury and was preparing to indict the singer. The website for *The New Yorker* published my story twenty-four hours later, on Valentine's Day. Prosecutors had a new videotape, albeit it one that dated from the time of the first tape for which Kelly had been tried and acquitted, and which featured the same then-fourteen-year-old girl, Reshona Landfair. It had recently been "discovered" by Avenatti, who turned it over to the state of Illinois.

Avenatti said he represented six clients, but he did not name them. He said two of his clients were victims; two were parents—Angelo and Alice Clary told me he represented them—and two were "whistle-blowers" he claimed had been close to Kelly. A prosecutor told me one of the latter was Charles Freeman, of "Chuck and Keith" fame from the first trial. Freeman had been the private investigator Kelly hired in the early 2000s but failed to pay in full to track down tapes "on the streets." One of those had been stolen by Lisa Van Allen, she testified during the trial. In 2008, Freeman had promised to "reveal all," and it seems as if he finally got around to it, a decade later, with help from the guy who brought the allegations by Stormy Daniels against the president into the national spotlight.

News of the pending indictments launched a media frenzy that made the ink and airtime spent on Kelly's crimes in the past pale in comparison. On February 21, my next piece for *The New Yorker* broke the scoop that the singer was also under investigation by three federal agencies. Based on probes by the FBI and the IRS, federal prosecutors had convened a grand jury in the Southern District of New York (the same office investigating Donald Trump), and it had issued at least one subpoena that I saw, to Kelly's former manager Derrel McDavid. The investigative division of the Department of Homeland Security planned to convene a second federal grand jury in the Eastern District of New York, a senior official told me, to hear evidence against Kelly for sex-trafficking and violating the Mann Act that felled Chuck Berry. I heard from women in four states who'd spoken to me for my reporting and who'd been visited by investigators from that agency.

Around 11:30 a.m. on February 22, I got a call from Jerhonda Pace. "They've got him!" she said. "They've finally got him!" Foxx's office held a mid-afternoon presser to announce the second time the state of Illinois indicted Robert Sylvester Kelly. I covered it for *The New Yorker*, still a journalist on a seemingly never-ending beat, and Abdon joined me because, he said, he just felt like he had to be there. Foxx spoke for two minutes and twenty seconds, and she did not take questions. The state charged Kelly with ten counts of aggravated criminal sexual abuse involving four victims, three of whom were minors, for incidents that took place between 1998 and 2010. Each of the ten counts carries a sentence of three to seven years in prison.

At that press conference and another twenty-four hours later, Foxx identified the victims only by their initials. Jerhonda told me she was "J.P." Foxx said that "R.L." had been identified in two scenes on a forty-five-minute videotape by her aunt "S.E." She was obviously talking about Reshona Landfair and Stephanie Edwards, Sparkle. Abdon and I felt an overwhelming sense of déjà vu.

Two investigators in New York told me they were frustrated that Foxx had "rushed" her charges, and that her office was not cooperating with them. They had hoped to issue joint state and federal indictments. "She was eager for the headlines," one said. But everyone I talked to at the law enforcement agencies involved agreed, this was just the beginning of the end for R. Kelly.

The singer turned himself in to Chicago Police at 8 p.m. on Friday, and he spent the night in Cook County Jail, waiting until bond could be set next door in the Criminal Court Building on Saturday afternoon. Media madness had descended on Twenty-Sixth and Cal. On Thursday, *Empire* actor Jussie Smollett stood in court and heard his bond set at $100,000 for charges that he staged a fake hate crime. That had been a circus, reporters and court personnel told me, but the crowd of a hundred journalists who swarmed for Kelly's bond hearing on Saturday was twice as big, and the scene was much, much weirder. For one thing, Michael Avenatti was there. For another, a middle-aged white woman ushered Joy Savage and Azriel Clary in and out of court, past the hungry cameras.

Joy and Azriel did not speak to the media, and Azriel never even looked at her parents, who sat several rows behind her in the courtroom. She and Joy stared straight ahead at Kelly, who displayed no emotion. The singer spent Saturday and Sunday nights in jail, too, while camera crews literally pitched their tents on the median strip across from the jail's exit, waiting for him to emerge. When Kelly finally got out of jail on Monday night, he and several scruffy members of what was left of his crew went to what had been the Rock 'N' Roll McDonald's on North Clark Street. As always, the star seemed defiant, confidant he was untouchable, oblivious to his troubles—and pathological. He'd gone back to the scene of one of his alleged crimes. I wondered what Patrice Jones and her cousin Shareese thought.

A few dozen fans who heard their hero was at the former Rock 'N' Roll McDonald's rushed to the parking lot and blasted his music from their cars. A quote from the singer resonated with me; he'd posted the video on his Facebook page in the spring of 2018. Cigar in one hand and what looked like a glass of cognac in the other, Kelly toasted a crowd of hangers-on at one of his his own never-ending parties. "Like a lot of you motherfuckers, I am handcuffed by my destiny," he said. "It's too late. They shoulda did this shit thirty years ago. It's too late. The music has been injected into the world."

That is a deeply troubling thought. No matter what happens to Robert Kelly in the years to come, the music of R. Kelly will continue to reverberate. It will echo at times in the soundtracks of our minds, it will still be heard at a few of those backyard barbecues and family gatherings, and it will be played in some of the clubs on Saturday night and maybe even in some of the churches on Sunday morning. And it will never be just music.

I must have been asked a hundred times by colleagues in the media scrums of those crazy days in late February if I felt "satisfied" that Kelly's moment of reckoning had come. I felt only a profound sense of sadness. It was all too little, too late. I'm eager to take off the investigative reporter's hat now and just be an investigative *critic* again, digging into the context, but mostly just listening. I've spent a third of my life reporting this story. I'll save the debates about separating the art and the artist for panel discussions and my classes.

On February 26, 2019, the headline for another media column by Margaret Sullivan of the *Washington Post* read, "Decades of investigative reporting couldn't touch R. Kelly. It took a Lifetime TV series and a hashtag." I don't see it that way. All three played a role, but even that powerful combination wouldn't have been enough if Kelly hadn't finally run out of money. Above all, it was those who spoke out so bravely for so long that made enough people finally care to stop him. It was the girls. For me, it was always about the girls.

When Tiffany Hawkins asked her lawyer Ian Alexander to contact the Illinois state's attorney on her behalf, the office chose not to pursue charges against a Chicago superstar based on the word of a girl who met him in her high school choir class. Alexander then filed a civil claim for Tiffany, the first to accuse the superstar of underage sex. Tiffany was the first girl to try to stop him, on Christmas Eve, 1996. If her name hadn't been in a single anonymous fax that arrived after I wrote a record review, I'm not sure Abdon Pallasch and I would ever have started our investigative reporting, or that I'd have been motivated to continue what became a very long journey.

Adopting the language of another literary-journalism hero, Randy Shilts, I always considered Tiffany "patient zero" in this story. Abdon had copied three pages from the Kenwood Academy yearbooks during Tiffany's time there, and for almost two decades, I kept her photos in a folder on my desk to remind me what this story was really about.

In mid-January 2019, Alexander still felt ethically bound by attorney-client confidentiality, but he didn't object when the client he'd represented twenty-three years earlier asked him to set up a meeting with a reporter. Two inches of snow had fallen the night before, but it was already melting as the thermometer climbed toward the mid-thirties under a bright, warm winter sun. The three of us met in a coffee shop on the Northwest Side on a Sunday afternoon. I arrived early, because I always do. It's a journalist thing, plus, I like to put the punk in punctual. Alexander showed up next. Then his client.

Tiffany Hawkins gave her attorney a big, warm hug, and their mutual affection was obvious. They'd kept in touch over all these years, sporadically trading greeting cards, emails, and phone calls. Pictures of the kids, that sort thing. They'd become part of each other's lives. "She's different than a lot of my clients," Alexander said. "I don't feel this way about all of them."

After Tiffany hugged her lawyer, she smiled and hugged me. I didn't know how to react. On December 21, 2000, Abdon and I put her name in a daily newspaper, reporting what a man ten years her senior had done to her when she was fifteen, and noting that she'd taken his money and signed a nondisclosure agreement. That had to be an incredibly difficult day for her. She had never talked about any of it, not when we called or rang her doorbell, and not when television producers working with Bunim/Murray and Lifetime dug it all up again and offered her $10,000. They told her they couldn't ethically pay people to appear in their docuseries, but they would pay for her photographs. She declined the offer. They used her photo anyway.

Tiffany was not eager to revisit that part of her life. She'd lost a lot, and she'd done things she was ashamed of. She regretted all of it, but she'd decided it was finally time to talk. Alexander informed her that as her attorney, he had to advise her that telling me what happened to her from 1991 to 1993, or talking about the lawsuit she filed in 1996 and settled in 1998, would break her NDA, placing her in legal jeopardy. Tiffany laughed a quiet, nervous laugh, then smiled wide, a gorgeous smile flashing bright white teeth. Then we talked for the first time, for two and a half hours, for the new digital recorder that replaced my old Sony Pressman.

I'd had some assumptions for almost two decades that turned out to be wrong. Tiffany had been a volleyball player; I'd assumed basketball, because that was *his* thing. She'd been a straight-A student who got into Kenwood Academy through its magnet program; I'd thought she'd struggled, since she eventually dropped out of high school. She'd been credited on *Age Ain't Nothing but a Number* as a rapper, but singing had always been her passion, and her strongest talent. As I went back to talk to some of her classmates again for this book, they said she had a voice like Whitney Houston's. Powerful. Beautiful.

I'd never known Tiffany toured as one of Aaliyah's backing vocalists, performing across the United States, as well as in London, Paris, and Amsterdam, a long way from the South Side of Chicago. She had never been jealous of Aaliyah. They'd become best friends, two teenage girls seeing the world for the first time, part of a great adventure, a new chapter in their lives—the Second Chapter, as they called their posse. "And when she left home, for them to get married, you know, she ran away," Tiffany said. "Her parents were on the phone with me, back and forth, and they're like, 'Aaliyah ran away, and the only place she would go would be to your house!'"

Tiffany split with him when she got pregnant at age eighteen. I will not use his name again, because she didn't, not very much, and because it doesn't need to be in this book one more time. She asked him to take a paternity test, because she wasn't 100 percent sure who'd fathered the child she was carrying. He refused. It turned out to be another boyfriend, not him, but the fact that he wouldn't take the test infuriated her. Every girl I interviewed had a different trigger that prompted her to leave. And like every girl I interviewed, Tiffany said she loved him, and she thought he loved her.

"I was really pissed off that he wouldn't take that test, and the whole spiel he gave me, you know, the mind tricks he tried to pull on me. I remember he was on tour with Toni Braxton. I'm on the phone with him, and I can hear the crowd waiting for him. The crowd is roaring and roaring. And I asked him to take the test, and, you know, he's like, *'No.'* He goes to me, 'You and me better both know that that is not my baby.' He said he didn't want to hear anything else about it. Then he said, 'Now tell me you love me.'"

Tiffany told me about the seven-and-a-half-hour deposition she gave to his attorneys, and about the horrible, invasive, and insulting questions they asked her about supposed lying, sleeping around, trying to shake down their client, and spreading venereal diseases. She also told me about the things she said.

"He used to call me 'Madam' and 'the Cable Girl,' because I used to hook him up, bring him girls, bring my friends. And you know what? That's exactly what I was at the time. I'm not even going to lie to you. It was like I wanted to be around and I knew what I had to do in order to stay around, you know? And I didn't want to do it, but there were girls who didn't mind doing it. So, it was kinda like, 'Okay, cool. All right, let's go.'"

Tiffany said she brought six underage girlfriends into his circle of intimates. She'd actually been the last of the seven teens to have sexual contact with him. "It got progressively worse. The more money and power he got, the worse he got. But I loved him. I wanted to be around him, you know? I looked at him in awe. You know, we would be in the studio, and he'd be writing something and singing, and I would just be like, *'This man!'* You know? 'I get to be around *this genius!'*"

He asked her to cut all her hair off. He asked her . . . well, he asked her to do a lot of things, and I'm not going to report another goddamn one of them. If the case has not been made to you by now, it never will be. I want you to meet Tiffany, like I did. On a sunny Sunday morning when even the endless Chicago winter didn't seem quite so daunting.

After she split from him, Tiffany tried to kill herself, taking a handful of pills. "I was at home, and my mother was there. She wound up taking me to the hospital, and I had to have my stomach pumped. And that was really hard. You know? It was *hard*."

I asked if she'd been disappointed that the state's attorney declined to pursue criminal charges. "I don't think it was disappointment . . . more like what I expected. I was a young black girl. Who cared?" She had quickly squandered the money she got from the settlement. She cashed her check, for two-thirds of $250,000 minus costs, and immediately went shopping at the mall. "The money . . . I wish I had done better with it, however I still have people to this day that believe the story about how he's the reason I live in a decent home, drive nice cars, and am able to travel frequently. *Not!* I just made the decision not to let my past define my future. I made my life what it is now, because I wasn't going to let anyone else do that for me."

With her own money, not his, Tiffany went to college downstate, "with the baby with me," and then to a Big-10 university, where she earned a degree in radiologic science. Then she got an online master's degree in management. She runs a hospital's ultrasound department now. Understandably, she doesn't want to say where, and she has a different surname these days. She's been happily married for going on six years, and she has two children. "My son is grown and gone, and I have a daughter, who is awesome." Her daughter is almost as old as she was when. . . .

"For a long time, no matter what I was doing, if I heard Robert's music or saw him on TV, my stomach would drop. It would be like, I don't know, reliving a nightmare. It was something for a long time that I couldn't get past, because his music was everywhere. And every time, I had to hear it. For a long time, I could not get away from him."

A hundred million albums sold, his own and those he crafted for so many other artists. Billions of dollars generated. The voice of a generation. Ubiquitous. Untouchable. But she finally, slowly began to tune it all out. To mute it. Tiffany not only survived, but eventually thrived. "I think, maybe . . . I don't know . . . I'm stronger than most?"

Tiffany gave me another big hug when we got ready to leave. I'd cried, she'd cried, her attorney had cried, and we'd all laughed a few times, too, because, hell, sometimes you just have to. She'd already told me she doesn't sing anymore. "I tried, later on, several years after that, but the passion just wasn't there." I thought of one more question as we were trading email addresses and phone numbers and taking iPhone pics. This one didn't come from the journalist, critic, professor, father, or husband. It came from the inner thirteen-year-old who fell in love with that Velvets song about a life saved by rock 'n' roll, who later did a fanzine called *Reasons for Living*, and who still lives to listen. After all the evidence I've compiled of damage done and young lives robbed, of all the painful and horrible things I've heard and seen, Tiffany's answer to that question breaks my fucking heart, every single time I think about it.

I know you can't listen to him, I said, but can you find joy in any music now?

"No," she said. "Not really. Not very much. No."

ACKNOWLEDGMENTS

Although it could seem very lonely at times, I was never the only journalist on the R. Kelly beat. I have diligently tried to credit the work of others who contributed to this story throughout the text, but several reporters—and editors, who rarely get public thanks—deserve special mention. These include Thomas Conner, Michael Cooke, Laura Emerick, and Don Hayner, when we worked together at the *Chicago Sun-Times*; Jessica Hopper, Max Blau, and Theresa Campagna, when we worked together for MTV News; Robin Amer, Maya Dukmasova, and Jake Malooley, when we worked together at the *Chicago Reader*; and my friends and colleagues at WBEZ, past and present, including Shawn Allee, Collin Ashmead-Bobbitt, Tricia Bobeda, Cate Cahan, Alyssa Edes, Monica Eng, Kate Grossman, Shannon Heffernan, Michael Lansu, Linda Lutton, Chip Mitchell, Natalie Moore, and Adam Yoffe.

During the fast-moving developments of early 2019, I am not ashamed to say I had to run to keep up with the next generation of intrepid young reporters, in the media scrums at Twenty-Sixth and Cal, and via their stories about the new round of indictments in Chicago. Those who provided welcome company as well as significant illumination included Megan Crepeau, Morgan Greene, Jason Meisner, and Tracy Swartz at the *Chicago Tribune*; Robert Chiarito, a contributor to the *New York Times* and other outlets; and my former student Sam Charles, now an ace reporter at the *Sun-Times*.

I proudly covered the most recent events for *The New Yorker*'s website, and I thank Michael Agger for his encouragement and deft editing, as well as David Haglund, Sean Lavery, Michael Luo, and David Remnick for their support, and Amanda Petrusich for the introduction and the cheerleading.

No one outside my family has endured my rants for longer or offered more encouragement and morale-boosting than my radio partner, Greg Kot, and my original nemesis, Bill Wyman. My gratitude to them extends to the crew at *Sound Opinions*, both past—especially Robin Linn, Jason Saldanha, and Matt Spiegel—and present, including Brendan Banaszak, Alex Claiborne, Ayana Contreras, and Andrew Gill. Thanks, too, to everyone who supports the show at WBEZ, not the least of whom are Steve Edwards and Goli Sheikholeslami.

When I called Mary Mitchell a goddess in one interview, I did not overstate my admiration, while Abdon Pallasch is quite simply my brother from another mother. I don't think I can ever repay him for allowing me to drag him into this for two decades, but I should start by giving him the collected works of Curtis Mayfield.

Damon Dunn, thank you for always having my back, and especially for keeping me out of Cook County Jail, though I must say, it would have been an honor to share a cell with you. You, too, Neil Rosenbaum.

The team at BuzzFeed News included some of the most impressive professionals I've ever worked with, until its corporate board ordered layoffs in January 2019. Thank you, Talal Ansari, Antonio Enriquez, Shani Hilton, Matt Mittenthal, Katie Rayford, Matt Schafer, Nabiha Syed, and Linzee Troubh. My primary editor, Marisa Carroll, was especially brilliant, hard-driving, unrelentingly ethical, and inspiring. She stands as a model for what journalism can and should be.

I am very grateful to be a member of the Department of English and Creative Writing at Columbia College Chicago, and I appreciate the support, encouragement, and feedback I get from all my colleagues there. Like Wayne or Garth, I'm not worthy. Special thanks to Laura Johanna Waltje for translating Goethe from the old German and capturing the poetry, no easy task.

A ridiculously talented fiction writer and sharp feminist thinker, Kate Wisel served as my intrepid research assistant and sounding board for the past three years. (Read her first book, *Driving in Cars with Homeless Men*, due to be published in October 2019.) I have long benefitted from the efforts of Jennifer Grandy, who started helping me as a college intern, became a top-shelf legal scholar and attorney, and still lends me her talents and support. Thanks as well to my former graduate teaching assistant Crispin Torres. Their advice, feedback, and hours of digging and transcribing were invaluable and helped save some measure of my sanity.

ACKNOWLEDGMENTS

For encouragement and assistance above and beyond, I am indebted to my friends Jamie Ackley; Lorraine Ali; Dino Armiros; Sheila Baldwin; Maud Berthomier; Joe Berton and Gloria Groome; Jessica Blank and Eric Jensen; Barry and Joan Biediger; Lyric Cabral; Louie and Mary Calvano; Stephanie Caparelli; Ann Marie Carlson; Mike and Mary Kay Cobb; Aaron Cohen; Steven Corey; Ken Daley; Kate Darling; Wynne Delacoma; Anthony DiMurro; David Dunton; Robert Feder; dream hampton; Susan Hamre-Keller; Cynthia Taylor-Handrup; Deborah Holdstein and Jay Boersma; Rick Kogan; Bob Kurson; Aviya Kushner; Joe Kvidera; Anders and Julie Lindall; Jennifer Lizak; Todd Martens; Dr. Charmaine Jake-Matthews; Jim Merlis; Keith Moerer; Mark Anthony Neal; Michael Nejman; Douglas and Pegeen Reichert Powell; Helene Stapinski and Wendell Jamieson; Tony and Brandee Tavano; Jim Testa; Kristi Turnbaugh; Tim and Katie Tuten; Jaan Uhelszki; Dr. Annmarie van Altena; Ken Weinstein; Sam Weller; Robin Whatley; my pals at the Military Miniature Society of Illinois; my in-laws, Joe and Marcia Carrillo; and my brother and sister-in-law, Michael and Mary Ellen DeRogatis.

Monika Woods believed in this book since she first emailed me in January 2014 ("Hello from a literary agent"), and she eventually convinced me that living with the darkness I knew it would require was not only important, but necessary. Then it took forever to find a home, but she persisted, and with Jamison Stoltz, we connected with the perfect editor. I mean, this impeccably dressed Oak Park native prints out PDFs, marks them up with a fountain pen, scans them, and sends them back. How fucking cool is that? To be sure, that is only one in a thousand ways he made this book better. Thanks also to Alicia Tan, Lisa Silverman, Anet Sirna-Bruder, John Gall, Devin Grosz, Kimberly Lew, Jennifer Brunn, Gabby Fisher, Mamie VanLangen, Hannah Babcock, Tricia Kallett, Michael Jacobs, Michael Sand, and everyone at Abrams.

Finally, how can I express my thanks for the support and faith I get from *mi alma y corazón*, Carmél Carrillo? It is beyond me, and I apologize for that, and for the many sleepless nights, tense days, and interrupted vacations during our marriage because of this story. Whenever my energy flagged, the frustrations mounted, or the cynicism threatened to overwhelm me, I thought of my love for my wife and soulmate, as well as my daughter, Melody (whose plays and musical recitals I too often missed), and my mom,

ACKNOWLEDGMENTS

Helene (who lived to hear I'd found a publisher, but not to celebrate that news at Sabatino's Italian Restaurant). Their love kept me pushing forward and reminded me that all the girls I've written about have people who love them that much, and who they love that deeply in return. So many suffered for so long because a soulless man perverted the art form that inspires me. I tried to shine a light on that, but it was the voices of these girls and their loved ones that finally stopped it.

Born in Jersey City, New Jersey, the year the Beatles arrived in America, Jim DeRogatis began voicing his opinions about music shortly thereafter. He is an associate professor of instruction in the Department of English and Creative Writing at Columbia College Chicago, and together with Greg Kot of the *Chicago Tribune*, he co-hosts *Sound Opinions*, the weekly music talk show heard on public radio nationwide, and at soundopinions.org via podcast. DeRogatis spent fifteen years as the pop music critic at the *Chicago Sun-Times* and is the author, co-author, or editor of eleven books, including *Let It Blurt: The Life and Times of Lester Bangs, America's Greatest Rock Critic*; *Staring at Sound: The True Story of Oklahoma's Fabulous Flaming Lips*; *Turn On Your Mind: Four Decades of Great Psychedelic Rock*; and *Milk It! Collected Musings on the Alternative Music Explosion of the '90s*. He has played in bands since age thirteen, but he jokes that he is a drummer, not a musician. His current trio, Vortis, recently released *This Machine Kills Fascists* on vinyl with Cavetone Records. He lives in Chicago with his wife, Carmél Carrillo, while his daughter, Melody, pursues her passion for musical theater.